Simon Gibbons has done a detailed, wide-ranging analysis of Harold, my father's, work. The book has enthused me with the will to join the dots between what I knew and what I only knew of by name. As a father, he was a hugely knowledgeable, funny, relentlessly questioning figure, jumping between earthy observation and scholarly viewpoints. This book matches my personal view in that it shows us Harold weaving his way between the concerns of the classroom teacher, the culture and language of school students and the downward pressure from those in charge of education. I'm both grateful for, and in awe of how Simon has synthesised all this into a coherent, accessible survey of Harold's life-work.

– **Michael Rosen**

Simon Gibbons has composed an authoritative account of and personal tribute to the work of one of the most influential thinkers, writers and activists in the world of English teaching and language and learning in the second half of the 20th century. Harold Rosen's intellectual legacy is as relevant now as his words and acts were ground-breaking in his lifetime; and, in the current context of the politics of education, yet more sorely needed.

– **John Richmond,** *Editor*

Harold Rosen and English in Education and the Language Arts

Simon Gibbons embarks on a detailed and groundbreaking study in this book, examining the profound influence of Harold Rosen, a pivotal figure who transformed English education in the latter half of the twentieth century. Gibbons offers the first comprehensive analysis of Rosen's revolutionary contributions to progressive English teaching methodologies that continue to resonate in classrooms worldwide.

Drawing on extensive research, including previously unpublished writings and interviews with Rosen's colleagues, Gibbons meticulously charts Rosen's multifaceted impact: his development of a new model for English teaching; his pioneering work on language, class and culture; his innovative approaches to narrative in education; and his advocacy for teacher agency. The book illuminates how Rosen's work at the London Institute of Education, alongside colleagues James Britton and Nancy Martin, fundamentally reshaped understanding of language across the curriculum while maintaining an unwavering commitment to educational equity. Gibbons makes a compelling case for the contemporary relevance and necessary rediscovery of Rosen's educational philosophy.

This volume serves as an essential resource for student teachers, practicing educators and academics in English and language arts while also offering valuable insights to educators across disciplines interested in language's role in learning. By reconnecting readers with Rosen's enduring legacy, the book provides both historical perspective and practical guidance for addressing current educational challenges.

Simon Gibbons is Reader in English Education at King's College London, where he is Director of Teacher Education. As a teacher and researcher, he has published extensively on the development of English as a school subject for over 30 years.

Key Thinkers in English in Education and the Language Arts
Series Editor: Andy Goodwyn

This truly global and all-encompassing series provides definitive knowledge about key thinkers in English language and literature teaching and research from around the world. Each volume is a key text to understanding the wider context to each thinker to the field, illustrating their continued relevance to contemporary approaches in English teaching and especially as it's applied to the classroom. Exploring key ideas and condensing complex theories in an easily digestible format, this series will be engaging, accessible and appealing to readers with a range of levels of interest in the field of English in Education and the Language Arts (EELA).

Titles in this series include:

L. S. Vygotsky and English in Education and the Language Arts
Peter Smagorinsky

Garth Boomer, English Teaching and Curriculum Leadership
Bill Green

Harold Rosen and English in Education and the Language Arts
Simon Gibbons

For more information about this series, please visit: https://www.routledge.com/Key-Thinkers-in-English-in-Education-and-the-Language-Arts/book-series/KTEELA

Harold Rosen and English in Education and the Language Arts

Simon Gibbons

LONDON AND NEW YORK

Designed cover image: © Getty Images

First published 2026
by Routledge
4 Park Square, Milton Park, Abingdon, Oxon OX14 4RN

and by Routledge
605 Third Avenue, New York, NY 10158

Routledge is an imprint of the Taylor & Francis Group, an informa business

© 2026 Simon Gibbons

The right of Simon Gibbons to be identified as author of this work has been asserted in accordance with sections 77 and 78 of the Copyright, Designs and Patents Act 1988.

All rights reserved. No part of this book may be reprinted or reproduced or utilised in any form or by any electronic, mechanical, or other means, now known or hereafter invented, including photocopying and recording, or in any information storage or retrieval system, without permission in writing from the publishers.

Trademark notice: Product or corporate names may be trademarks or registered trademarks, and are used only for identification and explanation without intent to infringe.

British Library Cataloguing-in-Publication Data
A catalogue record for this book is available from the British Library

ISBN: 978-1-032-96287-0 (hbk)
ISBN: 978-1-032-96282-5 (pbk)
ISBN: 978-1-003-58891-7 (ebk)

DOI: 10.4324/9781003588917

Typeset in Galliard
by Apex CoVantage, LLC

Dedicated to Leanne, Ruby and Louie

Contents

	Series Editor Foreword	*x*
	Acknowledgements	*xii*
1	Introduction	1
2	Harold Rosen and the Rise of the New English	21
3	Harold Rosen: Class and Cultures	49
4	Harold Rosen: Language and Learning across the Curriculum	75
5	The Importance of Story, Narrative, Autobiography and Memory	100
6	Harold Rosen: Activist and Advocate for Teacher Agency	120
7	The Enduring Importance of Harold Rosen's Work	141
	Index	*161*

Series Editor Foreword

It is with great pleasure that I introduce the third volume in this series, Key Thinkers in English in Education and the Language Arts, an international series that aspires to provide truly comprehensive insights into the significance of a major author's body of work and their lasting importance to this very special section of Education, but also to the development of the whole field and beyond. The series focuses on key figures who were of great importance to Education generally and who have had strong influences on English in Education and on other leading authorities who acted directly in the field itself.

Harold Rosen was a remarkable individual thinker and educator and part of a generation of highly influential colleagues and associates, often known as 'The London School', a group with a truly international significance. Rosen was a generous and supportive teacher and colleague and also gifted with a very distinctive presence and perspective. This book traces his life beginning with his remarkable upbringing in a Jewish immigrant family, growing up in the turbulent maelstrom of London's East End, part of an intensely political family committed to social justice. The intense nature of his early life stayed with him throughout his work in education and especially in relation to the subject of English as a radical and humane force for social change.

In 'The London School', he found many like-minded colleagues [see Gibbons, 2014, 2017] in the 1960s, 1970s and 1980s, and he was always collegiate whilst being distinctive in his particular radical perspective. He was one of the key representatives of progressive English to be invited to the seminal Dartmouth Conference in 1966 [see Goodwyn et al., 2018]. He was a stalwart champion for the working class and a fair and diverse society and particularly for the cause of an egalitarian approach to language. Later in his work, he explored the special significance of narrative in English but also more broadly in education, undertaking pioneering work about oral storytelling and autobiography.

The author of this volume, Simon Gibbons is perfectly placed to provide a comprehensive understanding of Rosen's life and work, having known him and his family personally and because of his own research and scholarship. His first major book [2014], *The London Association for the Teaching of English,*

1947–67: A History, is a remarkable piece of scholarship, intense and vivid, and capturing a key period in the development of the field. This was followed [2017] by *English and Its Teachers: A History of Policy, Pedagogy and Practice*, the most important study that we have of the evolution and struggles of the profession in England. Both texts make considerable reference to the work of Rosen and his significance and influence. These texts provide remarkably valuable histories of some of the key developments in English in Education in the twentieth century. We are fortunate that in 2017, John Richmond compiled an excellent anthology of Rosen's writing, making some of his work very accessible, *Harold Rosen: Writings on Life, Language and Learning 1958–2008*.

I was fortunate enough to read Rosen's work in my teacher training year and then to become well acquainted with his later work through his many publications and collaborations. As Gibbons makes clear, he was a stalwart activist and supporter of teachers and their associations. As a new Head of Department in the outer London Borough of Harrow in 1984, I was disappointed to find no local branch of the National Association for the Teaching of English and promptly set about forming the Harrow Association for the Teaching of English (perhaps HATE was not the most attractive of acronyms?) and was pleased to find other like-minded teachers to work with me. I rather tentatively contacted the now retired Harold Rosen as my ideal choice for our inaugural event – he graciously accepted, remarking, 'there is nothing more important than a NATE inaugural'. I happened to know he had also taught and lived locally. He spoke about the place of narrative and autobiography in the English classroom and of its significance for English teachers. His talk was full of passion and strong words about the negative developments in English in Education and the direction of travel of the education system in the 1980s and its impact on the disadvantaged students; he was properly radical as always. It is an abiding memory for me of a remarkable and distinctive key thinker.

Andy Goodwyn
August 2025

References

Gibbons, S. (2014) *The London Association for the Teaching of English, 1947–67: A History*. London: Institute of Education Press.

Gibbons, S. (2017) *English and its Teachers: A History of Policy, Pedagogy and Practice*. London: Routledge.

Goodwyn, A., Durrant, C., Sawyer, W., Zancanella, D. and Scherff, E. (eds.) (2018) *The Future of English Teaching Worldwide and its Histories: Celebrating 50 Years from the Dartmouth Conference*. London: Routledge.

Richmond, J. (ed.) (2017) *Harold Rosen: Writings on Life, Language and Learning 1958–2008*. London: UCL Institute of Education Press.

Acknowledgements

Although for significant periods of time it felt as though the writing of this book was a solitary enterprise, characterised by day after day sat alone with only a keyboard and screen for company, the truth, of course, is that I have many to thank that this work has come into being. The order in which I make the following acknowledgements should not be taken as indicating any particular hierarchy of importance; all named have been of enormous assistance in a variety of ways.

I should offer thanks primarily to the series editor Andrew Goodwyn, who invited me to submit a proposal for this text. Even as I enthusiastically accepted his invitation, I was acutely aware that there are others who would be as, if not more, qualified to take on this work. Andy's support through the writing process and his positive comments on the draft of the manuscript were enormously helpful. I am grateful for the faith Andy put in my skill and capacity; I hope he feels that faith has been rewarded by what follows.

I should confess it was something of a daunting prospect to take on the writing of a book about the work of a man who is held in such high affection and esteem by his family, friends and former colleagues and collaborators. Betty Rosen, Michael Rosen, Brian Rosen, John Richmond, Tony Burgess and John Hardcastle, all people with intimate knowledge of Harold Rosen's life and work, were unequivocal in their support of my efforts to produce this text, and for that I am hugely grateful. All generously spared time to talk or write to me about their experiences of living and working with Harold Rosen, and John Richmond offered incredibly helpful feedback on not one but two drafts of the manuscript.

Finally, I should thank my family. My wife, Leanne, was once again staunch in her support and encouragement as I wrote, and my children, Ruby and Louie, accepted, with varying degrees of grace, that there were times at which their father would have to be at his computer, rather than responding to their latest urgent requests for attention.

Chapter 1

Introduction

Once Upon a Time: A Memory

The person who is the subject of this book would, I believe, find it entirely appropriate that I begin with an autobiographical anecdote. Once upon a significantly long time ago, I was a newly qualified English teacher just lurching to the end of my first year in post, having survived nearly three terms in a community comprehensive school in East London. I use the word survived advisedly; it would be wholly misleading to claim that I had thrived. At the invitation of both my head of department and a senior teacher at the school – himself a former head of English – I attended the annual weekend conference of the London Association for the Teaching of English (LATE) being held at Corsica Hall in Seaford, near to Brighton, on the coast of East Sussex. It was July of 1994, just a few months since the death of James Britton, a founding member of LATE and a towering influence on the teaching of English in schools in the second half of the twentieth century. The title of the conference was 'Prospect and Retrospect', one borrowed from a collection of Britton's essays (Pradl, 1982) and the weekend was going to be an opportunity to reflect on the history of LATE as an organisation, on the development of English as a subject, and on Britton's contribution to that development, all in the context of the emergence of a new version of the English National Curriculum. I'm sure I had little or no idea at the time about LATE's fantastically rich history, and only a little more of an idea of the significance of Britton – the vestiges of the learning from my PGCE that had survived the turmoil of a year in the classroom. I also had little idea that the weekend in East Sussex would change, perhaps even dictate, the course of my subsequent professional life.

The first session of the conference, after dinner on the Friday evening, took place in a room at the front of Corsica Hall, with a view looking out to the English Channel. As the sun set, three influential figures from LATE's history – Nancy Martin, Alex McLeod and Joan Goody – each shared their memories of the activities of the Association, how it was founded, the work it undertook and its means of operating. I can remember little now of the content of those three talks, though in later years when researching LATE's

DOI: 10.4324/9781003588917-1

history I did rediscover and read one of them (Martin, 1994). I do remember, however, the feeling I had sat in that room with three people who I vaguely knew then, but grew to fully understand, were colossuses in the world of English education, whose influence spread to English-speaking jurisdictions across the globe. The atmosphere in the room was one of reverence and appreciation for the contribution Martin, McLeod and Goody had made to English teaching and of the extraordinary story of LATE. I was inspired by the tales I heard and the way they were told and began to appreciate, probably for the first time, the richness of the legacy I was inheriting as a fledgling teacher of English seeking to enact, to dubious effect I suspect, his own interpretation of what a humane, progressive model of the subject might look like. As the sun disappeared over the horizon, and the clock ticked evening into night, no one stirred to reach for the light switch, as if such a move might break the spell of the stories that were being told. By the conclusion of the talks, we sat in near darkness, yet through the gloom I felt I had seen the light.

Yet this evening was in fact just the appetiser for what, for me, became the main event. On the second evening of the conference, Harold Rosen gave a talk under the title 'The Story so far. . .', a title that promised to show 'how our successes help us face the present crises' (LATE, 1994). Rosen spoke about the past in a way that brought the battles to forge a new progressive model of English into the present. The political climate at the time was perhaps the most hostile it had ever been for English teachers; the first boycott of Standardised Attainment Tests (SATs) had been led by the profession in the previous year and the original, many felt relatively benign, English National Curriculum had almost been replaced by what many viewed as an impoverished and politically right-wing-inspired 'back to basics' version,[1] only for this to be shelved in the wake of the Dearing review.[2] In this context, when many browbeaten English teachers were feeling oppressed and battle-scarred, Rosen spoke with a passion for the education of all children that left me in no doubt as to the significance of the enterprise with which I had chosen to engage. And he spoke with a sharp edge to his words that made it clear that, as English teachers, we were involved in nothing short of a political battle to ensure that children could be given the opportunity to change their world and the world around them, and this was a battle we must take up, no matter how challenging the circumstances. The stakes were simply too high to contemplate defeat. Rosen has been described as a 'compelling talker' (Hardcastle and Medway, 2009, p. 5); he more than lived up to that description on that evening in Seaford.

The feelings that Rosen's words inspired – and beyond his contribution to *Language, Learner and the School* (Barnes et al., 1969), I had precious little idea at the time of Rosen's enormous contribution to English in education – sustained me through the rest of that first year and into the decades of teaching and teacher education that followed. Over a decade later, they were hugely influential in my decision to undertake a study of LATE as the focus of my PhD; I wanted the story I heard told in that room in Seaford to be made public (such PhD theses can be seen as public documents). They led me to active involvement in LATE and in the National Association for the Teaching of English (NATE), ultimately as Chair of NATE. They reinforced something I, at best, only dimly knew at the time; specifically, what it was that English teaching was really all about, and why what I and my colleagues were doing was, arguably, the most important job in the world. It was my one and only encounter with Harold Rosen as a man, and it was perhaps the most important piece of professional development I ever experienced.

How much of that recollection is true is, of course, debatable. That there was a LATE conference at Seaford in 1994 called 'Prospect and Retrospect' is a documented fact, and that document, in the form of the conference programme, indicates the contributions of the key figures I've mentioned. In addition to those already detailed, Rosen's wife, Betty, enchanted delegates with an evening of storytelling, something I would in time discover was characteristic of the way LATE events had historically always been so much more than mere classroom focused professional development exercises. The conference programme even serves as a reminder that a precocious newly qualified teacher (me) spoke on the final day of the conference under the title 'At the end of every story there is another beginning...'. I recall that the evening prior to this, I had, after a little too much Dutch courage, pronounced, ignorant to my mixing of French idioms, that my talk would be 'la crème de resistance' (nobody at the time pointed this error out, no doubt to spare me the embarrassment at my faux pas). That I, as a newly qualified teacher, had the audacity to speak at the end of a weekend where delegates had listened to Nancy Martin, Alex McLeod, Joan Goody, Harold and Betty Rosen tells you all you need to know of how little understanding I had of the company I was keeping.

That I listened to Rosen speak is also true. How I remember the event, how I felt and the significance I now attach to it is the result of the process of memory influenced by the professional and personal life I have lived in the three decades since, three decades working within the field of English education in the context, more often than not, of hostile policy environments that appear to have done all they can to expunge the work of Harold Rosen from the collective professional memory of English teachers. Rosen was acutely attuned to the importance of autobiography and anecdote and to the significance and effects of the acts of remembering and retelling and of doing that in language – be it spoken or written. I hope if he were able to read my anecdote, he would agree that the 'truth' of the events recalled is not really the most important thing; what is important is the way I remember what happened, the way I have retold the story to myself over the course of my career and the way I feel that this story has been instrumental in shaping my professional, and indeed personal, identity. These are the things which are ultimately important about my memory of that weekend in the summer of 1994. It was, to use a term Rosen employed himself when writing on memory, a flashbulb moment (see, for example, Rosen, 1998), an event that I return to frequently and which has assumed a particular significance in my own life history. This book, though its earliest roots can probably be traced to my first reading of *Language, Learner and the School*, in many ways really began in a room in Seaford in 1994, listening to Harold Rosen speak and honestly believing that what I was doing had the power to change the world.

Harold Rosen: A Key Figure in English in Education

In another volume in this *Key Thinkers* series on the work of Vygotsky, the author maintains in his conclusion that he 'set out neither to bury Vygotsky, nor to praise him' (Smagorinsky, 2024, p. 314). That tome on Vygotsky is a hugely impressive work, and I can only commend the author for the analytical detachment he professes in his approach to the assessment of the work of a man who is, for many, nothing short of one of twentieth-century education's most esteemed icons. It would be disingenuous of me to make similar claims to dispassionate impartiality and a deception if I asked readers to believe this stance. Beginning with a personal anecdote is a way to make clear to any reader that I am not writing as an impartial researcher. My work, and that of the vast majority of colleagues with whom I have shared my professional life – though they may not consciously know it – has been unmistakably influenced, profoundly for the better, by Harold Rosen's contribution to the field of English in education. Confessing my own admiration for Harold Rosen and acknowledging the importance of his work to my professional career and identity does not, I believe, mean that I cannot attempt to come to some critically sound judgements as to what it is in his work that is so important and what should, therefore, be preserved and represented to the English teachers of the future. This I will endeavour to do. But there is little point pretending that I believe Rosen's work is anything other than of critical importance to anyone engaged in the teaching of English. One could, of course, argue that the mere fact an individual has been selected to be the subject of a book in this series means a judgement has already been reached on his or her importance; it really would be a curious, paradoxical state of affairs to reach the conclusion of this book to discover that the subject did not deserve to be featured in a series of this name.

Unarguably, Harold Rosen was a key thinker in the field of English in education and the language arts. Arguably, in the development of the new, progressive model of English that emerged in the years following the Second World War, he was the single most important key thinker of them all. Often, those who think and write about the development of this progressive model of English turn to a handful of instantly recognisable names that are very often mentioned in the same breath as Rosen; primarily James Britton, Nancy Martin and Douglas Barnes, but also John Dixon, Margaret Meek Spencer and Tony Burgess. This is an indicative, and far from exhaustive, list and all of these people played a significant part in the story of the new English. Thankfully, in a series of books featuring those who merit a preeminent place in the history of the key thinkers in English education and the language arts, it is not necessary to create a ranking order. The development of the model of English that began in London in the 1940s and which spread and influenced the teaching of the subject across the English-speaking world in the decades that followed was nothing if not a collaborative enterprise; it began when English teachers in the capital came together to share the challenges they faced in classrooms that were undergoing seismic change in the wake of unprecedented developments in social and education policy. However, with respect to the evolution of the progressive model of English as a school subject, we can evaluate the unique contribution of individuals within a collaborative endeavour, and Rosen's contribution, given his particular background, beliefs and motivations, was unique. This book will go some way, I hope, to ensure that the work of Harold Rosen is both evaluated for its historical significance in changing English as a school subject and reassessed for its ongoing importance.

Perhaps the most succinct encapsulation of Rosen's importance in the field of English education appeared in the editorial to the edition of the journal *Changing English*, published shortly after his death:

> Harold Rosen, who died at the end of July 2008 at the age of 89, was central to developments in English teaching during the second half of the twentieth century. From the 1950s, when he taught English at Walworth School in South London to the day in 1984 when he retired as Professor of the Teaching of English from London University's Institute of Education in 1984, he found and promoted the most progressive and innovative work on language, literature and culture, much of it with colleagues and teachers who are to be found as writers and collaborators in this issue of *Changing English*.
>
> (Miller,[3] 2009, p. 1)

The intention of this volume is, if you like, to 'unpack' that overarching description of Rosen's work and to identify some of the specific details of his distinctive contribution to what was an undoubtedly collaborative enterprise – in effect the transformation of the way English was taught in schools in the post-war decades. In fact, Rosen's part in this transformation began a decade before Miller suggests and continued for many years past his official retirement. We can't say how this model of English would have developed without Rosen's particular influence and contribution, but we can say how that significant influence and contribution helped forge particular dimensions of this new vision of the subject.

In doing this, I hope it is obvious what one other key purpose of this volume is. It is not intended to solely celebrate and give due credit to the importance and influence of Rosen's work. There is value in that in and of itself, though it could be argued that John Richmond's[4] excellently edited collection of Rosen's writing has achieved that aim (Richmond, 2017) to a large extent, bringing together, as it does, many of Rosen's most important academic works alongside autobiographical and poetic pieces. Rather, a prime purpose of this book is to ensure that the work is discovered, or rediscovered, by English teachers – indeed all teachers – and its importance recognised by those working with young people today so that it exerts greater influence on the way in which those young people experience the subject of English and education more widely. Though this is a book in a series on key thinkers in English in education, I would argue that the scope of Rosen's work, particularly that on language and learning and language and class, means it has relevance to all teachers. Similarly, his advocacy of teacher agency and autonomy transcends subject or phase boundaries.

As a writer, one can only make guesses – however educated they may be – about the contexts in which readers encounter their work, and so it is impossible for me to assume what the education landscape – local or national – looks like for you – the reader – as you come to these words. I can, however, attest to the context in which I write, and in the United Kingdom of the mid-2020s, it is apparent that many of the insights of Rosen's work have either been forgotten or suppressed or, more likely perhaps, never known by the policymakers and practitioners involved in schooling. In *English and Its Teachers: A history of policy, pedagogy and practice* (Gibbons, 2017), I sketched out, admittedly in a hugely generalised way, what English typically looks like for young people in schools in England two decades into the twenty-first century. That sketch – which was informed by the experience of observing many hundreds of English lessons – seems to me no less accurate as I now write, nearly a decade on, and it is a picture of the subject widely divergent from that which Rosen helped to build. It is a subject that is seemingly 'done' to young people; a relatively narrow range of knowledge, content and skills is delivered, and whilst we might be persuaded to believe that this is done with nothing but the best motives of policymakers and practitioners – to ensure pupils have the knowledge and skills of English they need to negotiate assessment hurdles and thereby succeed in their adult lives, for example – it doesn't often seem that the pupils' own experience, language, concerns, hopes and fears have much impact on what is happening. This is not what education, and specifically English teaching, ought to look like in the mind of Rosen, where everything that is done in the classroom should start, at the very least, with the children, with their experience and their language.

It may well be that a majority of teachers, when questioned, continue to highlight the importance of a progressive, growth model of English (see, for example, Goodwyn, 2016) to their own work and indeed central to their reasons for becoming English teachers in the first place. Broadly speaking, this is the model that Rosen was central to developing, working with his colleagues in school and in higher education. However, in my experience, though English teachers may hold a belief in this version of the subject, a humane model that is sensitive to the needs of its learners, it all too seldomly translates into classroom practice. Let me be clear; this is not to blame individual English teachers or to suggest those who profess a belief in progressive English yet enact a seemingly contrasting model are possessed of ingrained hypocrisy. There are many reasons why any given teacher does not feel she has the freedom to enact the sort of practice that she would in conversation espouse. One set of reasons for this are clear and well known – the standards-based curriculum and assessment reforms and high-stakes accountability frameworks of many education systems within English-speaking jurisdictions over the past 40 years have, understandably, impacted on what teachers feel they can, or even want to, do in the classroom. With data as king and inspection bodies as overlords, the pressure to deliver examination results and to teach in apparently evidence-based ways is felt by school leaders and passed down, often unfiltered, to those in the classroom. Fear of failure is endemic, so risk aversion is the norm. More recently, advocates of a knowledge-based curriculum in English have had significant influence in places like England and the United States, and this has manifested itself in English classrooms with the introduction (or perhaps reintroduction) of what might be seen as a more traditional model of curriculum with an emphasis on the literary canon and on standardised language use. This traditional model may well be supported with 'new' arguments about cultural capital and vocabulary enrichment and the importance of these in terms of social mobility, and there may be the accompanying argument that so-called progressive education has benefitted only the middle classes, while the working-class and underprivileged children have been the victims of a self-indulgent left-wing conspiracy. A knowledge curriculum promises to solve the problem of the underachievement of working-class children by offering these children the stock of linguistic and literary knowledge they need to close the attainment gap. Whatever the argument given, however, it is a traditional model of English that emerges in the classroom nonetheless and, in practice, it often seems to take scant notice of the learners themselves – at least not that which they bring to the classroom. It focuses instead on that which they are supposed to lack. Though it's difficult to prove cause and effect, English – in England at least – is far from a popular subject with young people – increasingly so as they move up the years of secondary school.[5] The number of young people choosing to study English beyond the age of 16 in England has declined sharply in recent years (Ofqual, 2022, 2023), as have the numbers of undergraduates pursuing English studies courses in universities (British Academy, 2023). Whilst we might suggest that the decline in students studying English in the post-compulsory phase is a result of the global socio-economic context, where STEM[6] subjects are seen as having priority given their perceived value to the national economy and the potential rewards available to those who work in the related fields, and whilst we might accept that popularity of English should not necessarily be the aim for teachers of the subject, it ought at least to demand a pause to consider why this dwindling popularity and seeming perceived irrelevance of the subject is the case, and what impact that might be having on how young people experience the subject in school. Why are students seemingly not engaged with a subject that really ought to be offering pleasure and relevance as natural constituents of its content and teaching?

Rosen helped to lay the foundations of an English rooted in, and building from, learners' own language, experience, interests and concerns. It is a model of the subject that might, at the very best, be seen as endangered, and at worst, extinct. However, there is much in that model, and much in Rosen's work, that ought, I believe, to be rediscovered and re-evaluated to inform future development. Brian Simon remarked that the study of educational history allows us to see that 'things have not always been as they are and need not remain so' (Simon, 1991, p. 92). A book such as this that resurfaces and reviews Rosen's professional life's work of making English work for young people is intended to show, or remind, English teachers that things have been different and, unarguably in my view, should be in the future. With no false modesty or deference intended, I shall judge the success of this book not on any positive reviews or sales figures (though these would, of course, be welcome); I shall consider this book to have achieved its aim if it leads English teachers back to the work of Harold Rosen.

Harold Rosen: Some Selected Personal and Professional Biography

Given the importance that Rosen placed on the role of autobiography, it would be perverse not to at least sketch out some key aspects of his personal and professional background. This is not simply to acknowledge the importance of autobiography, but rather it is to allow for enhanced understanding of the influences and driving forces which shaped Rosen's professional endeavours. What is clear to anyone familiar with Rosen and his work is the deeply felt passion which inspired his beliefs on what education, and an education in English, should be and should do for young people. Rosen's upbringing – his family and community life and schooling – was critical in laying the foundations of his educational philosophy and thinking and continued to inspire him for over 60 years working in the field. As he wrote himself:

> Everything I've worked for in education I can trace back to its beginnings in my family and its fierce radicalism and dogged hope which themselves grew out of an East End humming with politics.
>
> (Rosen, 1993, p. 92)

John Richmond's introduction to the collection of Rosen's writing offers a very helpful overview of Rosen's early years (Richmond, 2017), and it is worth highlighting some of the key information which appears there in somewhat greater depth. Born in Brockton, Massachusetts – a fact that significantly affected his involvement in the Second World War – Rosen came with his mother, Rose, to the East End of London at two years of age. According to John Richmond, his upbringing in America had been one of 'extreme poverty' and similarly in London, the family, though they were 'not destitute by any means',[7] were financially poor. This was a distinctly working-class background, one that would set Rosen apart from many of those with whom he ultimately collaborated in his professional work and which therefore contributes to the distinctness of his influence on the development of progressive English.

Though he grew up in challenging financial conditions, other dimensions to his upbringing were rich. Rosen grew up in a highly political family environment; he himself recalled in an interview, 'My mother was on the committee of Stepney's CP (Communist Party). Before the First World War my grandfather had been a member of the Social Democratic Federation, which was about as left as you could get then' (Socialist Worker, 2008). Growing up in a communist and secular home within the context of an extended Jewish family and community in the deprivation of the East End worked to form Rosen's own beliefs, which were, for Richmond, 'to defeat fascism and to liberate working-class people from every sort of poverty' (Richmond, 2017, p. 1). It was also, significantly, a highly literate household in which he was raised, as Rosen recalled, 'But books just flowed in and out of the house' (Hardcastle and Medway, 2009, p. 7). Rosen's lifelong passion for the empowerment through education of the working class and his deep-rooted beliefs in the potentially enabling power of literacy fuelled his lifelong professional endeavours. Also highly significant was the linguistic context in which Rosen was raised. Harold's son Michael, the highly celebrated children's author, reflected that his father was

> from a bilingual, trilingual environment. At home people are speaking Yiddish – Eastern European vernacular language, spoken much more than it ever got written down. He's surrounded by people speaking Polish and Russian and on occasion German and Czech and some other languages.[8]

This rich linguistic context meant that Rosen had ample personal experience of the breadth and depth of language use in what others may have seen as an impoverished existence. This undoubtedly informed his work, making it natural for him to challenge prejudices about the experience of the working class and helping him to formulate ideas about the ways in which linguistic diversity should be recognised and harnessed as a resource for the classroom and how such diversity should provide fertile ground for the teacher of English.

Rosen himself became politically active at a young age. He joined the Young Communist League at the age of 15, and a year later, in 1936, took part in The Battle of Cable Street, what Rosen later called a 'red letter day in the left-wing almanac' (Rosen, 1998, p. 28), when Oswald Moseley and his fascist followers were prevented from marching through the East End's streets. There's no doubt this was a formative and enduring event for Rosen; it was one he returned to in his later writing, but he did not simply write about it to reflect on its significance as a major political event for the left in Britain; it also became an event he could recall to explore the importance and nature of personal and collective memory. It was through the Young Communist League that Harold met his first wife, Connie Isakofsky, beginning a personal and professional relationship that would span over 40 years until Connie's untimely death in 1976.

Following secondary schooling at the Davenant Foundation School, a state-run grammar school, and studying in the sixth form at Quintin School, Rosen read English at University College London (UCL). Though he claimed to enjoy the experience of being a university student, the study of English at UCL was 'a bitter disappointment' (Hardcastle and Medway, 2009, p. 7), due to the 'medieval' teaching methods – apparently the ideas of the highly influential Cambridge English academic F.R. Leavis had thus far failed to infiltrate the literature course at UCL so that Rosen 'came away with no awareness of all the innovations beginning to occur' (Hardcastle and Medway, 2009, p. 7). He then undertook teacher training at the London Institute of Education (IoE), where Perceval Gurrey and Maura Brooke Gwynne, founding members of the LATE, were lecturers in methods of teaching English. Though attending the IoE, Rosen actually did his final teaching placement on the course in Nottingham, due to the evacuation of the Institute from London in the war years. Gwynne was Rosen's tutor, and he recollects her being connected to the New Education Fellowship, an organisation founded in 1921 that critically promoted a progressive, child-centred approach to education, publishing a journal amongst its activities. This was without question an influence on Rosen's development as an English teacher in the earliest years of his training; well after retirement, Rosen recalled how Gwynne had made her students look at past copies of the New Education journal and that through this the notion of progressive education was promoted. According to Rosen's recollection, this was rooted in work in a number of private schools, causing him to remark in characteristic fashion, 'Very thoughtful people, but a bit up there, and they needed to be brought down'.[9]

Rosen's Teaching Career

After completing the teacher training course at the IoE, Rosen began his career in education. It is not entirely straightforward to give a completely accurate account of Harold Rosen's teaching career, as there are some anomalies in the historical evidence available – apparent contradictions exist, for example, between extracts from interviews with Rosen and other available documents. However, if we take his own CV, provided in support of an application for the post of Chair in Education at Bristol University (Rosen, 1970), as possibly the most reliable record of his employment, Rosen began his teaching career at The Gateway School, Leicester, in 1941, where he worked as an assistant master for around 18 months. It's likely that securing a position in Leicester, rather than London, was a direct result of the evacuation of the IoE. According to Rosen, The Gateway School was 'meant to be somewhat experimental. It wasn't in fact'.[10] A reference from the school's headteacher (White, 1943) noted that 'although he came direct from the London Institute of Education, he settled down very quickly and easily to do his work'. In this reference, Rosen's 'gift of exposition' was mentioned, as was his extracurricular contribution, including that Rosen had 'created a lively interest in the Drama' (White, 1943).

From The Gateway, Rosen moved to London to take up a post at Harrow Weald Grammar School – described as a 'progressive' school (Lofty, 2009, p. 31). Although he only worked there until 1945, this was a highly significant move in terms of the connections Rosen would make. Both James Britton and Nancy Martin worked, or had worked, at the school. Though some accounts (Lofty, 2009, p. 31) state that it was here that the career-long relationship between the three began, it is not actually the case that Rosen and Britton taught together, since the latter had moved into a job with the publishers, John Murray, several years earlier, in 1938, and was serving in the Royal Air Force at the time Rosen took up his post at the school. However, as Rosen said, he

> heard a lot about Jimmy (James Britton), and he had started the department, single handed, to begin with, because they built up from a one year intake. And I heard a lot about him, and met him when he came home on leave, and we hit it off.[11]

Rosen certainly worked with Nancy Martin at the school; however, and indeed it was Martin who interviewed Rosen for the post of English master, in what appears to have been a somewhat unconventional way:

> my most vivid recollection of Nancy was that when I went for the interview there was a kind of talk in a room interview, but then Nancy said – let's go for a walk. And we walked round and round the school field, a very nice spot, Harrow Weald was then, and I can remember, she was wearing red corduroy trousers.[12]

This recollection speaks perhaps to the somewhat unusual nature of the school, as Martin herself recalled, 'The whole atmosphere of Harrow Weald was just another world where I had come from. It was not stuffy. I'd say it was very populist' (Lofty, 2009, p. 31).

The relationship that began between Rosen, Martin and Britton at Harrow Weald School was to last for the rest of their personal and professional lives, and their collaboration was instrumental in the development of the new progressive English that emerged in London from the late 1940s.

Rosen clearly made a great impression on Martin, even if she left the school just a year after his arrival in 1944. In a reference, presumably, given the date, written for Rosen's application for the Head of English post at Walworth School, Martin refers to Rosen's time at Harrow Weald, revealing him to be a 'gifted teacher' and a man of 'strong and challenging personality' (Martin, 1954, p. 1). Tellingly, Martin also referred to his 'unfailing ability to take the individual pupil into account', and with reference to his work as a mentor for her PGCE students, she claimed to know of 'no other teacher of English who has given such skilful, sympathetic and intelligent assistance to the students in his care' (Martin, 1954, p. 1). References are, of course, by their nature generally complimentary, but there's no doubt that Martin held Rosen in high regard. The reference written by the Harrow Weald headteacher was similarly effusive in its praise, noting that Rosen's 'energy, his vitality and his genuine interest in his pupils made his subject a living one to the boys and girls whom he taught' (Barlow Butlin, 1947). Implicit in these references is the sense that the English Rosen was teaching was very much what we might call a child-centred version of the subject with the learner taking centre stage and that Rosen's concern was, first and foremost, for the child.

As a citizen of the United States, Rosen was called up to the military as the conclusion of the Second World War approached, and his teaching career was thus interrupted. During his time in the US Army, between 1945 and 1947, Rosen worked briefly at the short-lived Shrivenham American University,[13] served in the infantry and had posts as an Information and Education officer both in England and Berlin. On leaving the army, Rosen took up his first post-war teaching post at Greenford County Grammar School, where he worked, according to his CV (Rosen, 1970), until 1952 (although this date is somewhat contested since a Greenford School photograph purportedly taken in 1953 features Harold, and Douglas Barnes (Barnes, 2009) recalls meeting Rosen for the first time at a job interview in that year while he was still at the school).

Rosen clearly again impressed during his time at Greenford, though apparently his chances of internal promotion were negatively impacted by his political beliefs.[14] A reference written by the head for Rosen – presumably in support of his application to Kingsbury County Grammar School – commented on his 'abundance of energy' (James, 1952). This reference also noted that Rosen was one of 'the prime movers in the London Association for the Teaching of English' (James, 1952). LATE was formed in 1947, and, as the historical account of the Association details (Gibbons, 2014), Rosen was a founder member and instrumental to much of its pioneering work through the late 1940s, 1950s and 1960s. Rosen's work with colleagues in LATE was critical to the development of the new, progressive model of English that developed in London in the post-war decades. Chapter 2 of this text, in considering Rosen's contribution to the development of the new English, will explore the significance of his work within LATE as a key component of his endeavours.

Rosen spent two years at Kingsbury County Grammar School and then made what was almost certainly the most important move of his career in school teaching, to Walworth School in south London. Up to this point Rosen had taught in grammar schools, but Walworth School was one of the first experimental comprehensive schools set up in London in 1946, and thus this was Rosen's first experience of teaching in a non-selective school in the wake of the 1944 Education Act that had, in effect, made secondary schooling an entitlement for all children up to the age of 15. This context, as will be explored in the following chapter, was critical in enabling Rosen to develop, and, crucially, put into practice, his emerging thinking on what the subject of English should look like for children – what should curriculum and pedagogy look like in reality for all ability classrooms? Rosen was a passionate advocate of comprehensive education throughout his life; Walworth offered the context to experience the ideal in reality. Hugely significant, too, were the colleagues with whom Rosen worked at Walworth. The headteacher and former head of English was Guy Rogers, who himself was a significant figure in the early years of LATE, acting as secretary for the Association. According to Rosen, in terms of securing the post at Walworth, Rogers 'plucked me out', not that there wasn't some difficulty associated with taking the post, as apparently Rosen had previous dealings with an inspector of the Inner London Education Authority (ILEA).

> I had crossed swords with her on a number of occasions, and she didn't want me. I can't remember her name now. And she tried to get me on technical grounds, that I wasn't a British citizen, which she discovered, and also that I was a commie, which were two very good grounds.[15]

Rosen's politics were understandably problematic given the time; as Richmond noted, Rosen's 'career was impeded by the blacklisting of communists then practised in some circles' (Richmond, 2017, p. 1). Faced with the resistance of the inspector, Rosen argued that his schooling and teaching experience were entirely based in England, and he successfully secured his post of head of English at Walworth in 1954. Whilst there, Rosen worked with other hugely significant figures in the development of the new progressive English – John Dixon, who took over as Head of English when Rosen departed, was perhaps most notable among them, but other colleagues, who joined as Rosen left but inherited the work he had begun, such as Simon Clements and Leslie Stratta, equally have a unique place in the history of English's growth as a subject. At Walworth, he also first met the woman who would ultimately be his second wife, Betty, and her recollection of seeing Harold teach as a PGCE student in the school is striking personal testimony to Rosen's skill as a practitioner:

> It was the most important event of my professional life. The articulate telling of tales he elicited out of those wild working-class cockney kids made me feel I had had a deprived childhood. My naïve notion of English teaching was turned on its head.
>
> (Rosen, 2009, p. 26)

Though he spent only three years at Walworth, the significance of this time in the subsequent development of the new English was profound, as those he left at Walworth continued his legacy, armed with the innovative syllabus he wrote before his departure.

In 1957 or 1958 (there is a discrepancy in dates between Rosen's CV and a reference contained in the archive at the London IoE), Rosen moved from teaching to teacher education, taking up a post at Borough Road College, which was the first teacher training institution to be founded in the United Kingdom (White, 1958). Rogers' reference for Rosen noted his 'fearless and enthusiastic way' in meeting the challenges of teaching at Walworth and his 'faith in the innate abilities of the children' (Rogers, 1958, p. 1) and concluded that despite not wanting to see Rosen leave the school:

> I should be very selfish to try to keep him in the face of an opportunity for him to obtain a training post, where the fruits of his experience and his great gifts as a teacher would benefit not one school, but many.
>
> (Rogers, 1958, p. 3)

After four years at Borough Road College, Rosen made the final move of his professional career to the London IoE in 1962. In the English department here, he would unite with James Britton and Nancy Martin. The work of Rosen, Martin and Britton would ensure that the IoE secured both national and international recognition as a centre for the professional education and development of English teachers. The research that Rosen and his colleagues undertook at the IoE helped to shape the future of the subject across the English-speaking world. The work and writing that Rosen did in his time in higher education institutions were always directly related to contributing to the work of classroom English teachers; though he did write extensively and publish, he did not opt to pursue a personal research agenda that would, perhaps, have led to more obvious esteem in the academic world. He could have chosen to do this, but as his friend John Richmond observed:

> He was scornful of people who got into teacher education and went off on academic frolics of their own. He was absolutely clear. If you have the privilege of teaching teachers to teach, you must do that. You mustn't go and find safe little corners where you can do academic stuff which doesn't relate in some direct or indirect way to helping teachers, whether student teachers or practising teachers, do their job.[16]

Those who have written of their memories of being taught by Rosen at the IoE portray a vivid picture of committed, inspiring and empowering teacher educator. Peter Medway, who himself went on to become a noted teacher educator and researcher, recalled that on joining the PGCE at the Institute after studying Classics and English at an elite university, 'Nobody in my four years at Oxford made such an impression on me' (Medway, 2009, p. 61) and that 'Harold turned all our preconceptions about English teaching on their heads' (Medway, 2009, p. 62). Another IoE student, John Hardcastle, who would ultimately join the IoE English department himself, remembered that 'Harold engaged with you immediately, wanted to know who you were, what you were up to'.[17] Rosen took the PGCE students beyond the sorts of reading normally associated with a course in initial teacher education, introducing the work of 'Gorki and Makarenko and the autobiographies of Sean O'Casey, Bernard Kops, Clifford Hanley, Arturo Barea' (Medway, 2009, p. 62). Another PGCE student recalled being inspired by Rosen's 'unbridled and opinionated visions' (Hemming, 2009, p. 56), whilst another vividly recalled:

> the way he would sweep into a packed hall to give a lecture to a hundred or so students. You could tell he enjoyed it and loved to be challenged, somehow always taking the wind out of the challenger's sails by saying how glad he was that they had said that. That made him difficult to argue with.
> (Hewitt, 2009, p. 58)

Rosen went on to lead the department at the IoE and became emeritus professor on his retirement in 1984. He continued to work and write through his retirement years, until his death in July 2008.

A Note on Material, Organisation and Structure

In researching the content of this book, there were a number of sources of material. The obvious starting point is the consideration of Rosen's published work. Richmond's edited collection (Richmond, 2017) was of enormous help here, and I would recommend it heartily to anyone wishing to engage directly with Rosen's writing; it is an incredibly thoughtfully constructed combination of Rosen's academic and creative work.

Richmond's collection is selective, however, and further work by Rosen appears in various journals and publications cited in this text. In addition, the Rosen archive at the University College London IoE library is a huge collection of documents; it dates back to Rosen's military service and includes unpublished writing, notes for conference speeches, letters of application, CVs, references and more. Many details and records of Rosen's contribution to the work of LATE can be found in the LATE archive, similarly held in UCL IoE library; I catalogued a substantial amount of this material some years ago as part of the work for my PhD. Finally, I have drawn material from a series of interviews, some conducted as part of previous work on the history of LATE and the development of post-war English more generally, and some conducted specifically in preparation for this text. In total, this constitutes a prodigious amount of material with which to work.

The scope of Rosen's work, across more than 60 years of deep involvement in education, is staggering and this inevitably creates a challenge when trying to encapsulate it neatly within the pages of a text like this. A book which aims to evaluate the significance of Rosen's work and, hopefully, contribute to ensuring that this work retains its rightful place of relevance in the thinking of those teaching English – and indeed other subjects – today and in the future, inevitably must adopt some organising principles in its handling of the material. The chapters that follow seek to do this, with each focusing on a particular dimension of Rosen's thinking and work. Following this introduction, Chapter 2 considers the importance of Rosen to the development of the new model of subject English that evolved primarily in London in the post-war decades, considering both his contribution to the work of the LATE and his time as head of English at Walworth School (and the subsequent impact this had). Chapter 3 examines the scope and importance of Rosen's work on class and culture; issues of class reverberate through most, if not all, of Rosen's work, but this chapter considers particular ways in which this was articulated, including the particular focus on working-class language and then on the language of the increasingly diverse school cultures in London. Chapter 4 focuses on language, both within the subject of English and across the curriculum; Rosen's work here is central to the focus on language across the curriculum, which properly began to draw appropriate attention in the late 1960s and into the 1970s. Chapter 5 examines Rosen's work on the importance of story, predominantly narrative and autobiography, which can be seen to be major preoccupations later in his career, although, again, Rosen's interest in hearing pupils recount their own experiences in narrative was core to his work right from the start of his teaching career, as was his commitment to the importance of literature in English. Chapter 6 considers Rosen as an activist and advocate of teacher agency and autonomy; Rosen was very upfront about his own political beliefs, and these were fundamental to his own identity, but the more general push for teachers to have agency transcends political inclinations. The final chapter attempts to draw conclusions to underline precisely why Rosen's preeminent place as a key thinker in the sphere of English education and the language arts is unquestionable and makes the argument that his work and ideas are as important now, if not more important, than they ever were.

It should be acknowledged that these are, of course, my views – others may evaluate Rosen's work differently. In preparing this text, the views of some of Rosen's family and former colleagues have been sought, and it would be misleading to suggest there is uncontested consensus on all matters relating to the relative importance of different strands of his work. There was, however, consensus on the overarching principle that Rosen's contribution to the field of English in education is one that should be neither neglected nor forgotten.

There is some sense of the chronology of Rosen's work adopted in the organisational approach taken here, but this can only be helpful up to a certain point, and there would certainly be alternative ways to structure the text. The major concerns of Rosen's work as an English educator spanned his professional life, so whilst it may be true that in his later years his focus was primarily on the importance of story, Rosen organised a LATE conference on 'Narrative in and out of school' in 1950 (LATE, 1950). That focus on the significance of narrative for pupils and teachers was not absent at the beginning of Rosen's career. Equally, Rosen's interest in class, borne out of his own childhood and upbringing, was a lifelong one, though expressed in different terms in different times – for example, the common use of the phrase 'ordinary children' in the 1950s, which was seemingly functioning as a proxy term for the working class. Organisation into chapters might in one way suggest discrete areas of work – and one could reasonably suggest that a claim could be made to class Rosen as a key thinker in English education purely for his work on either curriculum, or language, or story, etc. However, pinning the different threads of his work together points to the larger tapestry created by Rosen's work, which is an overarching vision of a radical, political, progressive, humane model of English that maintains as its focal point the learners themselves: their experience, their language, their hopes, their concerns and their potential futures.

Notes

1 The government ordered a review of the original National Curriculum for English in 1992, within three years of its introduction. The architect of the original National Curriculum, Professor Brian Cox, saw this as a politically motivated move by Conservatives who wanted a greater emphasis on grammar and Standard English in the Orders, something they felt Cox had failed to deliver in his relatively progressive view of English (Cox, 1995).
2 In 1993, the then Secretary of State for Education asked Sir Ron Dearing to lead a review of the National Curriculum. Ostensibly this was intended to 'slim down' the curriculum, but the revision of the Statutory Orders for English that followed offered a reductive version of the subject in the view of many in the profession.
3 Jane Miller had been a PGCE student at the University of London Institute of Education when Rosen taught on the course. She later went on to work in the English department at the Institute alongside Rosen.
4 John Richmond was a great friend of Harold Rosen, their friendship starting when Rosen came to see the work Richmond was doing as a young teacher of English in Vauxhall Manor Girls School in London in the early 1970s. Interviews with John Richmond conducted for this book and for a previous publication (Gibbons, 2017) are quoted throughout the text.
5 See, for example, the YouGov Children's Omnibus Poll (2018) available at https://d3nkl3psvxxpe9.cloudfront.net/documents/YouGov_Childrens_Omnibus_-_subject_enjoyment.pdf accessed on 30/01/2025
6 STEM is the acronym standing for science, technology, engineering and mathematics and is used in many English-speaking educational jurisdictions when describing this group of related subjects.
7 Comment taken from an interview with the author.
8 The author had a series of conversations with Michael Rosen, facilitated by Frances Gilbert from Goldsmiths, University of London. In the interview quoted here – available on YouTube at https://www.youtube.com/watch?v=nZLMVd1LLQ8 – Michael reflected on his father's upbringing and its influence on his life working in education.

9 Comment taken from an interview with Harold Rosen conducted by John Hardcastle and Peter Medway as part of research for Medway, P., Hardcastle, J., Brewis, G. and Crook, D. (2014) *English Teachers in a Postwar Democracy: Emerging Choice in London Schools, 1945–65*. New York: Palgrave Macmillan.
10 Comment taken from an interview with Harold Rosen conducted by John Hardcastle and Peter Medway as part of research for Medway, P., Hardcastle, J., Brewis, G. and Crook, D. (2014) *English Teachers in a Postwar Democracy: Emerging Choice in London Schools, 1945–65*. New York: Palgrave Macmillan.
11 Comment taken from an interview with Harold Rosen conducted by John Hardcastle and Peter Medway as part of research for Medway, P., Hardcastle, J., Brewis, G. and Crook, D. (2014) *English Teachers in a Postwar Democracy: Emerging Choice in London Schools, 1945–65*. New York: Palgrave Macmillan.
12 Comment taken from an interview with Harold Rosen conducted by John Hardcastle and Peter Medway as part of research for Medway, P., Hardcastle, J., Brewis, G. and Crook, D. (2014) *English Teachers in a Postwar Democracy: Emerging Choice in London Schools, 1945–65*. New York: Palgrave Macmillan.
13 Set up as an establishment to educate American forces in August 1945, the Shrivenham American University only in fact existed until December of the first year due to the abrupt ending of the war in the Pacific (see https://www.shrivenhamheritagesociety.co.uk/listing.asp?listID=1005, accessed on 25th April 2025).
14 In email exchanges with the author, Harold's sons Brian and Michael both recollected that Harold has been 'blacklisted' from applying for the post as Head of English at Greenford due to his Communist Party links, and it was this that precipitated his departure to Kingsbury.
15 Comment taken from an interview with Harold Rosen conducted by John Hardcastle and Peter Medway as part of research for Medway, P., Hardcastle, J., Brewis, G. and Crook, D. (2014) *English Teachers in a Postwar Democracy: Emerging Choice in London Schools, 1945–65*. New York: Palgrave Macmillan.
16 Comment taken from an interview between the author and John Richmond. Richmond had a career that included English teaching and advisory work and work in the media; he was commissioning editor for Channel 4 schools programming before being a senior executive of Teachers TV from 2004 to 2010. Richmond first met Harold Rosen when he was a teacher at Vauxhall Manor School in South London. There, he led the school's Talk Workshop, a collaborative teacher action research group that produced work published as Becoming Our Own Experts (Eyers and Richmond, 1982).
17 Comment taken from an interview between the author and John Hardcastle. Hardcastle had been a student at the IoE before teaching in London schools. He ultimately worked in the English department at the IoE. Along with Peter Medway, he conducted a number of interviews with Rosen for a research project that led to the publication of *English Teachers in a Postwar Democracy: Emerging Choice in London Schools, 1945–65* (Medway et al., 2014).

References

Barlow Butlin, E. (1947) *Reference for Harold Rosen*, held in the Harold Rosen Archive at the University College London Institute of Education library.
Barnes, D. (2009) 'Learning from Harold'. *Changing English*, 16:1, pp. 355–356.
Barnes, D., Britton, J. and Rosen, H. (1969) *Language, the Learner and the School*. Harmondsworth: Penguin.
British Academy (2023) *English Studies Provision in UK Higher Education*, available at English-studies-provision-UK-higher-education-British-Academy-report.pdf (the britishacademy.ac.uk) accessed on 10th January 2025.

Cox, B. (1995) *Cox on the Battle for the English Curriculum*. London: Hodder and Stoughton.

Eyers, S. and Richmond, J. (1982) *Becoming Our Own Experts; Studies in Language and Learning made by the Talk Workshop Group at Vauxhall Manor School 1974–1979*. Trowbridge: Talk Workshop group, also now available online at https://www.becomingourownexperts.org/ accessed on 24th July 2025

Gibbons, S. (2014) *The London Association for the Teaching of English 1947–67: A History*. London: Institute of Education Press.

Gibbons, S. (2017) *English and its Teachers: A History of Policy, Pedagogy and Practice*. Oxford: Routledge.

Goodwyn, A. (2016) 'Still Growing After All These Years? The Resilience of the Personal Growth Model of English in England and Also Internationally'. *English Teaching Practice and Critique*, 15:1, pp. 7–21.

Hardcastle, J. and Medway, P. (2009) 'In his Own Words: Harold Rosen on his Formative Years, with Speculations on Working-Class Language'. *Changing English*, 16:1, pp. 5–14.

Hemming, J. (2009) 'Old Students Remember'. *Changing English*, 16:1, pp. 55–62.

Hewitt, M. (2009) 'Old Students Remember'. *Changing English*, 16:1, pp. 55–62.

James, L. (1952) *Reference for Harold Rosen*, held in the Harold Rosen Archive at the University College London Institute of Education library.

LATE (1950) *Narrative in and out of School*, LATE Conference programme, held in the LATE archive at the University College London Institute of Education library.

LATE (1994) *Prospect and Retrospect*, LATE Summer Weekend Residential Conference Programme, held in the LATE archive at the University College London Institute of Education Library.

Lofty, J. (2009) '"There is One Story Worth Telling": An Essay for James Britton and Nancy Martin'. *English in Education*, 42:1 pp. 29–60.

Martin, N. (1954) *Reference for Harold Rosen*, held in the Harold Rosen Archive at the University College London Institute of Education library.

Martin, N. (1994) '*Once upon a Time . . . How LATE began*' Unpublished text of speech to LATE Conference, Corsica Hall, Seaford, 8th July 1994, held in the LATE archive at the University College London Institute of Education library.

Medway, P. (2009) 'Old Students Remember'. *Changing English*, 16:1, pp. 55–62.

Miller, J. (2009) 'Editorial'. *Changing English*, 16:1, pp. 1–3.

Ofqual (2022) *Provisional Entries for GCSE, AS and A Level: Summer 2022 Exam Series – GOV.UK* (www.gov.uk) accessed on 10th January 2025.

Ofqual (2023) *Provisional Entries for GCSE, AS and A Level: Summer 2023 Exam Series – GOV.UK* (www.gov.uk) accessed on 10th January 2025.

Pradl, G. (ed.) (1982) *Prospect and Retrospect: Selected Essays of James Britton*. Montclair New Jersey Boynton/Cook Publishers.

Richmond (ed.) (2017) *Harold Rosen: Writings on Life, Language and Learning 1958–2008*. London: UCL Institute of Education Press.

Rogers, G. (1958) *Reference for Harold Rosen*, held in the Harold Rosen Archive at the University College London Institute of Education library.

Rosen, B. (2009) 'Breakfast, Sometime in the Nineties, and More of his Wife's Tale'. *Changing English*, 16:1, pp. 25–28.

Rosen, H. (1970) *Application to the Post of Chair of Education*, University of Bristol, held part of the Rosen Archive held in University College London Institute of Education Library.

Rosen, H. (1993) *Troublesome Boy: Stories and Articles by Harold Rosen*. London: English and Media Centre.

Rosen, H. (1998) 'A Necessary Myth: Cable Street Revisited'. *Changing English*, 5:1, pp. 27–34.

Simon, B. (1991) *Education and the Social Order*. London: Lawrence and Wishart.
Smagorinsky, P. (2024) *L.S. Vygotsky and English in Education and the Language Arts*. Oxford: Routledge.
Socialist Worker (2008) *Harold Rosen: A Rebel from the East End*, available at https://socialistworker.co.uk/obituaries/harold-rosen-a-rebel-from-the-east-end/ accessed on 28th January 2025.
White, E. (1958) *An Outline History of Borough Road College 1809–1958*, available at Hamilton-An-Outline-History-of-BRC-1809–1958.pdf accessed on 25th October 2024.
White, E. C. (1943) *Reference for Harold Rosen*, held in the Harold Rosen Archive at the University College London Institute of Education Library.

Chapter 2

Harold Rosen and the Rise of the New English

Introduction

It is worth recalling the context, or contexts, in which Harold Rosen returned to civilian life and took up what would be his life's work in the years following the Second World War. The contexts – historical, geographical, political and educational – are critical to understanding why the development of a new model of English was nothing short of a necessity. The contexts demanded a different vision of the subject, but whilst this necessity might be said to have been a product of the time and the policy context surrounding education, there still needed to be English teachers ready to recognise this and able to begin the work of constructing this new model. Among these teachers, Rosen was absolutely at the forefront, working in school and with colleagues from across the capital in the newly formed London Association for the Teaching of English (LATE) to forge a radically different vision of English.

The Need for a New English

In part, policy created the need for a new model of English, in the secondary school in particular. The Education Act of 1944 – often known as the Butler Act in acknowledgement of its architect, the then education minister, Rab Butler – made statutory secondary education for all young people up to the age of 15 (Board of Education, 1944). This was perhaps the most significant single shift in educational policy in England in the twentieth century. The 1944 Act followed the earlier Norwood Report (Board of Education, 1943) and Spens Report (Board of Education, 1938), which had recommended that students in the secondary phase of education[1] should attend one of three types of school – grammar (for the academic children), technical (for pupils focusing on mechanical and scientific subjects) or modern (for the majority of pupils). Significantly, however, the 1944 Act did not mandate that all such schools had to be available in any given part of the country – it in effect set up the architecture of local education authorities and left it to these bodies to submit a plan as to how to best organise secondary education in their areas. In the event, probably as a result of financial considerations, relatively few technical schools were opened, with most local authorities opting for a system of grammar and secondary modern schools, a two-tier system where perhaps 15–20% of those judged to be most academically able by the 11+ exam would be educated separately from the majority of young people in the grammar schools.[2]

In very simple terms, it seems obvious that one impact of the implementation of secondary schooling for all would be the need to think again about both curriculum and assessment. The traditional grammar school curriculum had hitherto been providing for perhaps 15–20% of the now secondary school-age population, and something was needed for the new pupils finding themselves in education until the age of 15, whichever kind of school they might happen to be attending.

With respect to the subject of English, Burgess (1988) noted that 'a changed map of English as a subject . . . was the immediate task' (p. 158) in the light of the educational change following the Butler Act. Within the work of those who have written about the development of subject English in schools (see, for example, among others, Shayer, 1972; Mathieson, 1975; Ball, 1987; Sawyer, 2004) there is at least some shared consensus that the pre-Butler Act grammar school version of the subject was one that had literature as its foundation and was hugely influenced in the pre-Second World War years by the work of Cambridge scholar F.R. Leavis and his followers, including those he taught as undergraduates who went on to become teachers of the subject in schools. In the literature on the subject, this model of the discipline is often referred to as the 'Cambridge School' of English teaching or 'English as Literature', and it is often starkly contrasted with the model of the subject that began to emerge in the post-war years that had at its core the language and experience of the pupil. This contrasting model is variously called 'London English', 'English as Language' or 'personal growth' English and has been characterised as a progressive model of the subject as opposed to the traditional Cambridge model. Such generalisations are in fact only helpful up to a point, and there is much that goes unappreciated about the development of school English and those who have been critical to it in the construction of a history composed of two sharply opposing paradigms. One only needs to consider the case of Douglas Barnes[3], who was a student of Leavis at Cambridge but who, along with Rosen, was critical to the development of the new English, to see that the neat construction of opposing schools of thought very quickly fails to hold. Even to suggest there is some agreed definition of either 'Cambridge' or 'London' English would be erroneous and create a simplicity that does not stand up in the face of the available evidence. What is generally beyond argument, however, is that, whatever the intricacies of its genesis, a new English did begin to emerge in the post-war years, and it was in London that this new English began to ferment, and it was this progressive model of the subject that Rosen did so much to forge that went on to have enormous reach across English speaking jurisdictions across the globe, particularly in the United States, Canada, Australia and New Zealand.

It was in London, where Rosen worked, that the very obvious need for a new English was most apparent, as a result of the landmark decisions taken by the London County Council (LCC) in response to the Butler Act. The LCC eschewed the recommended tripartite school system model and instead included in its plan for schools the aspiration for:

> a system of Comprehensive High Schools throughout the Administrative County of London, providing for all pupils equal opportunity for physical, intellectual, social and spiritual development, which, whilst taking advantage of the practical interests of the pupils, should make the full development of personality the first objective.
> (London County Council, 1947, p. 230)

Although the Butler Act made such an ambition acceptable, it has been observed (by, for example, McCulloch, 2002) that London was one of the few local authorities that took such an approach. More than that, as Rubinstein and Simon (1973) noted, whilst there were a few other areas that moved towards comprehensivisation, it was only London that framed this as part of a wider project for social unity. For Simon (1991), London's response to the Butler Act was exceptional, and Jones (2003) suggests that London was perhaps 'the most innovative of local authorities' (Jones, 2003, p. 24). Certainly, to place 'the full development of personality' as the 'first objective' of the education system is striking; it is a view of the purpose of education as something far more than academic attainment or equipping students with the skills they need to become economically active. London was emerging from the carnage of the Second World War, having suffered the brutality of the Blitz; to accompany the physical rebuilding of the capital, there was to be a reshaping of society built on an education offering equality of opportunity for all. To divide young people at the age of 11 would be counterproductive in an effort to forge a just and equal society.

Such a radical plan as that articulated by the LCC would obviously take time to implement, and as Maclure (1970) observed in his historical account of schooling in London, the 25-year period after Butler was a continuous period of trying to enact these big ideas. Indeed, it should be noted that even now, over two decades into the twenty-first century, there are still a significant number of grammar schools spread across various London boroughs. However, following the publication of the London Plan, there were almost immediately eight experimental comprehensives founded, and one of these was Walworth School, where Rosen would become head of English in 1954. An interim or experimental comprehensive from 1946, Walworth still had grammar schools in its environs, but its intake was diverse, and with its mixed pupil cohort, it was exactly the environment that needed an alternative to traditional

Cambridge English. In fact, by the time Rosen joined Walworth in 1954, he had already spent almost a decade laying the foundations to construct this new model in, to an extent at least, a comprehensive environment.

In the immediate post-war years, Rosen was deeply involved in the initial shaping of the new English that would be required for the schools in London – and indeed throughout the country, where tens of thousands of pupils would be experiencing secondary English for the first time. The need to develop something new for these pupils, and the motivation for London English teachers to find this, were instrumental in creating the conditions for the formation of the LATE in 1947. The significance of this organisation in providing a mechanism for London's English teachers to collaborate in responding to the new conditions created by the Butler Act and the London School Plan is well documented (Gibbons, 2014), and Rosen's involvement in LATE from its very beginning highlights the critical and particular nature of his contribution to the evolution of the new progressive English. A consideration of some of Rosen's particular activity within LATE in its first decades informs an understanding of his significance to the development of a model of the subject that would become globally important within a few short decades.

Rosen and the Early Work of LATE in Developing the New English

When LATE was founded in 1947, the records show that Rosen, along with his lifelong collaborators James Britton and Nancy Martin, was a founding member. Interestingly, the first LATE membership list indicates that Rosen was working at Kilburn Grammar School, an establishment that curiously is absent from his own CV (Rosen, 1970) (this may be an error in the LATE record or perhaps it was a short-term post where Rosen worked before taking up his appointment at Greenford County Grammar School; the first LATE meeting was on 1st July 1947, and Rosen took up post at Greenford in September of that year). Also, founding members were Percival Gurrey and Maura Gwynne Brook, Rosen's PGCE tutor, from the Institute of Education (though Gurrey very soon departed the United Kingdom to take up an academic post in Africa; Hardcastle (2014) offers an interesting perspective on Gurrey's particular significance in the development of the new English, which is often forgotten). The extensive LATE archives[4] show, however, that Rosen was not simply a member of the new organisation, he was a driving force, soon becoming organising secretary for the numerous conferences the Association convened each year, contributing actively to such conferences and LATE meetings, and leading on the writing of influential early publications that emanated from the Association. Gibbons (2009) offers an overview of how central Rosen was to the work of LATE in its early years.

The historical account of the work of LATE in its first 20 years (Gibbons, 2014) shows how the Association worked on all areas of English pedagogy, curriculum and assessment. The Association did this through meetings, conferences, classroom-based research and publications, always taking the concerns of English teachers as the starting point in the drive to develop a model of the subject that would work in the interests of all children. The story is a remarkable one of teachers with agency, collaborating proactively with one another to face the challenges that came from their own teaching in their own classrooms. The vast majority of these teachers had been, indeed many still were, grammar school teachers, and they were increasingly facing very different cohorts of children in their classrooms. Many had been rapidly trained in the post-war years; many would not have been what we now consider specialists in terms of their own qualifications in English. They were teachers brought together by a shared need for professional development. It's important to state that LATE did not seek to devise a policy or philosophy for the subject that it then invited members to adopt; it was a genuinely bottom-up organisation, with members in study groups carrying out small-scale projects, with resulting ideas and insights shared in meetings and conferences; from this collaborative enterprise, a new model of the subject emerged. Thus, the new English was not formed by putting a set of theoretical ideas into practice; it took shape from the practical activities of teachers seeking new and different ways to respond to the needs of learners. The practical work of teachers in study groups would be informed by the input of leading thinkers at LATE conferences; discussions in those study groups would then inform ongoing work in classrooms. The evidence suggests that there was a genuine dialogue between research and practice – neither one leading the other – resulting in fundamental changes in the way English was experienced by young people.

During its first decade, a number of key LATE activities show how the new English was evolving through the Association's work, and Rosen was evidently a driving force in the developments. The minutes of the 1953 LATE annual general meeting, for example, noted that the Association's organising committee met 24 times 'under the chairmanship of Harold Rosen' (LATE, 1953). Simply a line in a record of a meeting, it is perhaps worth pausing for a moment to reflect on this and consider the commitment and endeavour it reveals; if we think of an academic year to be around 40 weeks, this means that the organising committee was meeting more frequently than fortnightly for what were meetings above and beyond its members' everyday working commitments (and for Rosen this would have been in addition to other political group meetings he would no doubt have been attending). It may well be we are considering a context where the notion of directed time for teachers (school and departmental meetings, and the like) was not part of their contractual obligations, and so they may have had somewhat more capacity for this work than a teacher today, but it is still nonetheless remarkable for that. The frequency of the meetings and the scope of work that was undertaken point without question to the urgency these teachers felt to develop practice that would genuinely meet the needs of learners in the classroom.

The range of conferences for which Rosen was organising secretary in LATE's first years included *English and Examinations* (1951); *English – Two Subjects or One?* (1952); *Spoken English* (1953); *Books in the Life of the Teacher and the Pupil* (1954); *The Literature Question* (1955); *English and the Urban Child* (1958); *Television: A Weekend's Viewing and Discussion* (1960); *Learning by Discussion* (1961) and *Changing Concepts of the Curriculum: The School, Society and the English Teacher* (1962). The list speaks to the importance of Rosen's work in LATE and to his energy and endeavour – anyone who has organised a conference as an extra-curricular project to a full-time day job will recognise the amount of work involved. Organising venues, producing and mailing out programmes (in the days before websites and emails), arranging speakers, and all the other associated duties that conference convening implies may be somewhat mundane tasks, but they take time, huge effort and significant commitment, and they are the tasks that keep an intellectual agenda going. LATE was a collaborative organisation, and the workload was no doubt shared, but the frequency with which Rosen's name appears on meetings and conference programmes leaves one in no doubt that his energy was critical to this collaborative endeavour.

The list of those conferences – which is only a selection of the range of work undertaken by LATE – also illustrates the scope of activity that was going on as the new English was being forged. All aspects of English as a subject were up for discussion – the distinctions between language and literature, the teaching and assessment of composition and comprehension and the role of talk in English all featured as central topics. Many of the conferences were weekend residential conferences held at Beatrice Webb House in Surrey, which had been purchased to use as a conference centre by the Webb Memorial Trust for the 'advancement of education and learning with respect to the history and problems of government and social policy'.[5] It was these weekend conferences that, for John Dixon at least, had the most profound effect, as he recalled that 'the big Beatrice Webb Conferences changed us every year'.[6]

Perhaps the most significant early work of LATE was its attempt to develop an alternative GCE O Level syllabus and examination,[7] a highly ambitious project made possible by the regulations that allowed schools to submit their own arrangements for O level, provided they were deemed by the established examination boards to be of comparable quality and rigour. There was much dissatisfaction within LATE with the existing O level examinations at the time; these were, after all, examinations that had been developed primarily to assess young people at the age of 16 who had reached the end of their grammar schooling, and whilst they might, arguably, have been appropriate for some children, they were certainly never designed to cater to a large comprehensive intake. The disquiet of LATE members emerged strongly in conferences held in the late 1940s and early 1950s. The Association resolved to go about working for change in the system.

The LATE project to develop an alternative O level developed into nothing short of a battle with the London Board that extended over a period of five years (Gibbons, 2009). It was a fight to have a curriculum and assessment system in place that would be more appropriate to the needs of all children, and Rosen was at the very heart of this collaborative endeavour. The importance of his contribution is clear in the records of the project and perfectly illustrates some of his overriding concerns with respect to how assessment in English should be responsive to the learners. It was Rosen who had carefully scrutinised ten years' worth of past O level papers in preparation for a LATE meeting in 1952 with representatives from the examination board, and he used the knowledge he had accrued to launch a stinging attack on the examination in the presence of the deputy secretary of the School Examinations Board of London University. Rosen's attacks on the various aspects of the existing exam – the topics for composition, the precis exercise and the grammar questions in particular – illustrate his own concerns that children's experience needed to be central to work in English, and therefore should equally be central to how they were examined. Rosen suggested only a very small number of children were in the examiners' minds when they came up with topics for composition – 'children who visited pen friends abroad, who were chairmen of school dramatic clubs, and who arranged private dances' (LATE, 1952). These were not the 'ordinary' children that Rosen was concerned for. In reporting the meeting, the Times Educational Supplement noted how Rosen had questioned the value of the 'deeply entrenched ritual' (TES, March 1952) of the precis exercise and on grammar he had scathingly suggested, 'it must be supposed that this exacting and unpractical business of clause analysis was thought the peak of grammarian glory by the university, for, having achieved advanced standard in the art a student need never analyse another sentence' (TES, March 1952). Rosen also suggested that in reinstating a context question to the literature O level paper, the Board had 'daringly seized the opportunity of a new examination to put the clock back' (TES, March 1952). This was no faux indignation; Rosen's scrutiny of the past papers had cemented a deeply held sense of an injustice being visited upon masses of young people. Rosen recalled many years later,

> the precis paper was reduced to a third of its length.[8] What is magic about a third? And I had found out by then it is because the Civil Service do it and if somebody has to go through papers and present them to their boss, they reduce them by a third. And a lot of kids in grammar schools went on to be civil servants. So I went on doing the demolition job. And I was furious actually.[9]

For Rosen, it was self-evident that this assessment system was set up to favour certain kinds of young people and that it was constructed to serve the needs of the establishment. Rosen's anger and his willingness to challenge the established figures of the examination boards illustrate perfectly the passion that drove his desire to change the way the subject was taught and assessed.

Rosen's contribution to the LATE O level campaign makes abundantly clear his commitment to a model of the subject that would be responsive to all children, not the grammar school elite, and that would be rooted in the values and concerns of the children themselves. For Rosen, this was a vision for the subject informed by his socialist politics, and therefore seemingly in tune with the grand notions of the London Plan for education with its ambitions for equality of opportunity. LATE itself was not overtly a political organisation; it could scarcely risk being so, given its membership was anything but radical in its makeup, but Rosen, and a few other members, did not hide their motivations. Douglas Barnes described Rosen as 'the most political person of the leadership'[10] within LATE, and John Dixon felt, 'Harold was probably the most consistently left wing in his trajectory and his perspective and I would be a follower in some respects compared with him'.[11]

Ultimately, the campaign that Rosen led to offer an alternative to the existing O level succeeded. LATE's alternative O level paper, with Rosen as co-writer, was taken by students at Queen Elizabeth Girls' Grammar School in 1955. With only one school taking the paper, it might be said that LATE's victory was more symbolic than anything else, but it did have the very real effect of causing the examination boards to make some changes to their offerings, given the pressure brought to bear on them and the threat of the potential loss of their client base. It was a campaign that stretched over five years, with many collaborating schools dropping out along the way as the exam boards responded to various specimen syllabuses and papers submitted by LATE with challenges and obstacles. There is no doubt, though, that this campaign did have a significant impact on the thinking of those exam boards as they adjusted their papers in the attempt to take the sting out of the objections raised. There is equally no doubt that the work of Rosen was critical in the campaign leading to a successful conclusion.

If the model of English that was developing through LATE's work could be seen in the lengthy campaign to reform the O Level, this vision of the subject that LATE was developing was perhaps most interestingly, and perhaps fully, articulated for the first time in a document prepared in response to a request from the British Council, titled *The Aims of English Teaching*. This document was commissioned to be sent to teachers and training colleges in schools in India to describe 'the aims that lie behind current practice in teaching the mother tongue' (LATE, 1955, p. 2). In a sense, the document is the first full articulation of the new English that had been developed through LATE's work in its first decade. This vision of English can be seen in the document's opening section, which boldly asserts, 'Experience comes first. . . . The aim of the English teacher should be to assist the development of language adequate to the child's experience' (LATE, 1956, p. 2). The articulation of the relationship between language and experience is then further developed:

> The effect of language upon experience, in our view, is to deepen it, order it, and make it accessible. By language we acquire a measure of control over our own experience and thereby are able to learn from it. It is a commonplace that language helps us to think: our formulation implies also that language similarly helps us to perceive and feel and act.
>
> (LATE, 1956, p. 2)

Though collaboratively written, the influence of Rosen on *The Aims of English Teaching* can be quite clearly detected when we compare it with the groundbreaking syllabus Rosen would pen just two years later as head of English at Walworth School. Starting from the learner, from her language and experience, was at the heart of Rosen's notion of what English should be. This is abundantly clear too in a document written by Rosen several years later, as LATE's response to the committee collecting submissions in advance of the publication of the Newsom Report:[12]

> Room must be found in English lessons for pupils to express sincerely their experience, to consider the problems which arise from it. . . . We would expect English work to be rooted in the concerns, hopes and fears, and daily lives of the pupils. . . . The work is not easy for us. Our academic education often does not fit us for the kind of awareness and sympathy demanded.
>
> (Rosen, 1962, p. 1)

Rosen's contribution to the work of LATE in its first decade was immense, both in terms of pushing forward the thinking of the Association and in purely practical and organisational matters. By the end of LATE's first decade in existence, one can see the articulation of the new, progressive English as an unashamedly child-centred subject, with the language and experience of the learner at its core, and as a subject that is growing in scope and range, embracing new kinds of literature and the mass media as part of its content so that young people are encouraged to see its relevance to their own lives. In the collaboratively written *The Aims of English*, and in his draft submission to the Newsom Report, Rosen's vision of subject English emerges. It is this vision that is an articulation of the new, progressive English that would ultimately command attention internationally. Rosen's centrality to the work of LATE from 1947 meant that by the time he took up the post of head of English at a comprehensive school, he was ready, in effect, to implement this new version of the subject in a pioneering and, very probably, unprecedented way.

The New English and the Walworth Syllabus

An overview of the work emanating from LATE from 1947 clearly shows a new model of English emerging. Central to this new model is placing the child, her experience and her language as the foundation for the development of curriculum and pedagogy. Rosen was at the forefront of shaping this vision and it was when he assumed control of the department at Walworth, one of London's first experimental comprehensive schools, that he was truly able to put this into practice. Rosen trained at what had previously been the London Day Training College (LDTC) and based on his research, Hardcastle has suggested that 'On the evidence of lecturers' memories of the LDTC, it seems that the principle of starting with the children's lives and interests was not specific to English and it was established before the war, not after it' (Hardcastle, 2014, p. 161). Indeed, the suggestion is that when Rosen articulated the vision of a new English at Walworth, 'he was continuing a tradition in educating urban working-class children that has its roots in nineteenth-century progressive education' (Hardcastle, 2016, p. 114). This tradition:

> underlined the importance of starting from what children already know, working with their concerns and interests to a point where – and this is often wilfully overlooked by the detractors of child-centred approaches – it becomes both appropriate and necessary to broaden out into the domains of systematic (school) knowledge.
>
> (Hardcastle, 2016. p.114)

What is most significant, however, is that 'Rosen was the first English teacher to turn the principle into viable practice with working-class children in a London school' (Hardcastle, 2014, p. 161). Significant, too, is the particular importance that the new English placed on the child's language; the idea that children should leave their own language at the school gate and adopt the accepted discourses of school was particularly antithetical to Rosen, infused as he was with the linguistic richness born from an upbringing in London's East End.

The most striking documentary evidence of turning this vision of a new English from principle into practice is the 1958 Walworth English Syllabus. The 1958 Walworth Syllabus is a practical document for teachers in the English department for the implementation of the new English. It's difficult to say with any surety to what extent this document was unique for its time, but it is equally difficult to find any contemporary document with which it can be compared. The nature, tone and content of the 1958 Walworth English syllabus represent a remarkable vision of the subject, and one that was in some senses both of its time, whilst also being well in advance of it.

The opening paragraph of this syllabus is bold, striking and confident, demonstrating Rosen's beliefs in what made effective English teaching with unambiguous directness and clarity. It begins with the primacy of pupils' experience and language, 'The teaching of English at Walworth calls for a sympathetic understanding of the pupils' environment and temperament. Their language experience is acquired from their environment and from communication with the people who matter most to them' (Richmond, 2017, p. 208). Though the call is specific to the teaching of English at Walworth, Rosen is articulating the wider principles of this new progressive English. The syllabus then immediately addresses the now well-trodden ground of the difference between the language of the home and the language of the school, with the pupils' own localised language 'likely to stand out in their own minds in strong contrast to the language experience being consciously presented in the framework of English lessons in particular, and school work in general' (Richmond, 2017, p. 208). The wisdom of previous prominent government reports on the teaching of English (most notably the seminal Newbolt Report (Departmental Committee of the Board of Education, 1921) had been that it was the teacher's job, unequivocally, to purge children of the pernicious habits of speech that had been brought from home. Rosen's view could not be more clearly opposed to this, for he saw that the difference between the language of home and school was likely to cause conflict and disaffection (what he termed 'aversion to poshness' (Departmental Committee of the Board of Education, 1921)). The syllabus is clear that 'Whatever language the pupils possess, it is this which must be built on rather than driven underground' (Departmental Committee of the Board of Education, 1921) and in an implicit warning against the assumptions teachers might be prone to make about pupils with whom they may share little in common, Rosen declares:

> However narrow the experience of our pupils may be (and it is often wider than we think), it is this experience alone which has given their language meaning. The starting point for English work must be the ability to handle effectively pupils' own experience.
> (Departmental Committee of the Board of Education, 1921)

The use of 'starting point' is vital; we know from Rosen's work on language and curriculum that he had no intention of limiting pupils' experiences – he was clear and ambitious about the potential good English teaching had to widen the linguistic and cultural knowledge of pupils, but for pupils to advance and to move beyond their own worlds, 'Oral work, written work and the discussion of literature must create an atmosphere in which the pupils become confident of the full acceptability of the material of their own experience' (Departmental Committee of the Board of Education, 1921).

It's difficult to appreciate the radical nature of this kind of statement of syllabus intent summarised so succinctly in this opening paragraph without remembering the context. The notion of a core syllabus to determine the content of English for all children was out of step with conventional thinking, even in a London that was proposing to implement a fully comprehensive system. The memories of the Walworth teachers who inherited Rosen's syllabus reveal this only too clearly:

> The prevailing assumption is that you test at 11+, select say 20% for a grammar school curriculum and the established five-year course to GCE, leaving the rest to follow courses still being thrashed out, and ending after four years without a qualification. The idea of teaching them all together in the same school is hotly contested; the idea of a common syllabus for all of them verges on the incredible.
>
> (Clements and Dixon, 2009, p. 1)

The pursuit of a common syllabus was something Rosen had been exploring with colleagues within LATE before the writing of the Walworth document. In 1957, he convened a study group for LATE with Walworth headteacher Guy Rogers on 'English in the Comprehensive School', the work of which was reported in LATE's annual report:

> Whatever tasks they may ultimately take on, they are at present at the stage where the pooling of experiences in discussion provides what they want. What is exciting about these discussions is that they have the whole range of children's ability to consider and I believe this fact enables them to dispense with certain restrictions, gives a sense of unity of the task of English teaching, and so takes them with unusual directness to the fundamental issues.
>
> (LATE, 1957, p. 2)

John Dixon later recalled (Hodgson, 2017) that it was at this study group that he first met Rosen, and they bonded over their shared left-wing credentials. Dixon at the time was teaching at Holloway School in North London, which itself had become comprehensive in 1955, and went with friends to a meeting of the LATE Comprehensive study group, 'I went along . . . I always remember, we said, "Well, if they're no good, we'll take it over" . . . we were very Bolshie young people!'[13] In fact, Dixon found that the group was 'bloody good actually' and he formed a friendship with Rosen – this was the basis on which ultimately Rosen recommended Dixon should apply for the post of head of English at Walworth on his departure from the school. The work of the LATE Comprehensive study group fed into the Walworth syllabus, so the collaborative thinking was there, of course, but the syllabus itself is unarguably Rosen's work.

The syllabus was radical and was as much policy statement as curriculum; it has been suggested that it marked:

> not just the beginning of a new era at one school but a radically different conception of English curriculum and pedagogy, a conception that was not merely attentive to local circumstances, to the language, culture and experience of the pupils, but rather sought to construct a version of English from these foundations.
>
> (Yandell, 2014, p. 405)

This is a remarkable claim for the Walworth syllabus, one that points to the significance of the document not just in terms of articulating a vision for a common curriculum in a single school, but in the evolution of an overarching rationale for the new English. Researchers that investigated English in three London schools in the post-war years leading to the publication of *English Teachers in Post War Democracy: Emerging choice in London schools 1945–1965* (Medway et al., 2014) suggest that the commitment expressed in the Walworth syllabus to building a curriculum on the everyday language and experience of the children was 'stronger than anything we have found in earlier writers' and that the implied pedagogy was, 'Start from experience and not words, and if you focus on it intently enough the words will look after themselves' (Medway and Kingwell, 2010, p. 756). Rosen's syllabus was apparently unique, pioneering and groundbreaking, a bold statement of his vision of what English should be for learners.

Beyond the strong and strident opening remarks of the syllabus, which make the case for a subject rooted in children's language and lived experience; there are other aspects worthy of consideration. In terms of reading, Rosen's syllabus does not contain lists of books that teachers should use with pupils; rather, in the reading section, there are instructions that both teachers and pupils should bring books of their own choice to the classroom to talk about. Teachers are urged to find suitable reading material to encourage the reading habit, and they should ask the head of department if they are struggling to find such material. There follows a line with is unmistakably Rosen's, 'No real help can be given to an English teacher unless he is prepared to read children's books from time to time' (Richmond, 2017, p. 209). The fact that 'Literature' (with a capital 'L') is not mentioned in the syllabus raises interesting questions about the way that this new progressive English stood in relation to what we might call the traditional canon. Some have suggested that London English – as we can safely say the Walworth syllabus articulates – was actively hostile to literature, or at least saw it as something tied to the traditional Cambridge model of the subject. Sawyer, for example, suggested that members of LATE 'reacted against the influence of Leavis and the Cambridge school' (Sawyer, 2004, p. 28), and another account claims, 'the critique of the Cambridge Leavis position was based on an alternative conception of experience and its relation to meaning, rooted in the immediacy of language rather than traditions of literature' (Ball et al., 1990, p. 58). Such accounts have led to the suggestion that the advocates of the new English discarded the Canon in favour of relevant texts, with the word relevant perhaps used pejoratively to suggest this meant something as crass as only offering children reading that explicitly reflected their own experience. This is a huge simplification and one that implies the new English denied access to the cultural hinterland of the elite. This, for Rosen at any rate, was simply not the case. Rosen, in fact, sought ways to enable the working-class children of Walworth to engage with traditional literature by allowing pupils to see its relevance to their own experience – this was the way in. Indeed, when his son Michael reflected on this idea of relevance as Rosen saw it, he said:

> When people like Harold and others talked about relevance they didn't simply just mean that they were going to find stuff that only applied to the lives of the children. What they noticed was that those children and students – call them working class, marginalised or whatever – their lives had been excluded, had been marginalised so they said no, let's bring it in so that their lives are not seen as inferior to the lives of the people that appear in Jane Austen. They reclaimed Dickens, they reclaimed scenes in Shakespeare, they weren't by any means saying exclude it. I often give the example – what was the first piece of drama that my dad turned to when he went to work in a comprehensive school in Walworth in the East End . . . in the Old Kent Road . . . was *Anthony and Cleopatra*. Because he said there were passions and excitement going on in there that these students – the sixth formers, O level going into sixth form – could relate to. So there was no question of chucking out Shakespeare and then bringing in dime novels[14]

Traditional literature, then, was important to Rosen, but the aim was to reclaim this, to take ownership of it, to see it not as the property of the elite, but as relevant to and reflective of the experience of the ordinary children of South London. Rosen himself gave an account that illustrates this perfectly when talking about the teaching of *Great Expectations* in Walworth school:

> I discovered that, used with discretion, Dickens is their author, you know, in spite of those long, you know, posh bits. And I remember we'd got to start off this opening . . . the encounter with Magwitch, the convict, which is a fantastic piece, I've always thought it was quite incredible.
> (Medway and Kingwell, 2010, p. 754)

This is clearly a gripping extract of the text, but it is what Rosen recalls doing next with the class that underlines the key element to the approach – that is, how he enabled the pupils to connect the great literature with their own lives and experience. After some drama work, the class:

> explored the idea of being frightened, and being frightened of certain kinds of adults. Well, I can remember being fantastically chuffed because . . . they couldn't stop talking about frightening adults, quite different kinds, of course, and I was surprised at how often they were people encountered in the markets, and who grabbed hold of them and so on, tried to get money from them. And then, of course, they could, if they wanted to, write about that, and they did, and there were a lot of good pieces.
> (Medway and Kingwell, 2010, p. 754)

The importance and place of traditional literature in the new progressive English in Rosen's view at his time at Walworth is important. It gives the lie to the stereotype of the progressive English teacher excluding Shakespeare and Dickens in favour of teenage fiction and television. There is empowerment for ordinary children here, and that is critical for Rosen, but it comes not through treating those children as empty vessels to be given the gift of being filled with a dollop of elite culture; it comes through an active connection between the lives of the children and the ideas of literature so that they can see it is for them as much as it is for the children in the grammar school. This seems to me to be fundamentally different from a view that sees great literature as some form of cultural capital that some children, not having access to it from their upbringing, need to have given to them. It appears that for advocates of a knowledge curriculum, working-class children are at a deficit, lacking the cultural and literary knowledge of the elite. Whilst such advocates of bestowing this knowledge on children might claim the object in offering a diet of the classics is for their benefit and in the noble aim of enhancing social mobility, allowing them to compete on a level footing with their middle-class peers, it does work on a deficit model – something that was anathema to Rosen, whose starting point was the richness of ordinary children's lived experience. For Rosen, starting with their own language and experience, with their stories, ultimately enables them to reclaim the language, experiences and stories of others. There was no sense that Rosen's vision of English was limiting or restricting; starting from the learner was the only way to enable these learners to encounter, embrace – or challenge – other cultures and views. Though it's true, too, that Rosen wanted to find the space in the English curriculum for other literary voices, as Michael Rosen said, at the same time as enabling young people to take ownership of the classics, the aim was:

> to dig down to discover literature by people like Sid Chaplin and Bill Naughton . . . people who had been marginalised who had written about working-class life with the same gamut of emotions and feelings as anybody else. It was also reclaiming world literature . . . constantly finding powerful texts that spoke to the students.[15]

Here is another indication of the innovative nature of the work Rosen pioneered as Head of English at Walworth – diversifying the reading diet to include literature from other classes and other cultures.

Rosen's vision of English, the new progressive English perhaps put into practice in the comprehensive school for the first time, as articulated in the Walworth syllabus and in his own memories, is political. Of this there can be no doubt. It is a syllabus that unashamedly promotes the lives and experiences of working-class children and so is a challenge to the traditional values of English espoused in the Newbolt Report and embodied in the Cambridge model of the subject. Rosen's English was not designed to suppress the working class or to convince them that their best chance in life was to embark on a forlorn quest to somehow learn to be middle class. This English was designed to acknowledge and validate the experience of ordinary children and to offer them the chance to question, challenge and – ideally – change their world and the world around them.

Though Rosen left Walworth for the teaching training post at Borough Road College after a few short years, and so arguably didn't have much time for the implementation of his new syllabus, the significance of his work there and the influence of his syllabus can clearly be traced in subsequent seminal moments in the articulation of the new English, most obviously perhaps in the publication of the groundbreaking English resource *Reflections*, and its accompanying *Teachers' Book*, published in 1963 (Clements, Dixon, Stratta). John Dixon had taken over as Walworth's head of English on Rosen's departure, and with colleagues Simon Clements and Leslie Stratta joining at the same time, he worked from the basis of Rosen's syllabus to create a course for the fourth- and fifth-year pupils in the school (what would now be Years 10 and 11). Clements remembers that on his very first day at Walworth, after a conversation with the headteacher, Guy Rogers, 'Harold's syllabus was put in my hands' and that even though Rosen had left, it was still known as 'Harold's syllabus and Harold's department'.[16] Rosen's syllabus had the stipulation that composition work across the years should take the form of 'magazines', where pupils would work on a particular theme over the course of a term or terms, producing related written work. The overarching themes suggested in the syllabus include such things as 'Out of School', 'the Street' and 'the District' with suggested titles for individual pieces of work like 'My Family', 'Evening in the pub' and 'Local characters' (Richmond, 2017, pp. 216–217). Inheriting the syllabus, Dixon and Clements later observed:

> Harold used the umbrella word 'magazines', which we interpreted as students' best work or cumulative folders. . . . In effect, writing over a term or year was given a certain coherence, by following themes through, starting from local (personal) experiences in an early mag and building out towards wider horizons.
>
> (Clements and Dixon, 2009, p. 19)

When Rosen left Walworth, Clements, Dixon and Stratta took this magazine approach forward when constructing the syllabus for students in their final two years in school, and this, in turn, was published as *Reflections* and the accompanying Teachers' Book (Clement et al., 1963). The themes identified as the focus for pupil work in *Reflections* – 'Family, the Community and Work', 'the mass media' and 'questions of our time' (Clement et al., 1963) – clearly align with, and are probably inspired by, those in Rosen's syllabus and the continuity of approach is evident. As West (1998) shows in his re-evaluation of *Reflections*, the book was commercially successful, selling out its initial print run of 10,000 copies in its first year of publication, and it is suggested that:

> *Reflections* drew together many of the new ideas which were then in circulation in English teaching, and demonstrated how these new ideas could be put into practical effect. Through *Reflections*, progressive teachers committed to the comprehensive school ideal finally had a course book which they could feel comfortable using in the classroom; and a new generation of pupils could benefit from its enlightened pedagogy.
> (West, 1998, pp. 41–42)

In a sense, *Reflections* brought Rosen's vision of the new English to a national audience. Few beyond Walworth would likely have seen or read a copy of his syllabus, but the sales figures for *Reflections* attest to a large-scale adoption of this model of the subject, such that, in the view of West:

> *Reflections* was, indeed, the first breakthrough for the new English: it represented the point at which a particular movement in English teaching, a movement which had its origins in the previous decade, gained for the first time a degree of recognition amongst teachers of English and the teaching profession as a whole.
> (West, 1998, p. 42)

In his own recollections of *Reflections*, it is interesting that Dixon observed:

> I thought you might like to know that in the teacher's book to *Reflections* we say in the preface 'While many of the ideas in this book come from the traditions of Walworth school, and from many exciting discussions with colleagues and friends in the London Association or the Teaching of English, etc. . . . we could not enumerate our debts, they are too many, but it must be said that the encouragement of Miss N Martin and Mr J Britton have made this book possible.' So that's what we said then. We should have said Harold, I don't know why we didn't.[17]

This is indeed a curious omission. When read alongside the Walworth syllabus, with its description of pupils producing magazines centred around various themes, it is hard to escape the conclusion that *Reflections* is a direct result of the approach to English embodied therein, both in terms of philosophical thinking and practical application. In a sense, the Walworth syllabus is a manifesto for the new English, and *Reflections* is both manifesto and practical handbook for its enactment. One can certainly say that the new English that Rosen was so influential to forging had its origins before the Second

World War. The LDTC was clearly promoting a progressive view of English. Indeed, progressive ideas about education have a centuries' long history. And there are those who would argue that child-centred progressive English is, in some sense, certainly traceable to the Romantic period, if not earlier. These are interesting discussions; for my purposes, it is sufficient to make the case that it was in the Walworth syllabus and in the subsequent publication of *Reflections*, that the new English was articulated as a vision and put into practice. West argues *Reflections* that 'was not simply a new course book for the comprehensive school, but a new course book at the heart of which was a new pedagogy' (West, 1998, p. 36). This pedagogy was that which Rosen had initiated at Walworth when he wrote the English department's syllabus, and which had grown from his own beliefs in what English should be and from a decade of collaboration with colleagues in LATE to refine the vision.

The popularity of *Reflections* points to the fact that the new progressive English, which Rosen had been working on for over a decade, was becoming widespread, certainly nationally. The international reach of the new English would be secured shortly afterward as a result of the 1966 Dartmouth Conference.

Rosen and Dartmouth and the New English Orthodoxy

The 1966 Dartmouth Conference, held at the college of that name in New Hampshire in the United States, retains a unique place in the history of English as a school subject. Officially titled the 'Anglo-American Conference on the Teaching and Learning of English' and proposed in 1965 by the Chair of the National Council for the Teaching of English (NCTE), the month-long meeting of American and English academics and teachers had lofty aims: 'the results of such a seminar . . . could change the shape of English instruction for the next two decades' (Squire, 1965, p. 2). Rosen and his wife Connie were among a British delegation to the seminar that also included James Britton, Douglas Barnes and John Dixon, meaning that at least a quarter of the English representatives were heavily involved in LATE and at the forefront of the thinking about the new progressive English that had been shaped in London. Though the English delegates were effectively representing the relatively recently established National Association for the Teaching of English (NATE), the evidence of the formation of the NATE just three years earlier (see Gibbons, 2014) demonstrates that Barnes, Britton, Dixon and Rosen were fiercely protective of the endeavours that had shaped London English, and it is this vision that would undoubtedly have informed their contributions to debates at Dartmouth.

Dartmouth has assumed almost legendary status in the history of the development of the subject English, and it's all but inconceivable to imagine a similar event ever being repeated. The notion of a charity (in the case of Dartmouth, this was the Carnegie Foundation) ever again funding 40 teachers of English to spend six weeks debating the nature of their subject is fanciful. There are, however, widely and wildly different accounts and recollections of what happened at the seminar, and much has been written on the subject. A decade after the event, one of the foremost English delegates declared that the event had been a 'debacle' with 'much raising of elbows' but 'very little meeting of minds' (Whitehead, 1976, p. 13), whilst a leading American academic in attendance said, 'the entire conference was shattered into myriad pieces by a common subject and discipline' (Miller, 1969, p. 2). The evidence suggests that the key to the problems at Dartmouth were the different starting points of the groups from either side of the Atlantic, in part, at least, as a result of contemporary political contexts. The Americans were in the midst of huge educational change with the launch of Sputnik, shocking policymakers who saw the Russians moving ahead in the post-war space race. The result of this was some fundamental changes to education policy, leading to the development of new structured and functional programmes in maths, science and English, which, the policymakers hoped, would underpin an education system that would produce the kind of educated generation that would ensure the US would not fall behind the Russians in terms of global influence. They were, in effect, moving away from so-called progressive notions of curriculum and assessment to a more structured and traditional approach to pedagogy, curriculum and assessment. In contrast, the English delegation came with progressive ideas about a child-centred version of the subject; this was seemingly true not just of those coming from the London context, but also those, like Frank Whitehead, Boris Ford and Denys Thompson, who are traditionally seen to represent the 'Cambridge' view of English. NATE had only recently formed, in 1963, and this association was, in one sense, an alliance of sorts between those involved in the Cambridge-aligned 'Use of English' study groups and LATE and its sister regional groups. There were tensions between these groups in the formation of NATE and on the agreement of its constitution and modus operandi (see Gibbons, 2014, for detail on this; additionally, the significant role Rosen played in arguing for a 'bottom up' rather than 'top down' model for the new national association is considered in Chapter 6), but there was some coalescence around the idea that English should enable and empower the learner and that the learner should be at the foundation of the development of curriculum and assessment.

The result of this apparent difference in starting position for one delegate was that

> The opening session at Dartmouth was surrealistic in the sense that the British sounded to the Americans like themselves (their other progressive selves), and the Americans sounded to the British like their discarded authoritarian selves. In short, the British seemed to be the progressivists, while 'the Americans' talked like classicists.
>
> (Miller, 1969, p. 7)

Expectations had apparently been confounded. Reporting back to a LATE meeting shortly after the seminar, John Dixon claimed that agreement had been achieved at Dartmouth, as the case for a structured curriculum had been 'brilliantly demolished' by Frank Whitehead (LATE, 1966, p. 1) and that consensus had been reached over the importance of an English curriculum that focused primarily on children's own experience and the use of language to order and explore this experience. Whether any such consensus was reached is highly debatable given the evidence to the contrary, but in a sense that is somewhat unimportant when set against the publication that became the official write-up of the conference for the profession, John Dixon's *Growth through English* (Dixon, 1967). Only 40 people attended Dartmouth; many thousands of English teachers would read Dixon's account as the agreed outcomes of the proceedings, so in many ways this account has become the accepted version of the discussions that took place at the seminar. According to Douglas Barnes, a delegate at Dartmouth, 'NCTE weren't unwilling to accept that as a version of what happened. You still meet American teachers who know the truth is very different'.[18] In one account of the development of subject English in the twentieth century, the events at Dartmouth were characterised, somewhat simplistically perhaps, not merely as significant in the adoption of a child-centred model, but as the moment when the London model of English defeated the Cambridge model (Ball, 1985).

Two official reports were to be written from the seminar – one for the public, Herbert Muller's *The Uses of English* (Muller, 1967), and one for the profession that Dixon had been charged with producing. *Growth through English* was, and remains for many, the watershed moment in the articulation of the new progressive English. The very title itself cemented the term 'personal growth' as one that would go on to resonate with English teachers for decades to come. There's some irony in this given Dixon's own recollection of the meeting at which the title was decided:

> I said I thought of calling it something like Language and Operation. You see not a very brilliant title. So somebody – in fact one of the most reactionary north Americans – said, well it's about growth why don't we call it Growth through English?[19]

That personal growth stuck was perhaps both a blessing and a curse; it offered a title that progressives could champion, yet it invited criticism for the suggestion of self-centredness. As Rosen wrote later, in using the term personal, 'we have made English sound like the greatest ego-trip ever invented' (Rosen, 1975, p. 55). For Rosen, the experience of learning English was a social, collaborative process with the ultimate aim being change; it was not, for him, intended merely to be a journey of self-discovery.

In terms of the vision of English articulated in *Growth through English*, it is far easier to see it as a manifestation of the views of the participants from the English delegation rather than a result of a negotiated consensus. The concepts of participant and spectator in relation to language, which appear in the text, for example, are originally ideas of Denys Harding,[20] a delegate at Dartmouth, ideas which were taken forward and further by a fellow delegate in his work within the field of English, James Britton. And at its heart, *Growth through English* proposes the model of English rooted in the learner's language and experience that Rosen had defined in the Walworth School English syllabus. Putting the two documents side by side provides an interesting comparison:

> In English, pupils meet to share their encounters with life, and to do this effectively they move freely between dialogue and monologue, between talk, drama and writing; and literature, by bringing new voices into the classroom, adds to the store of shared experience. Each pupil takes from the store what he can and what he needs. In so doing he learns to use language to build his own representational world and works to make this fit reality as he experiences it.
>
> (Dixon, 1967, p. 13)

> The starting point for English work must be the ability to handle effectively pupils' own experience. Oral work, written work and the discussion of literature must create an atmosphere in which the pupils become confident of the full acceptability of the material of their own experience.
>
> (Richmond, 2017, p. 218)

The similarities between the two extracts are striking. Both put the case strongly for an English rooted in the learners' experience and language. There is much more to *Growth through English*, but at its heart is an articulation of a model of English that in so many ways echoes that presented by Rosen to his staff in Walworth in 1958, a model that Rosen was able to define after a decade of working in schools in London and collaborating with members of LATE on so many conferences, projects and campaigns. It was the model that Rosen left for Dixon in the Walworth syllabus and which formed the basis of the material in *Reflections* (Clements et al., 1963). For Dorothy Barnes, 'Growth through English was what LATE stood for'[21] and according to Douglas Barnes, growth English was 'very much the LATE line from the 50s onwards'.[22] It seems to me not too far a stretch of the imagination to see *Growth through English* as the key moment of definition for the new progressive English, to trace its roots back to 1947 and to identify clearly the critical position of Rosen in shaping that vision through his work within LATE and in writing the Walworth English syllabus to articulate this model of English for practice in the comprehensive school. *Growth through English* established London English as an orthodoxy and was critical in the establishment of this vision of the subject in English-speaking jurisdictions globally. The model has, according to the evidence, retained a preeminent place in the minds of English teachers internationally. According to the results of a survey conducted with 260

English teachers and education academics at the International Federation for the Teaching of English (IFTE) conference in 2013, it was justifiable to claim that 'the Personal Growth model, certainly in England but also internationally, retains its pre-eminence as the preferred ideology of the majority of teachers of English' (Goodwyn, 2016, p. 19). In England, official status was proffered on the model when it was included as one of the five suggested models for the teaching of English in the first version of the National Curriculum (Department of Education and Science, 1988). Though there was no hierarchy for these five models suggested in the national curriculum, the fact that personal growth was cited first is perhaps significant in terms of its importance to the profession. From its origins in the first activities of LATE, through the Walworth syllabus, *Reflections*, the Dartmouth Seminar and the publication of *Growth through English*, this English – be it termed, London English, English as Language, or Personal Growth English – was indelibly influenced by the thinking and work of Rosen.

Conclusion

A new English was developed in the 20 years following the second World War. Whether we term this London English, English as Language or personal growth English is, to some degree, immaterial, as is the extent one might wish to place it in opposition to Cambridge English or English as Literature. And whilst it might be convenient to see *Growth through English* as a written encapsulation of this new English, it's problematic to suggest that there was a fully defined, universally agreed conception of how this new English should be expressed and what it might actually look like in practice. There were disagreements, or at least differences in emphasis, even between key figures in the development of the new English. Often James Britton, Harold Rosen, Douglas Barnes and Nancy Martin are almost spoken of as a single entity with a homogenous view of the subject; evidence suggests this was not the case.[23] Each of these critical contributors to the development of the new English had particular areas of interest, which meant the scope of the subject was always growing and intersecting with ideas from the worlds of psychology, sociology and linguistics; with increasing cultural diversity and the seemingly endless rise of the mass media the boundaries of the subject have never ceased to expand.

What is clear, though, is that certain fundamental principles lie at the core of this new model of the subject and unite those who thought and wrote about, and practised, it. These are principles that remain central to many involved in English education, in many parts of the globe, to this day. English should start from the learner, not from content, and it should have at its heart the language and experience of the child. Starting from the child, validating her language and experience opens the way for the exploration of different ways of speaking and writing and exploring different experiences through literature. This conception of the subject is vividly recalled in Douglas Barnes' memory of Rosen bringing a group of PGCE students to see him teach a poetry lesson in Minchenden Grammar School. When Barnes himself had failed to elicit responses to the poem, Rosen stepped in to try, inviting the children to share personal anecdotes that might help them find meaning in the verse:

> I had always begun by reading a poem or prose passage with a class and then inviting the pupils to comment. They could if they wished mention experiences of their own that were relevant, but I seldom asked for them explicitly. It seems unbelievable now, but this was the first time it had ever occurred to me that one could start with their experiences, and later introduce the literature as another voice contributing to the conversation that was the lesson.
> (Barnes, 2009, p. 356)

Barnes' succinct anecdote of the classroom illustrates how Rosen revealed both the power and the simplicity of this model of English in the straightforward activity of inviting pupils to share their language and experience as the starting point for an encounter with literature. Barnes' incredulity at not thinking of this for himself reveals how this has, over time, become an orthodox way for English teachers to work.

The new English, which was rooted in London, spread nationally through the publication of *Reflections* and internationally following Dartmouth and the publication of *Growth through English*. It flourished in English-speaking jurisdictions, with a growth model of English becoming something of an orthodoxy in England, Australia, Canada and the United States by the 1980s.

That the development of this new English was a collaborative pursuit is clear from the documentary evidence and the recollections of those intimately involved, but collaborations are the result of the joint working of individuals. Harold Rosen's importance to the development of the new English was critical on a number of levels. In one very practical sense, the huge contribution that he made to the early work of LATE in terms of organising and chairing meetings and study groups, and in convening conferences was critical in the sheer scope of activities that the Association took on in its first decade and more, when the new English was just beginning to emerge. It's difficult to see how so much could have been done without this level of commitment. John Dixon remembered that 'through the late 50s Harold was the great energy in the Committee'.[24] All the evidence supports this evaluation.

The power and passion of Rosen's character and argument, his righteous indignation at the treatment of ordinary children, leap off the pages of the documents that tell the story of the reform of the English language 'O' level, a touchstone in bringing the need for a new English to be recognised by the authorities. And, uniquely among his celebrated peers, he took this new English – essentially an English for all – and put it to work in the context of Walworth, a comprehensive school. Arguably, one can trace the legacy of what happened at Walworth through the publication of *Reflections*, on to Dartmouth and the publication of *Growth through English*; this is the evolutionary path that the new English followed.

What's clear, too, is that in contributing so significantly to the development of the new English, the key concerns that would be central to his subsequent work as a researcher and teacher educator were always present, always beginning with the learner and her experience and language, telling and hearing and reading stories as an essential part of being human, and the politically rooted belief in the importance of the education of the working class.

Notes

1 In England the primary phase of education covers children between the ages of 5–11 years old. The secondary phase is schooling between the ages of 11–16 years old.
2 According to Childhood Policy Milestones (British Academy, 2019), around 20% of children ultimately attended grammar schools in the wake of the Butler Act. Five per cent attended technical schools, with the remaining 75% in modern schools. In fact, the proportion of pupils at grammar schools in the immediate years after the Butler Act was much higher, at 'just under 38%' in 1947 (Danechi, 2020, p. 4). The reason for the relatively high percentage after the Butler Act was that many grammar schools already existed and so could fill places quickly.
3 Douglas Barnes was a key figure in the London Association for the Teaching of English and, along with Harold Rosen and James Britton, wrote Language, the Learner and the School (Barnes et al., 1969). He had been a student of Leavis at Cambridge but went on to become a leading figure in the development of the new, progressive English in London. He is one example of why it is not necessarily helpful to conceive of Cambridge and London English as opposing paradigms. It was Barnes position, with, one might say, 'a foot in both camps', that perhaps led to him being critical in the meetings that were held to form the National Association for the Teaching of English (NATE) in 1963.
4 The extensive archive of documents relating to the London Association for the Teaching of English is held at the library of the University of London Institute of Education. It includes membership lists, conference programmes and reports, meeting minutes, etc. . . . and includes documents dating from the foundation of the organisation in 1947.
5 From the history of the Webb Memorial Trust, at https://www.rethinkingpoverty.org.uk/about-the-trust/ accessed on 11/2/2025
6 Comment taken from an interview with John Dixon conducted by the author as part of PhD research. John Dixon took over the Head of English role at Walworth from Harold Rosen. He had a distinguished career in teaching and academia and was a key member of LATE in the 1960s in particular. He is probably most widely known internationally for his book Growth through English, which was a report of the 1966 Dartmouth Seminar.
7 The General Certificate of Education (GCE) Ordinary – or 'O' level – examination was introduced in 1951. Generally speaking, it was a qualification aimed at the top 20% of pupils in terms of academic attainment. It was replaced in 1987 by the General Certificate of Secondary Education (GCSE), which was an assessment designed for pupils of all abilities.
8 By this, Rosen meant that the task required candidates in the examination to reduce a text to a third of its original length.
9 Comment taken from an interview with Harold Rosen conducted by John Hardcastle and Peter Medway as part of research for Medway, P., Hardcastle, J., Brewis, G. and Crook, D. (2014) *English Teachers in a Postwar Democracy: Emerging Choice in London Schools, 1945–65*. New York: Palgrave Macmillan.

10 Comment taken from an interview with Douglas Barnes conducted by the author as part of PhD research.
11 Comment taken from an interview with John Dixon conducted by the author as part of PhD research.
12 The Newsom Report (Central Advisory Council for Education, 1963) was titled *Half Our Future* and was the work of a Committee asked by the then Conservative Education Minister, David Eccles, to advise on the education of 13–16 year olds of average and less than average ability. Among its principle recommendations was the raising of the school leaving age 16, which was implanted a decade later.
13 Comment taken from an interview with John Dixon conducted by the author as part of PhD research.
14 The author had a series of conversations with Michael Rosen, facilitated by Frances Gilbert from Goldsmiths University. In the interview quoted here – available on YouTube at https://www.youtube.com/watch?v=nZLMVd1LLQ8 – Michael reflected on his father's upbringing and its influence on his life working in education.
15 The author had a series of conversations with Michael Rosen, facilitated by Frances Gilbert from Goldsmiths University. In the interview quoted here – available on YouTube at https://www.youtube.com/watch?v=nZLMVd1LLQ8 – Michael reflected on his father's upbringing and its influence on his life working in education.
16 Comment taken from an interview with Simon Clements conducted by the author as part of PhD research.
17 Comment taken from an interview with John Dixon conducted by the author as part of PhD research.
18 Comment taken from an interview with Douglas Barnes conducted by the author as part of PhD research.
19 Comment taken from an interview with John Dixon conducted by the author as part of PhD research.
20 Denys Harding was both a professor of psychology and a literary critic. He had studied under Leavis at Cambridge and worked as an editor of Scrutiny alongside him. However, he also had connections with LATE, having spoken at a LATE conference in 1958. Harding is one figure who brings into question the sharp division some make between Cambridge and London English.
21 Comment taken from an interview with Dorothy Barnes conducted by the author as part of PhD research.
22 Comment taken from an interview with Douglas Barnes conducted by the author as part of PhD research.
23 Douglas Barnes, for example, has expressed his unease with the concepts of language in the participant/spectator role, as put forward by James Britton. In an interview with the author, Barnes recalled arguing with Britton at Dartmouth, saying, in an interview with the author, 'I think observer/participant distinction doesn't work. That both poetic language and engaged political language can be both and I wanted a different definition of the distinction as I didn't think his definition worked'.
24 Comment taken from an interview with John Dixon conducted by the author as part of PhD research.

References

Ball, S. (1985) 'English for the English since 1906' in Goodson, I. (ed.) *Social Histories of the Secondary Curriculum*. Sussex: Falmer Press.
Ball, S. (1987) 'English Teaching, the State and Forms of Literacy. Research on Mother Tongue Education' in Kroon, S. and Sturm, J. (eds.) *An International Perspective:*

Papers of the Second International Symposium of the International Mother Tongue. Enshde: International Mother Tongue Education Network.

Ball, S., Kenny, A. and Gardiner, D. (1990) 'Literacy Politics and the Teaching of English' in Goodson, I. and Medway, P. (eds.) *Bringing English to Order.* Sussex: Falmer Press.

Barnes, D. (2009) 'Learning from Harold'. *Changing English*, 16:3, pp. 355–356.

Barnes, D., Britton, J. and Rosen, H. (1969) *Language, Learner and the School.* Harmondsworth: Penguin.

Board of Education (1938) *Report of the Consultative Committee on Secondary Education with Special Reference to Grammar Schools and Technical High Schools* (commonly known as The Spens Report). London: His Majesty's Stationery Office.

Board of Education (1943) *Curriculum and Examinations in Secondary Schools* (commonly known as The Norwood Report). London: His Majesty's Stationery Office.

Board of Education (1944) *The Education Act* (commonly known as The Butler Act). London: His Majesty's Stationery Office.

British Academy (2019) *Childhood Policy Milestones: Chronologies*, available at https://www.thebritishacademy.ac.uk/documents/225/The-British-Academy-Childhood-Policy-Milestones-Chronologies.pdf accessed on 2nd April 2025.

Burgess, T. (1988) 'Cultural and Linguistic Diversity and English Teaching' in Lightfoot, M. and Martin, N. (eds.) *The Word for Teaching is Learning: Essays for James Britton.* Oxford: Heinemann.

Central Advisory Council for Education (1963) *The Newsom Report: Half our Future.* London: Her Majesty's Stationery Office.

Clements, S. and Dixon, J. (2009) 'Harold and Walworth'. *Changing English*, 16:1, pp. 15–23.

Clements, S., Dixon, J. and Stratta, L. (1963) *Reflections.* Oxford: Oxford University Press.

Danechi, S. (2020) *House of Commons Library Briefing Paper: Grammar School Statistics*, available at https://researchbriefings.files.parliament.uk/documents/SN01398/SN01398.pdf accessed on 2nd April 2025.

Department of Education and Science (1988) *English for Ages 5–16: Proposals of the Secretary of State for Education and Science and the Secretary of State for Wales.* London: Her Majesty's Stationery Office.

Departmental Committee of the Board of Education (1921) *The Teaching of English in England* (commonly known as The Newbolt Report). London: His Majesty's Stationery Office.

Dixon, J. (1967) *Growth through English.* Oxford: Oxford University Press.

Gibbons (2009) "To know the world of the school and change it' An Exploration of Harold Rosen's Contribution to the Early Work of the London Association for the Teaching of English'. *Changing English*, 16:1, pp. 93–101.

Gibbons, S. (2014) *The London Association for the Teaching of English 1947–67: A History.* London: Institute of Education Press.

Goodwyn, A. (2016) 'Still Growing After All These Years? The Resilience of the Personal Growth Model of English in England and Also Internationally'. *English Teaching Practice and Critique*, 15:1, pp. 7–21.

Hardcastle (2014) "Coherence at Last': Percival Gurrey's Contribution to English'. *Changing English*, 21:2, pp. 159–170.

Hardcastle (2016) "The Dramas Themselves': Teaching English in London in the 1970s'. *Changing English*, 23:2, pp. 112–127.

Hodgson, John (2017) 'A Conversation with John Dixon'. *English in Education*, 51:3, pp. 238–254.

Jones, K. (2003) *Education in Britain: 1944 to the Present.* Cambridge: Polity Press.

LATE (1952) *Report of Meeting on GCE Examinations in English, 11th March 1952*, held in the LATE archive and the University of London Institute of Education Library.
LATE (1953) *Report of Annual General Meeting, 13th October 1953*, held in the LATE archive and the University of London Institute of Education Library.
LATE (1955) *Report of Autumn Term Meeting*, held in the LATE archive and the University of London Institute of Education Library.
LATE (1956) *The Aims of English Teaching*, held in the LATE archive and the University of London Institute of Education Library.
LATE (1957) *Secretary of Studies Report to the Annual General Meeting*, held in the LATE archive and the University of London Institute of Education Library.
LATE (1966) *Report to LATE of the Dartmouth Conference 1st December 1966*, held in the LATE archive and the University of London Institute of Education library.
London County Council (1947) *London School Plan*, available at https://www.education-uk.org/documents/lcc1947-lsp/1947-london-school-plan.pdf consulted on 3rd September 2025.
Maclure, S. (1970) *One Hundred Years of London Education: 1870–1970*. London: Penguin.
Mathieson, M. (1975) *The Preachers of Culture: A Study of English and Its Teachers*. Oxford: George Allen and Unwin.
Medway, P., Hardcastle. J, Brewis, G. and Crook, D. (2014) *English Teachers in a Postwar Democracy: Emerging Choice in London Schools, 1945–1965*. London and New York: Palgrave Macmillan.
Medway, P. and Kingwell, P. (2010) 'A curriculum in its place: English teaching in one school 1946–1963'. *History of Education*, 39:6, pp. 749–765.
McCulloch, G. (2002) 'Local Authorities and the Organisation of Secondary Schooling 1943–1950'. *Oxford Review of Education*, 28:2/3, pp. 235–246.
Miller, J. (1969) 'What happened at Dartmouth? (A Query by One who was there)'. Address at Illinois Association of Teachers of English Meeting, Urbana, Oct. 17, 1969, available at https://files.eric.ed.gov/fulltext/ED039249.pdf consulted on 6th February 2025.
Muller, H. (1967) *The Uses of English*. New York: Holt, Rinehart and Winston.
Richmond, J. (2017) 'The Walworth School English Syllabus' in Richmond, J. (ed.) *Harold Rosen: Writings on Life, Language and Learning 1958–2008*. London: UCL Institute of Education Press.
Rosen, H. (1962) '*Response to Secondary Schools Examinations Council*'. Unpublished draft, held in the LATE archive and the University of London Institute of Education Library.
Rosen, H. (1970) *Application to the Post of Chair of Education*, University of Bristol, held part of the Rosen Archive held in University College London Institute of Education Library.
Rosen, H. (1975) 'Out There or Where the Masons Went' in Richmond, J. (ed.) (2017) *Harold Rosen: Writings on Life, Language and Learning 1958–2008*. London: UCL Institute of Education Press.
Rubinstein, D. and Simon, B. (1973) *The Evolution of the Comprehensive School 1926–1972*. London: Routledge and Keegan Paul.
Sawyer, W. (2004) 'Seminal Books on English Teaching' in Gold, E. and Sawyer, W. (eds.) *Reviewing English in the 21st Century*. Sydney: Phoenix Education.
Shayer, D. (1972) *The Teaching of English in Schools 1900–1970*. London: Routledge and Keegan Paul.
Simon, B. (1991) *Education and the Social Order*. London: Lawrence and Wishart.
Squire, J. (1965) *Proposal for an International Seminar on the Teaching and Learning of English*, available at https://wac.colostate.edu/repository/exhibits/dartmouth/selection-of-13-documents/4-proposal/ consulted on 5th February 2025.

Times Educational Supplement (1952) 'English Examinations', 14th March 1952, held in the LATE archive and the University of London Institute of Education Library.

West, D. W. (1998) 'The Moment of 1963: Reflections and the New English'. *Changing English*, 5:1, pp. 35–43.

Whitehead, F. (1976) 'The Present State of English Teaching: Stunting the Growth'. *The Use of English*, 28:1 pp. 11–17.

Yandell, John. (2014) 'Changing the Subject: English in London, 1945–1967'. *Changing English*, 21:4, pp. 402–408.

Chapter 3

Harold Rosen
Class and Cultures

Introduction

It is abundantly clear from Rosen's work as a teacher and head of department and from his significant contributions to LATE that the education of working-class children was always at the very heart of his thinking. Unquestionably, Rosen's own upbringing influenced this thinking, as did his socialist politics; indeed, his upbringing and politics were inextricably intertwined. For Rosen, education for the working class was a critical part of creating a more equal society and an effective schooling in English should ensure that all children, but most particularly those from outside the elite cultures, should be highly literate, able to question, critique and challenge the inequities baked into England's class system. His work to pioneer the new, progressive English was rooted in his concerns for working-class children, and this inevitably meant building a subject that had the language and experience of the child as its foundation. Rosen's belief was that as a teacher, 'If you can't do something with working-class kids it isn't worth doing' (Medway and Kingwell, 2010, p. 756).

That his concern for the education of the working class was rooted in his own upbringing is perhaps one thing that sets Rosen apart from the other pioneers of the new English. His background, growing up in poverty in the East End of London, was not something shared by colleagues like James Britton and Nancy Martin, and for John Richmond, 'he absolutely understood from his own social class background about the importance of engaging with the culture and language of the child'.[1] From his own upbringing and schooling, Rosen had experienced the reality of having one's own language and culture excluded; he had been, intentionally or not, the victim of prejudice. However, he simultaneously, one could say instinctively, knew about the potential depth and richness of working-class language and life. He made the classrooms he taught in spaces for working-class pupils to share their stories, something perhaps most vividly brought to life by Betty Rosen's only partially fictionalised account of the lesson she saw as a student teacher on a visit to Walworth School. Using the pseudonym Mr Rees to conceal Rosen's identity, Betty Rosen wrote

DOI: 10.4324/9781003588917-3

in her autobiographical work of 'the lesson that had the most profound influence of my professional life' (Rosen, p. 10). She recalled that after introducing the topic of the lesson as 'Neighbours', the fourth-year (now year 10-, 14- and 15-year old students) pupils spoke in such a way that she 'had never heard, before or since, such a half hour's amazing medley of character sketches and hilarious encounters' (Rosen, p. 10). Observing the lesson, Betty Rosen was taken into a different world, that of the pupils, and saw the shift from speech to writing; 'They spoke – and soon afterwards wrote brilliantly – of a community life unknown to my family' (Rosen, p. 10). The effect on the young student English teacher was profound; 'That morning I discovered that to see behind the faces meant opening oneself up to other people's life stories – which were as valuable as any literature I might bring to the classroom. More, these stories themselves often became literature' (Rosen, p. 10). It is a striking sketch of a lesson that reveals in an instant what it meant to build the subject on the experience of children and the belief that their stories were as valuable as literature. It is one that would probably be revolutionary to many English teachers now, leave alone those working in schools in the late 1950s. Indeed, it was the placing of gossip and children's autobiographical writing on the same spectrum as the great works of literature that was one thing that caused advocates of the Cambridge model of English such disquiet. The embrace and harnessing of working-class culture and experience was Rosen's innovation, the significance of which can scarcely be overestimated. This was put into practice in the context of the comprehensive classroom in Walworth, but through his work in LATE and his subsequent work and writing as an academic, Rosen was one of the key figures in shifting the thinking about the education of the working classes, always seeing children from these groups as having something to bring to the classroom, rather than as coming to school lacking something their more affluent peers possessed. Rosen pioneered the thinking of difference, rather than deficit, when considering the education of those from the working class. Such thinking has had profound implications for educators across the English-speaking world, albeit that it might be more common in other jurisdictions to talk about underprivileged or marginalised pupils or to use the term 'socio-economic status' as opposed to class.

Rosen's Role in Bringing Working-Class Children, Their Language, Culture and Experience to the Heart of the LATE Work on Developing English

It's interesting to note that although for Rosen the education, experience and language of the working class were always central to his work, the evidence suggests that in his endeavours in the early years of his career, the explicit references to working class as a term are not obvious. In, for example, the LATE campaign to reform the O level, the references are often to making the assessment system more appropriate for the needs of ordinary children. The term working class is inherently political, whereas 'ordinary children' is not, or at least not as obviously in the same way. We could speculate that the term working class was side-stepped to avoid creating an explicitly political atmosphere. Although Walworth was an experimental comprehensive and may well have attracted teachers with a particular commitment to an inclusive education, the vast majority of teachers that collaborated within LATE were still teaching in grammar schools in the Association's first decade or more in existence – and the schools involved in the alternative O level campaign were most certainly of this type. We know, too, from the memories of those involved that though Rosen and colleagues like John Dixon did not hide their socialist credentials, far from all LATE members shared these political views. From the difficulties that Rosen experienced with the local authority inspector before securing his post at Walworth, it is clear that there was deep suspicion of teachers who were perceived to subscribe to radical left-wing political views. If LATE was to be inclusive and involve as many English teachers as possible in the work that was shaping a new progressive model of the subject, it was probably necessary to avoid overt political stances. 'Ordinary children' functioned as a proxy term for 'working-class children' in the discourse of LATE in its first decade. As time passed, however, the apparent reluctance to employ the term working class receded.

Towards the end of the 1950s and into the 1960s, perhaps reflecting the increasing pace in the shift in London towards comprehensivisation, it's clear that a more overt political agenda emerged in some LATE activities that very firmly placed the education of the working class at the centre of attention. This can be seen in two notable conferences – both organised by Rosen – that LATE held at the end of the 1950s and the beginning of the 1960s. These conferences clearly highlight the specific focus on the education of the working class that was so central to Rosen and are worth some brief consideration for the way that they demonstrate Rosen's efforts to put the experience of working-class children at the very centre of the agenda as the new English was being formulated through the work of LATE.

The first of these conferences, held in 1958, was entitled 'English and the Urban Child'. Significantly, the keynote speaker at the conference was not an English specialist; as John Dixon remembered, 'he (Rosen) invited someone from Leicester, no from Liverpool, who talked about dead patch areas in inner cities and the life of the dead patch areas in Liverpool'.[2] The invited speaker was John Barron Mays. Having studied an English degree, Barron Mays moved into sociology, and at Liverpool University, he helped to pioneer an approach to sociological research that 'was a concerted effort to link theory and methods with pragmatic issues, and to collaborate with the communities under study' (Hill, 2006, p. 112). Such an approach to research was certainly aligned with Rosen's, who echoed the sentiments later when writing that the need to develop an awareness of the lives of the working and middle classes would need 'the active informed help of the very people whose language is being studied, and this presupposes a very different approach to research altogether' (Rosen, 1972, p. 19).

It's likely that Barron Mays' publication *Growing Up in the City: A study of juvenile delinquency in an urban neighbourhood* (Barron Mays, 1954) brought him to Rosen's attention, and a contemporary review of the work points to why Rosen, teaching in inner-city London, would have been interested; the book was 'one of the most instructive inquiries carried out in the country on the causes and treatment of juvenile crime' and was based on research carried out in a part of Liverpool noted for its 'poverty, bad housing, casual employment, educational backwardness among the children, a strange mixture of races and a clash of culture and religious beliefs' (Burt, 1955, p. 604). It might well be that Rosen recognised in this description something of the experience of his own upbringing. Given the available evidence, the organisation of this conference marked a significant departure for LATE, in inviting Barron Mays to speak. Rosen was taking the Association, and its thinking about English, into new territory, explicitly addressing ideas of class and culture in the lives of inner-city children. This territory, as the report of the conference shows, brought into focus the significance of the gulf between the class and culture of the teacher and that of the pupils:

> If the upbringing and home background of the teacher differ fundamentally from those of the pupil, even values held in common maybe be totally unrecognised because of their different manifestations.
>
> (LATE, 1958, p. 1)

Rosen's upbringing meant that he could justifiably claim to understand the values of the pupils of inner-city London, but he was clearly in a minority in this respect within the LATE community. In organising this conference, Rosen was, however, drawing attention to the class and cultural mismatch between teacher and taught as fundamental in thinking about the subject of English. The area of reading material emerged as a central concern at the conference, with the conference report noting that a result would be the need for English teachers to encounter texts that were important to children, those 'of a kind we may never have had to consider in framing grammar school syllabuses' (LATE, 1958, p. 1). Here we can see one key result of Rosen's work in convening this conference: the explicit acknowledgement that the traditional classroom literary canon would need to be expanded to include texts that would resonate with the lives of working-class children. Ultimately, according to the report, there should be one question that is posed to teachers in choosing texts and in designing the English curriculum more widely: 'What do these people care about?' (LATE, 1958, p. 1). There is certainly a clumsiness in the language here, a sense of the working class as some kind of alien 'other', but this is perhaps forgivable given that the members of LATE were taking tentative steps onto unchartered ground.

'English and the Urban Child' was a critical conference, as the issues surrounding the teaching of English in the comprehensive school became central to an increasing number of LATE members; Rosen was seeking to ensure that in searching solutions to the problems posed by the challenge of teaching in the inner-city comprehensive, teachers should begin with the experience and concerns of working-class children. There was no other starting point for an English pedagogy and curriculum that would address the needs of this group.

A second Rosen-convened LATE conference four years later highlights again how the experience of working-class children was being promoted as core to LATE's work in developing the new progressive model of English for the comprehensive school. Titled 'Changing Concepts of the Curriculum: The School, Society and the English Teacher', the conference keynote was Brian Jackson. Jackson, with his colleague Dennis Marsden, was the author of the influential *Education and the Working Class* (Jackson and Marsden, 1962). This groundbreaking publication was the product of research into the education of eighty-eight working-class children in grammar schools in Huddersfield and is often interpreted as having poured cold water on the belief of the extent to which grammar schools functioned as an engine of social mobility in England. The research suggested that the fate of genuinely working-class children travelling through the grammar school system pointed to the fact that easy ideas about social mobility were far from supportable. What might be required of children in somehow moving away from the families and communities of their upbringing might well have the potential for negative, rather than positive, impacts on their later life. Rosen's own educational experience would likely have chimed with the sentiments of the book. For Rosen, an education that truly had the experience and concerns of working-class children at its heart would not be one that required an abandonment of those very experiences and concerns in some kind of spurious attempt to 'become' middle class. The results of such an enterprise, essentially reinforcing and affirming existing inequalities, would often leave those working-class children as 'homeless' adults, no longer part of their own culture and community, yet not comfortably part of another. Equally, such an education was simply reinforcing the norms and values of the status quo, not offering any validation to the lives and experiences of the working class, nor offering any hope of genuine change.

At the conference Jackson drew on the statistical evidence of his research to suggest that despite the 'commonly held view that educational opportunities were equal', the fact remained that 'only a small proportion of the working class were getting higher education and most children were streamed at an early age' (LATE, 1962, p. 1). He went on to deliver scathing criticism of traditional methods of education in English, seeing them as 'anti-creative' and insisting 'too much stress (was) put on the decorous syntax of the day (grammar) and on the current printers' cliches (punctuation)' (LATE, 1962, p. 2). There should be, he advised, 'less training in approved codes and manners and recognition of the "Classics" orthodox taste in literature' (LATE, 1962, p. 2).

Such sentiments would have directly echoed the thinking of Rosen and his colleagues seeking to move English away from its traditional model and methods.

Rosen gave a talk after Jackson at the conference. The record of this contribution reveals that Rosen was characteristically direct in his criticisms of the O level examinations in particular, claiming that 'the relevance of this type of education to the needs of pupils in modern society is . . . nil' (LATE, 1962, p. 3). Clearly, for Rosen at least, LATE's efforts to reform the O level examination had in effect achieved very little; radical changes were still required if English curriculum and assessment were genuinely to be meaningful for working-class children.

These two LATE conferences – 'English and the Urban Child' and 'Changing Concepts of the Curriculum' – were events that placed the experience of working-class children at the very centre of the Association's thinking and show how Rosen, in the context of increasing comprehensivisation in the capital, was leading English teachers beyond the subject into the area of sociology to confront the ways in which the working class were being failed by the education system. LATE was a collaborative organisation, but there is no doubt that this shift towards a direct focus on the education of working-class children was led by Rosen, and it was a highly significant shift in terms of the direction of LATE work in the years leading up to the formation of NATE and the Dartmouth Seminar.

Taking on Bernstein: The Importance of Language and Class

That, historically, working-class children had failed in terms of academic attainment in the English system – and indeed in systems globally – was clear. In being at the forefront of refashioning English, Rosen demonstrated the belief that the problem was not with the children, but with the system. The system and its architecture of pedagogy, curriculum and assessment needed to change in order to offer a reasonable chance of success for 'ordinary' children. It's arguable, however, that for those interested, for whatever reason, in the maintenance of the status quo, the responsibility for the underachievement of the working class is put not at the door of the establishment but cited within the group of underachievers themselves; that is to say, that the reason for the failure of working-class children is due to something in their background, upbringing or indeed in their very nature. To make such an argument without simply sounding prejudicial, however, one requires some sort of evidence. For a time, following the advent of intelligence quotient (IQ) tests,[3] a view was put forward that, put simply, working-class children were less intelligent than their middle-class peers and that this genetic inheritance explained the relative attainment of differing social classes in the school system. The strength of such dubious claims, however, was increasingly called into question in the decades following the Second World War. Fortunately, for those who would not want to consider that the failure of working-class children was in some way the responsibility of the establishment, a new intellectual argument emerged to take the place of the IQ tests. At the beginning of the 1960s and into the 1970s, the work of Basil Bernstein emerged as an alternative way, seemingly supported by robust arguments grounded in sociolinguistics, to interpret the failure of working-class children.

Bernstein's work is extensive, and the ideas expressed therein evolved and shifted over time. His central concepts of the different linguistic codes used by different social classes were highly influential in arguments around the contrasting fates of the working-class and middle-class children in education. Broadly speaking, Bernstein initially theorised that two linguistic codes were in use – the restricted code and the elaborated code. The restricted code was characterised as being language used in a particular way and context-dependent, understanding being based on shared knowledge of participants in communication with each other. The range of syntax and vocabulary is limited within the restricted code. Elaborated code, in contrast, is language used in a universalistic way, with understanding not dependent on shared context or knowledge; meaning is detailed and explicit for all to understand. To take one of Bernstein's earliest definitions: 'Two general types of code can be distinguished: elaborated and restricted. They can be defined, on a linguistic level, in terms of the probability of predicting for any one speaker which syntactic elements will be used to organize meaning' (Bernstein, 1971, p. 58). From this definition, Bernstein suggested that 'In the case of an elaborated code, the speaker will select from a relatively extensive range of alternatives and therefore the probability of predicting the pattern of organizing elements is considerably reduced' (Bernstein, 1971). However, the reverse was the case with the restricted code, where 'the number of these alternatives is often severely limited and the probability of predicting the pattern is greatly increased' (Bernstein, 1971).

Crucially, Bernstein's hypothesis was that the acquisition of these codes was dependent on upbringing and socialisation, with the home and family being the most important contexts in this respect. He posited that:

> Children socialized within middle-class and associated strata can be expected to possess both an elaborated and a restricted code, whilst children socialized within some sections of the working-class strata, particularly the lower working-class, can be expected to be limited to a restricted code.
> (Bernstein, 1971, p. 107)

Bernstein did explicitly seek to suggest that he was not making value judgements about the two codes:

> Clearly one code is not better than another; each possesses its own aesthetic, its own possibilities. Society, however, may place different values on the orders of experience elicited, maintained and progressively strengthened through the different coding systems.
> (Bernstein, 1971, p. 106)

This seems unambiguous enough on a surface reading, but it is perhaps difficult to escape at least one line of thinking that suggests if society places value on experience elicited in a particular coding system than this would be the elaborated code. From there, it is not leap to a conclusion that one code is in fact better than another.

Critically, Bernstein's suggestion was that the elaborated code was the code of the education system, of the school and of the teacher, and this was at the heart of why working-class children fail in school in disproportionate numbers. Working-class children 'have access to no other code; their only code is the restricted one' (Bernstein, 1971, p. 107). Having access to the elaborated code through their upbringing and socialisation means that the middle-class child is, in a sense, already acclimatised to the world of the school before arriving there; it is a familiar linguistic environment which offers continuity from that of the home. There is no divide, no gap to bridge. This is not the case for the child from a working-class background, 'between the school and community of the working-class child, there may exist a cultural discontinuity based upon two radically different systems of communication' (Bernstein, 1971, p. 111).

So in Bernstein's view, the experience of schooling is radically different for working-class and middle-class children. It becomes more than simply a linguistic challenge; it becomes a cultural one. For those who come to school in possession of the elaborated code, there is no potential 'clash of cultures' that might inevitably lead to problems of access or engagement. There is some sense of continuity; there is no necessity to deal with the challenges that ultimately, and inevitably, arise from change:

> Where a child is sensitive to an elaborated code the school experience for such a child is one of symbolic and social development; for the child limited to a restricted code the school experience is one of symbolic and social change.
>
> (Bernstein, 1971, p. 107)

Faced with 'symbolic and social change', it would be little wonder that school might present such difficulty for the working-class children that Bernstein suggested were limited to the use of the restricted code. The obvious conclusion from this line of thinking is that there is a need for working-class children to acquire the language of the school in order to have a chance to make progress and escape their fate of seemingly inevitable under attainment. As Bernstein puts it:

> If a child is to succeed as he progresses through school it becomes critical for him to possess, or at least to be oriented towards, an elaborated code. The relative backwardness of lower working-class children may well be a form of culturally induced backwardness transmitted to the child through the implications of the linguistic process.
>
> (Bernstein, 1971, p. 107)

This idea reflected what has been described as the 'common sense' of teachers, as Hardcastle and Yandell suggest in their account of the development of subject English in the post-war years:

> Perceived linguistic 'deficiency' was used widely to explain working-class educational underachievement. Well-meaning teachers aimed to equip their students, especially working-class students, with the language they 'needed' to succeed in education.
>
> (Hardcastle and Yandell, 2018, p. 567)

For some, Bernstein's ideas inevitably lead to the conclusion that there is something 'wrong' with working-class children that is a product of their upbringing, family and socialisation. Their shortcoming is the failure to have acquired the linguistic code necessary for success in school. Even if teachers are well-meaning, they are starting from the position that the fault lies in the child, not elsewhere – there is no questioning of the system in this formulation. It is difficult not to interpret the word 'restricted' without it carrying with it a pejorative sense. As previously mentioned, however, Bernstein did claim that he was not making value judgements about the two codes, and he indeed made the argument that schooling for working-class children should not be seen as 'compensatory' and not viewed as seeking to make up for a deficit the working-class child brings with them to the school gates. In one particularly notable section of his writing, for example, Bernstein suggests:

> It is an accepted educational principle that we should work with what the child can offer: why don't we practise it? The introduction of the child to the universalistic meanings of public forms of thought is not compensatory education – it is education. It is in itself not making children middle class.
>
> (Bernstein, p. 154)

This seems highly reasonable, and indeed the idea that it is an accepted principle that teachers should work with what the child should offer seems to be progressive in many ways. One could even begin to think, as Bernstein continues, that his reasoning might have appealed to Rosen:

> We need to distinguish between the principles and operations, that is our task as teachers to transmit and develop in the children, and the contexts we create in order to do this. We should start knowing that the social experience the child already possesses is valid and significant, and that this social experience should be reflected back to him as being valid and significant.
>
> (Bernstein, p. 154)

This seems clearly to suggest that the experience of the child should be the starting point for the work of the teacher, apparently the very argument Rosen had been making throughout his time as a teacher. Bernstein optimistically suggests that in creating classroom experiences that do indeed work to validate the experiences of children, 'possibly schools might become exciting and challenging environments for parents, children and teachers' (Bernstein, p. 154).

Passages such as this, however, with their seemingly progressive rhetoric, did little to pacify Harold Rosen. He was evidently incensed by the ideas Bernstein articulated about the language of the working class and its implications for their education. Rosen undoubtedly felt that notwithstanding Bernstein's claims, the model was indeed a deficit model; the failure of working-class children in school was as a result of their lacking something – the elaborated code of the middle class. It was another attempt to place the blame for failure at the door of working-class children and working-class communities. Rosen was inspired to respond to what he saw as another attack on the working class, an attack seemingly supported by powerful evidence from the field of linguistics, giving it an apparent intellectual foundation. The result was one of Rosen's most powerful and influential publications advocating for working-class children, *Language and Class: A Critical Look at the Theories of Basil Bernstein* (Rosen, 1972). It was a paper that began as a talk at History Workshop No. 6 at Ruskin College, Oxford. It was precipitated, as Rosen remembered, by a conversation he had with a leading academic historian at the time:

> It is just that I remember Ralf Samuels[4] saying to me, this is how it began, a little pamphlet, he said – I have got a problem, I have got wonderful working-class students that give the lie to Bernstein, but they all say – you can't expect us (to put it crudely) to write essays because we all speak restricted. And they had bought it hook line and sinker. And he said – will you come and give a talk at history workshop? And I did. And it was crammed with all these bright young sociologists, and the talk was virtually this pamphlet.[5]

Within this memory is an indication of the influence of Bernstein's thinking on language and class and a suggestion of one of its potentially most pernicious impacts – working-class students seeing themselves as somehow unable to fulfil the requirements of academic writing due to their socialised use of language. Perhaps it was this, the sense that Bernstein's influence was leading to working-class students accepting something of the inevitability of their fate, that particularly enraged Rosen, for *Language and Class*, is, without doubt, an angry polemic.

The paper is bold and uncompromising in its approach, infused with Rosen's political thinking as he critiques both Bernstein's work and the way in which it can be used by those in power to vindicate their positions, those 'who, in the effort to guard their privileges and power within the educational system, seek tirelessly for new and better theoretical positions' (Rosen, 1972, p. 2).

In the paper, Rosen notes how impactful Bernstein's ideas have become, to the extent of reaching classrooms rather than simply being in the sphere of academia, and the way in which both those on the left and the right of the political spectrum use the ideas to justify their respective positions.

A central criticism that immediately emerges from the text is what Rosen clearly considers Bernstein's inadequate conceptualisation of the notion of class. This includes the homogenisation of both the working class and the middle class to two discrete and singular groups and to the curious absence of the ruling class; Rosen's Marxist beliefs underpin the statement that 'A thorough attempt to analyse the relationship between class and language would require us to examine the relationship of the dominant culture of our society to the culture of the dominated' (Rosen, 1972, p. 6). There is nothing of this sort in Bernstein's work, and in this absence, there is, for Rosen, a central flaw in the conceptual thinking.

Rosen takes issue with the way Bernstein apparently focuses only on the family as the prime socialising agency, ignoring ways in which workers have changed society so that

> the working-class child, marooned in the family with his authoritarian father and status-oriented mother, appears by omission to be denied for ever access to an elaborated code and it benefits, since he is alienated from the only agency which could give it to him, school.
> (Rosen, 1972, p. 7)

One can sense Rosen's ire at what he sees as the stereotypical portrait of the working-class family, with each member fulfilling a particular role. He knew only too well from his own upbringing that this was a grossly inaccurate portrayal of at least one working-class family.

Focusing almost exclusively on the family and ignoring the work experience of the working classes means that Bernstein, in Rosen's view, neglects to consider the implications of differences in the language and experience of different groups of workers and fails to appreciate how the collective action of workers is rooted not in some sort of herd mentality but in individual uses of language to inform debate that results in such action. Rosen's view is that Bernstein's generalisations and omissions result in a 'relationship of the theory to the texture of reality [which] is at best tenuous' (Rosen, 1972, p. 10). This tenuous relationship is further exemplified for Rosen by the fictitious examples of language use Bernstein imagines to illustrate his theories in action – for example, the fictional conversation between the invented middle-class couple and their imaginary friends (Rosen, 1972, p. 10). These are not real uses of language by real people in the real world; they are dreamt-up interactions to lend weight to an argument that Rosen sees as fatally flawed in its inability to explore language genuinely in operation amongst real working- and middle-class people.

Rosen is dismissive of Bernstein's attempts to maintain that his theories are not in themselves denigrating the working class. Whilst Bernstein might powerfully argue that his ideas are not aligned with ideas around compensatory education designed to address a linguistic or cultural deprivation, labels which, in his own words, 'do their own sad work' (Bernstein, 1971, p. 192), Rosen argues,

> You cannot protest very convincingly about the harm done by the label, 'linguistic deprivation', when your own theory points to a deficit, indeed when you have actually stated elsewhere that 'the normal linguistic environment of the working class is one of relative deprivation' (Bernstein, 1971, p. 66) and that the codes are 'highly resistant to change' (op sit p. 91). The labels 'restricted' and 'elaborated' also 'do their own sad work'.
>
> (Rosen, 1972, p. 15)

For Rosen, Bernstein's ideas are rooted in a deficit model; the attempt to disguise this is, for him, defeated within the work's own internal contradictions and by the inevitable connotations readers draw from the terms restricted and elaborated. One could suggest it is curious that Bernstein, as a linguist, could ignore both the pejorative implication of 'restricted' and the conversely positive connotations of 'elaborated'.

Rosen ends the critique not claiming that 'working-class speech is as fine an instrument as could be devised for communication and thinking, and that middle-class speech is pretentious verbiage'. This would be 'absurd romanticism' (Rosen, 1972, p. 19). There is potential value in the acquisition of the different uses of language across the school, but there is nuance to such a belief. Rosen's conclusion is that

> There are aspects of language usually acquired through education which, given favourable circumstances, give access to more powerful ways of thinking; but given the conditions of life of many strata of the middle class, the language acquired through education can conceal deserts of ignorance.
>
> (Rosen, 1972, p. 19)

In this depiction of the fate of the middle class, and in his damning assertion that 'The middle class have often to pay a price for the acquisition of certain kinds of transactional language, and that is a loss of vitality and expressiveness, and obsession with proprieties' (Rosen, 1972, p. 19), one can almost feel that Rosen has a sympathy for those that, according to Bernstein, are predetermined to succeed within education. It is, for Rosen, far more complex than that. As is, for Rosen, the whole concept of different uses of language; he claims there is no 'sharp dividing line' (Rosen, 1972) between working-class speech and other speech, but that there are 'infinite variations in the deployment of resources of language' (Rosen, 1972). The polarisation of elaborated and restricted code offers nothing in terms of exploring the ways in which children from different backgrounds move along the linguistic spectrum and how and why they may do this in different circumstances, both in and out of school. After what is a withering and confident assault on Bernstein's thinking, Rosen ends *Language and Class* with a somewhat disarming, self-deprecating admission about what he has written, suggesting that despite his admonishment of Bernstein's ideas, the fact remains that 'we do not know much about the relationship between language and class. It is time to find out' (Rosen, 1972). It's fair to say that such an ending is not uncharacteristic of Rosen's academic writing; his thinking often does not provide easy solutions but points instead to the problems that exist and to the work that is still to be done.

One can argue whether Rosen is fair to Bernstein in *Language and Class*. As indicated, Bernstein does make numerous attempts to explain that his position is not to denigrate the language or experience of the working classes, and Rosen effectively dismisses these out of hand. Just as Rosen criticises Bernstein for the selective nature of his evidence, one could level the self-same accusation at Rosen. It is also the case that Bernstein's views did evolve and shift over time, as demonstrated in his writing, so that, as Burgess noted, despite the strength of Rosen's critique:

> It may be said that the general, underpinning theory of codes survived the force of Harold's critique; and Bernstein went on to develop the theory through a series of remarkable analyses of curriculum and pedagogy.
> (Burgess, 2009, p. 44)

Indeed, there have been arguments that deploy Bernstein's ideas as the basis for the construction of relatively radical visions of English curriculum and pedagogy (see, for example, Lambirth, 2011). Whether we fully agree with Rosen's critique of Bernstein's text, and the extent to which we feel it effectively negates the concepts of linguistic codes as expressed therein are, in some sense, not entirely the points. Whatever one's view, it is impossible not to acknowledge the enduring significance of *Language and Class*. What Rosen does in this punchy pamphlet is arguably forcefully and passionately for a shift in the discourse and thinking about the education of the working class. As Burgess suggested, *Language and Class* 'helped to make the themes of deprivation and deficit that it addressed central within English teaching' (Burgess, 2009, p. 44). If true, this alone speaks to its enduring significance. A reader of *Language and Class* can feel Rosen's anger and indignation at what he sees is implied by Bernstein's ideas – not simply the denigration of their language, but – as this language use is a result of their families, communities and work – a denigration of the working class as people. Even if Bernstein protests against this in a convincing way, it would be easy for the establishment to take the work as intellectual backing for the view that working-class children are doomed to fail until they learn the ways of the middle class.

Language and Class, at the very least, should make educators recognise and refrain from generalisations about class when making arguments about education or educational failure. A reading of the text powerfully argues the case that the working class – and for that matter the middle class – are far from a homogeneous mass about whom assumptions could or should be made about language use, with such assumptions being almost entirely based on probably uniformed notions of their home experience. This was an idea that Rosen continued to argue, writing a decade after *Language and Class*, for example:

> I would want quite simply to assert that those children are powerfully affected not only by the shared economic position of their parents but also by the lengthy history of education and the varied location of their parents in the social system; by the different histories they inherit, their degree of class consciousness, their ethnicity and their sex. Working-class children are not an undifferentiated cohort.
>
> (Rosen, 1986, p. 125)

To generalise, William Blake said, is to be an idiot, and there is a strong message for teachers and educators in *Language and Class* to avoid stereotypical assumptions and to appreciate the complexity in what is bound up in the term working class.

There are also powerful statements that warn against assumptions about what the so-called elaborated code of the school can do (or, indeed, is good for). Rosen quite correctly makes the point that:

> We are informed repeatedly by Bernstein that 'schools are predicated upon the elaborated code' (Bernstein, 1971, p. 186). No attempt is made, in fact, to examine how language is really used in schools most of the time.
>
> (Rosen, 1972, p. 18)

By the time of writing his critique of Bernstein, Rosen had been involved in the writing of *Language, the Learner and the School* (Barnes et al., 1969) and was involved in research with colleagues at the Institute of Education on pupils' writing. In addition to his own experience as a teacher and teacher educator, he had heard numerous examples of the oral language of the classroom on tape recordings and the written language in countless examples of writing. In this context, Rosen had knowledge of real classroom language use that Bernstein simply couldn't claim to possess. Rosen's view is that 'Some of us who have been studying tapes of language in school would say that very frequently, especially in the secondary system, there is an actual reduction in the range of pupils' language in many school lessons' (Rosen, 1972, p. 18). For Rosen, the simple characterisation of school language as elaborated code was another generalisation to the point of meaninglessness: 'There are many other things one would want to say about the way in which language is used and unused in school, but one thing is certain – Bernstein's alluring descriptions of the elaborated code do not fit it' (Rosen, 1972).

An indication of the impact of *Language and Class* can be gleaned from the immediate reception Rosen remembers receiving when delivering the initial talk at Ruskin College. He anticipated challenge from the listeners, perhaps a stout defence of Bernstein given the pervasiveness of his ideas, but instead he remembered:

> I thought they would all come diving in. Not a word. And I waited. And I said – this is interesting. What we could do with is a sociology of your silence. What have you been doing? Either swallowed the stuff or swallowed your misgivings. Anyway, Jeremy came up to me and said – the age of pamphlets is back, can we make that into a pamphlet? And we did. And it sold thousands and thousands. Nothing I have ever published before or since sold like that.[6]

The sales of the paper suggest an impact far beyond the world of academia, and certainly *Language and Class* survives as, arguably, Rosen's most powerful written contribution to the debates about the education of working class. *Language and Class* contributed to other critiques of Bernstein's work, so that by the 1980s, Rosen was able to make the claim that: 'It is no longer possible with any intellectual honesty to treat elaborated and restricted codes as though we were dealing with uncontentious objective aspects of language use' (Rosen, 1986, p. 127). Whether or not he had crushed Bernstein's claims, or whether they indeed survive the critique, Rosen did enough to ensure that the generalisations about language and about class that were encapsulated within the notions of restricted and elaborated codes were challenged and questioned. Rosen remained deeply critical of Bernstein's ideas for the remainder of his professional life; in an interview published in 1982, when Rosen was asked if he believed there to be anything of merit in Bernstein's work, he replied, 'Nothing whatsoever. The more I had acquaintance with it and its effects, the less I think there is in it. I think it's rather the biggest con that's ever been pulled' (Anderson and Butler, 1982, p. 28). A harsh evaluation perhaps, but one that underscores the potential damage Rosen saw in the propagation of ideas about restricted and elaborated codes. In his challenge to this potential damage, Rosen left us with arguably his most important single work on education, class and language, one to which contemporary linguists have returned when examining new iterations of deficit thinking in relation to the language of young people (see, for example, Cushing, 2023).

Multiculturalism

Rosen's focus on the education and language of the working class was understandably somewhat monocultural in its initial focus. The classrooms in which he worked during his teaching career would not have been ethnically diverse to any genuine extent. In the 1950s, London was only just beginning to see the mass immigration that would, within a very few years, mean that the capital's classrooms would become genuinely multicultural. As this shift took place, Rosen, perhaps inevitably, turned his attention to the implications for English teachers of working in multicultural classrooms. Rosen contributed significantly to the advancement of thinking in this area, particularly in his work on the language of the multicultural classroom. Rosen's contribution here is clearly of huge relevance to the field of English education, but the work in which he was involved has implications for teachers far beyond the specialism of English.

There is a clear indication of a turn in the direction of language and multiculturalism in *Language and Class*. Here, Rosen turned to the work of the American linguist William Labov to support his critique of Bernstein. Labov is an academic that Rosen draws on often in his own writing, unsurprisingly since his research is seen to offer groundbreaking insights into the language of the underprivileged. In his detailed analysis of black working-class language,[7] Labov powerfully called into question ideas about verbal deprivation, revealing the potentiality and richness of the Black English Vernacular. Labov's attention to the real language of groups of disadvantaged young people so struck Rosen that he questioned, 'Why is there no English Labov?' (Rosen, 1972, p. 18). For Rosen, a significant dimension of his critique of Bernstein was the plea for much greater research in England of the ways in which language is used by young people of different classes; in increasingly diverse classrooms it was almost inevitable that this research would need to consider the ways in which young people from different ethnic backgrounds, and users of English as a second or third language, would be using the vernacular.

Perhaps in part in response to his own plea for an English Labov, Rosen, in collaboration with Tony Burgess, ultimately led a research project that resulted in the publication of *Languages and Dialect of London School Children* (Rosen and Burgess, 1980). This groundbreaking project makes a significant contribution to the debates around multicultural education through an analysis of the linguistic diversity in a selection of the capital's schools. Twenty-eight schools were involved in this project, with data collected on a total of 4,600 11–12-year-old pupils. The project ostensibly was based on the collection of data, but its aim was not simply to produce figures about numbers of speakers of languages other than English, 'The focus was the diversity of languages and dialects at classroom level, regarding all pupils as contributing to this diversity, not simply a head counting exercise of overseas languages' (Burgess, p. 46). Significantly, the process by which the data would be collected was innovative in terms of research design. Rosen and his co-researchers worked alongside classroom teachers, and pupils were involved in group interviews and discussions as part of the compilation of the data. The aim was for the project to be a collaborative exercise between researchers, teachers and pupils so that the outcome of the survey was not simply to provide information but to 'serve as an instrument of in-service education sensitizing teachers to the configuration of diversity, improving their knowledge of their own pupils' language and setting in train a reconsideration of policies and practices' (Burgess, p. 3).

Languages and Dialect of London School Children was innovative of its time and now stands as a fascinating historical record of the linguistic diversity present in the capital's schools in the late 1970s. It's without doubt that the picture in the twenty-first century, should such an enterprise be repeated, would be even more diverse. The text offers fascinating insights, particularly when discussing and interpreting the various dialects present in schools, particularly around what the researchers term 'London Jamaican'. Distinctions are made between code switching and code sliding in terms of the choices children from West Indian backgrounds make in their language use, and language use is conceived in terms of 'continuums'. Thus, the language of these children:

> Emerges from the interaction of two quite different continua. There is the Creole continuum (ranging from one of the West Indian Creoles to a West Indian standard). And there is the London continuum (ranging from a full Cockney to standard British English). These two continua are in dynamic interaction.
>
> (Rosen, 1982, p. 69)

Although the explicit focus of *Languages and Dialects of London School Children* is linguistic diversity and the implications it presents are broadly concerning the area of multicultural education, it's entirely feasible to argue that the focus on social class that was always central to Rosen's thinking is never far from the surface. Harris (2009), for example, suggests that

> One of the remarkable things about LDLS was the way in which it kept the focus on class at a time in the 1970s and 1980s when the key preoccupation in debates on educational inequalities had shifted sharply from social class to race and ethnicity.
>
> (Harris, 2009, p. 83)

This suggestion is based on aspects such as the framing of questions in the survey, which implicitly imply that non-standard varieties of English would probably be the norm in classrooms, and on the prevalence given throughout to the influence of Caribbean dialects in the emergence of London Jamaican. Rosen was explicit about this relationship between language, class and diversity; for him, teachers that were simultaneously struggling with issues of the place of working-class language and the increasing diversity of classrooms were confronting the reality that, 'these two matters were in essence different facets of the same question' for 'language and cultural diversity is language and class writ large' (Rosen, 1982, p. 67).

The concluding chapter of *Languages and Dialects of London School Children* discusses the potential implications for schools, noting that 'multi-cultural education has struggled its way on to our national educational agenda' (Rosen and Burgess, 1980, p. 95) and asserting that 'it is only recently that we have come to realize that the whole curriculum for all children must change in the light of cultural diversity' (Rosen and Burgess, 1980). After addressing areas including examinations and tests, in-service teacher education and language maintenance, the text ends with a call 'for a change in how we perceive children so that school is seen by them as a place which is theirs' (Rosen and Burgess, 1980, p. 140). This would seem to be at least one definition of a truly multicultural education – one where the institution is seen to be truly inclusive.

However, Rosen saw the complexities of the notion of a multicultural education and that there were no easy answers to be had, and in his articulation of these difficulties, we can see the importance of his contribution to the debate. From Rosen's preoccupation with class, it's clear that he knew the pitfalls of monolithic conceptions of working or middle class. Classes are not homogeneous masses. The work that produced *Languages and Dialects of London School Children* revealed the complexities and intricacies of language use amongst pupils in school, and with language linked inextricably with identity and culture, it is self-evident that similarly complex conceptions about different cultures need to be at the heart of any discussion of multicultural education. Rosen was scathing of those who failed to see this complexity; with reference to David Holbrook's *English for Meaning* (Holbrook, 1979), in which the author seemed to suggest – in only one paragraph addressing the diversity of classrooms – that simply good reading and writing was the solution, Rosen legitimately made the point, 'What is this good writing and good reading which can be conjured out of processes which have nothing to do with the lived culture of the children?' (Rosen, 1982, p. 60). Knowledge of pupils and of their language, culture and community had been the cornerstone of Rosen's thinking about high-quality English teaching; in classrooms that were welcoming increasing diversity of language, culture and community, the priority was for teachers to develop their knowledge. Falling back on the easy adoption of 'good reading and writing' was not approaching a response to the challenge. Equally, Rosen rightfully saw the deceit implicit in the idea of some policy pronouncements that suggested there was some simple way to create harmonious multicultural classrooms, whilst ignoring the larger context of a society that was the site for cultural conflicts of various kinds. Such conflict is everywhere, is an inevitable product of class and culture within any given society, and presents a further level of complexity when we consider multicultural classrooms that may be home to young people from different countries. For Rosen sees that culture:

> is not a monolithic entity, an integrated diversity of significant meanings and practices, nor a common core of democratically shared life. There is

dominant culture and dominated culture both in the countries which have received new minority groups and in the countries from which they come.
(Rosen, 1982, p. 63)

Far from a monolithic entity, cultures are not just sites for conflict; they are dynamic and shifting, so that, 'Under our very eyes we can see cultures changing as they embody new orders of experience' (Rosen, 1982).

The notion of multicultural education being the offering of some sort of stable national British culture to those coming from other cultures was, for Rosen, ludicrous. Similarly, some kind of simple promotion of multiculturalism through the inclusion in the curriculum of texts from authors from around the world was no solution. A straightforward embrace of 'other cultures' ignored the complexity of the fact Rosen was only too aware of; there were – within any cultures – values that, as an English teacher, one would simply not want to be embraced.

Rosen, then, saw that whatever one wanted to mean by the term culture, it was not something that was stable, definable and quantifiable. Cultures were changing, and there were sites of conflict within and between cultures. Thus, the simple idea that the classroom should be a place that harmoniously embraced the cultures of the different children was utterly misleading. With reference to the Bullock Report blandly stating the idea that children should not be expected to experience school as a totally separate culture from their own, Rosen argued: 'it is possible, following this rubric, for schools to be the arbiters of what constitutes the culture of the home, to trivialise it in paternalistic fashion, seizing upon obvious differences of food, custom and ceremonies' (Rosen, 1982, p. 64). Again, the risk is of stereotyping and generalising, and whilst this might on the surface make decisions about curriculum straightforward, it ignores the fact that

> The culture of the pupils arises from lived understandings, and its meanings are not simply to be had for the asking. Bland and uncontroversial selections are likely to omit all those cultural practices which embody resistance and fracture the desired harmony.
> (Rosen, 1982)

Such a bland and benevolent conception of multicultural education, selecting accepted cultural norms from different communities, ignored a number of elephants in the classroom in England – for example, the legacy of colonialism and the lived reality of racism. In Rosen's words: 'It is a straight lie to claim that with steel bands and calypsos in the school concert we can produce racial harmony' (Rosen, 1982, pp. 64–65) because 'a concept of education which does not look racism in the eye is a mockery' (Rosen, 1982, p. 65). Typically, in considering ideas about the teaching of English in multicultural classrooms, Rosen did not present teachers with answers; rather, he was clear about the complexity of the questions that had to be resolved. Arguably, it is only in recent years with the advent of thinking about decolonising, rather than diversifying, education, that the kinds of questions Rosen posed have begun to be properly addressed.

All of the complexities of attempts to define or compartmentalise culture or cultures led Rosen to a view that rather than seeking to develop multicultural education, the aim should be 'intercultural' education, an enterprise that

> must be based on the active expression and exploration by the pupils of their sense of their lives in the here and now, of their intercultural experience. In the absence of real equality we need to give scope to the expression of tension and conflict, not to muffle its discordant and strident notes.
>
> (Rosen, 1982, p. 65)

This appears to be a genuine challenge to teachers and, indeed, to an education system; that is, to allow pupils ways in the classroom that enable them to reflect on the tensions that are the reality of a multicultural society. What, for Rosen, did this mean for teachers of English? Simply opening up the classroom for all forms of linguistic diversity in the attempt to foster some kind of harmony was a wholly unrealistic enterprise. For Rosen, the premise that one could happily proclaim equality of dialects was confounded by the evidence, which suggested, 'the speaking of dialects may constitute different kinds of acts for different speakers' (Rosen, 1982, p. 70). Such acts might include intentional resistance to the attempts by an institution to impose a standard language. Rosen suggested that this resistance was manifested in the classroom in pupils' responses to authority: 'In inner city schools what most pupils share is frustration and often anger, expressed, as we know, in anything from surliness to overt rebelliousness' (Rosen, 1982). Rosen's conclusion was that for pupils for whom Standard English – (whatever that means; as will be discussed in the next chapter, Rosen found this term anything but unproblematic) – was not a mother tongue:

> It will not be enough to allow them to use their dialect in school; they will need to be convinced that they can use it to say the most important things they have to say in writing as well as speech.
>
> (Rosen, 1982)

For the teacher of English, this is a challenge indeed – then as it is, arguably as much, now. It is one thing to make the English classroom a space where pupils feel empowered to use their own language in speech – the ephemeral nature of most oral activity in classrooms might well make this somewhat more achievable – but to extend this to the written context is a further, significant, challenge. Schools, and this was fundamental to much of Rosen's important work on writing and on language across the curriculum, as we will see in the next chapter, have accepted ways that things can be said but arguably even more rigidity in terms of the acceptability of the ways in which things can be written. This rigidity is undoubtedly strengthened by the workings of assessment frameworks and examinations. Rosen felt the task facing the English teacher in the multicultural classroom, to be not impossible, but 'demanding, delicate and exploratory' (Rosen, 1982). Rosen saw this sort of teaching and learning happening in classrooms in London, where:

> the best English teaching in recent years has been an attempt to tear down all those barriers which made the pupils invisible – invisible to themselves, to each other and ultimately to the world; an attempt to call a halt to all those verbal exchanges in English classrooms in which what was not said was more important than what was said.
>
> (Rosen, 1982)

Despite the undoubted challenges Rosen saw for English teachers seeking to adopt genuinely 'intercultural' approaches to their teaching, then, he remained optimistic for the potential effects of these endeavours. This optimism, bolstered by the work of those like Chris Searle[8] in Stepney, was characteristic of Rosen, who wanted teachers to see the possibilities open to them and to their pupils through effective English work; notwithstanding the many barriers the nature of the institution placed in the way, he was anything but defeatist. In the poetry of the children taught by Searle, Rosen suggested that one could see that sparks were flying, as children were empowered to express what was important to them in the ways they wanted to express these things, and that if all minority children might be given the same opportunity, there might be 'sparks galore' (Rosen, 1982).

Rosen presented one model of how this kind of multicultural education might be developed through work on the language curriculum in the fourth chapter of *Languages and Dialects of London School Children*. The account (Rosen and Burgess, 1980, pp. 119–126) describes how one school's involvement in the research via a working party and conference led to the development of a set of materials produced by a number of schools in a booklet under the title Languages. The materials produced for the classroom were designed to encourage an exploration of the diverse range of children's languages and dialects and the sharing of these in the classroom. The approach taken, inviting children to share stories in their own languages, for example, meant, according to Rosen, that for the teachers involved, that work on linguistic diversity was of critical importance for education in a multicultural society, bringing with it the potential 'to combat racism and prejudice generally' (Rosen and Burgess, 1980, p. 126). Being rooted in children's own language and experience, the approach 'forges links between school and community which can only enhance the curriculum' (Rosen and Burgess, 1980).

Conclusion

Rosen's work in the area of the education of the working class is a critical element of his legacy, and one central reason why he deserves to be considered a key thinker – not just within English and the Language arts, but within education more broadly. Working within LATE in the 1950s and 1960s, he brought the education of the working class to the forefront of the Association's agenda. He did this initially, as seen in the previous chapter, through his central role in the campaign to reframe O level assessment and then, far more explicitly, through the planning of conferences and the invitation of speakers from disciplines beyond English. As a head of department at Walworth, he was at the very forefront of the capital's drive to comprehensivisation and began to put into practice the reality of an English curriculum attuned to the needs of 'ordinary' children. This meant changing practice so that English classrooms became a welcoming space for the experience and language of working-class children, where they could talk and write about their lives, their families and their communities. He took this passion for the education of the working class into his long career in academia. In writing *Language and Class*, Rosen took on Bernstein's influential ideas and changed the debate around class, language and education. Taking working-class language as the focal point of debate, he called into question easy generalisations about social status and challenged many aspects of the arguments around deficit which beset the prevailing thinking about working-class children and their relative under attainment in schools. In his writing about the education and language of the working class, Rosen brings fundamental issues to the forefront of teachers' minds for working-class children:

> may accept the class-based judgment passed on their language and strive to adapt and adopt the meaning system which school presses upon them. If they do so, they sever themselves from their own meaning system or even develop a contempt for it. If they reject the language the school offers they retain the class identifying power of their own language but lose the opportunity of mastering much of the understanding which enables them more effectively to change their condition.
>
> (Rosen, 1986, p. 129)

This is the iniquitous position a traditional education puts the working-class child in; she must seemingly abandon her own language and culture or retain it but thereby sacrifice the opportunity to transform her world. Reading Rosen's writings and thoughts on education and class, one cannot help but be struck by the passionate empathy for children and how they are positioned by the system. Repeatedly in officially sanctioned government reports, dating back to Newbolt (Board of Education, 1921), the language of the working class had been denigrated, and for Rosen the establishment and teachers' views of the working class were only further vindicated by the work of Bernstein: 'It didn't need Bernstein to make teachers contemptuous of working kids' language. They always have been. What he did was to give academic respectability to it' (Anderson and Butler, 1982, p. 28).

Rosen was fired by a belief in the potential of the working class and the possibility that education might genuinely empower them. This was an optimistic view; Rosen did not share the defeatist view of some on the left of politics that the education system simply plays its part in the hegemonic capitalist system and can only ever reproduce and sustain inequalities. Late in his life, Rosen, reflecting on this pessimistic view that education only works to keep the established system going, to 'feed the appropriate numbers into the appropriate slots', stated this to be:

> Rubbish, of course, because they don't know the appropriate slots. As though capitalism has got it all worked out, successfully, which it manifestly has not. But it is a bit like going very fundamental and saying – what do you teach kids to read for? They will only read capitalist stuff. Well, the answer is, once you teach kids to read you don't know what he or she will do with it. You just don't know. And it is an incredible, potential weapon.[9]

This was a belief in the potential of education for the working class that was in no small way borne out of his own life story; he was a working-class boy from an impoverished urban background. He had experienced the prejudice that came with that background and succeeded within an education system that was, at best, inhospitable. But Rosen's view was also informed by a particular strain of political thinking that recognised the history of left-wing intellectualism:

> I think it was Marx, or Engels, who said what was remarkable about the working class he encountered, one of them, was their extraordinary reading. And he said they are reading unexpurgated texts which the intelligentsia, upper class, don't read.[10]

Rosen was well versed in the alternative, intellectual history of what he called 'the great working class of our country' (Rosen, 1975, p. 339), so that for him it was simply a socially established assumption to proclaim they are 'nothing but a deprived inarticulate herd' (Rosen, 1975). A proper appreciation of working-class history shows us that

> millions of people throughout Europe in the late nineteenth and early twentieth centuries won their way to literacy from homes which were totally illiterate. Theories about the cycle of deprivation, glibly cited by politicians, have lurking beneath their surface an unhistorical notion that generations passively reproduce cultural attitudes
>
> (Rosen, 1975)

Rosen's optimism for the potential of education, however, was not just that capitalism hasn't 'got it all worked out'; he articulated powerfully that the nature of schools meant that there was reason to believe that change, to the benefit of the working class, was possible:

> Because schools in our society are so diverse, because they are never controlled in total fashion, because teachers themselves are not uniform, mindless zombies nor uncritical transmitters of the dominant ideology, because pupils are beginning to exert powerful pressures within the system, because politics in the community can break into sealed institutions, schools themselves are the arenas where genuine battles over contending practices are fought out. To turn our backs on them, to write them off as parts of the controlling apparatus and no more, is to refuse to participate in life itself.
>
> (Rosen, 1986, p. 127)

Rosen insisted, however, that for schools, and specifically for the English teachers within them, to genuinely create an environment where the working class had some equity of opportunity, there would need to be significant changes in attitude and approach:

> So much has already been achieved by pioneering English teaching, but if it is to take, to bite deep, then we must engage with working-class life and learn to apply our educated ears to its voice, with the same respect, awareness of nuances and human warmth we have applied so readily elsewhere. This is really the next bold step for English teaching.
>
> (Rosen, 1975, p. 340)

In extending his own work and thinking beyond the language and culture of the working class and into questions of multiculturalism and multilingualism, Rosen signalled further bold steps that would be necessary for educators to take.

Notes

1 Comment taken from an interview between John Richmond and the author as part of research for this book.
2 Comment taken from an interview with the author as part of PhD research.
3 IQ tests were developed in 1904 by the French psychologist Alfred Binet. Following the 1944 Education Act (Board of Education, 1944), IQ tests were used within the 11+ tests that were used to determine which children would attend grammar schools (see *IQ: A hundred* at https://www.theguardian.com/education/2004/jan/20/schools.uk1 accessed on 3rd March 2025).
4 Rapheal Samuel was a leading British historian. According to the website of the Bishopsgate Institute, 'He was Professor of History at the University of East London at the time of his death and also taught at Ruskin College from 1962 until his death. He also took a leading part in founding the History Workshop movement

which powerfully influenced the development of the approach to historical research and writing commonly called "history from below"'. Available at https://www.bishopsgate.org.uk/collections/raphael-samuel-and-history-workshop-archives accessed on 28th February 2025.
5 Comment taken from an interview with Harold Rosen conducted by John Hardcastle and Peter Medway as part of research for Medway, P., Hardcastle, J., Brewis, G. and Crook, D. (2014) *English Teachers in a Postwar Democracy: Emerging Choice in London Schools, 1945–65*. New York: Palgrave Macmillan.
6 Comment taken from an interview with Harold Rosen conducted by John Hardcastle and Peter Medway as part of research for Medway, P., Hardcastle, J., Brewis, G. and Crook, D. (2014) *English Teachers in a Postwar Democracy: Emerging Choice in London Schools, 1945–65*. New York: Palgrave Macmillan.
7 Labov's Language in the Inner City: Studies in the Black English Vernacular (1972) was a groundbreaking publication and well known to Rosen.
8 In 1971, Chris Searle was a probationary teacher in a school in Stepney, East London. Against the wishes of his school's governing body, he published an anthology of his pupils' poems under the title Stepney Words. He was subsequently dismissed, an act which prompted the walkout of 600 pupils who insisted they would not return to school until Searle was reinstated. He was eventually reinstated, albeit after two years.
9 Comment taken from an interview with Harold Rosen conducted by John Hardcastle and Peter Medway as part of research for Medway, P., Hardcastle, J., Brewis, G. and Crook, D. (2014) *English Teachers in a Postwar Democracy: Emerging Choice in London Schools, 1945–65*. New York: Palgrave Macmillan.
10 Comment taken from an interview with Harold Rosen conducted by John Hardcastle and Peter Medway as part of research for Medway, P., Hardcastle, J., Brewis, G. and Crook, D. (2014) *English Teachers in a Postwar Democracy: Emerging Choice in London Schools, 1945–65*. New York: Palgrave Macmillan.

References

Anderson, S. and Butler, S. (1982) 'Language and Power in the Classroom: An Interview with Harold Rosen'. *The English Journal*, 71:3, pp. 24–28.
Barnes, D., Britton, J. and Rosen, H. (1969) *Language, the Learner and the School*. Harmondsworth: Penguin.
Barron Mays, J. (1954) *Growing up in the City: A Study of Juvenile Delinquency in an Urban Neighbourhood*. Liverpool: University Press of Liverpool.
Bernstein, B. (1971) *Class. Codes and Controls Volume 1: Theoretical Studies Towards a Sociology of Language*. London: Routledge.
Board of Education (1921) *The Teaching of English in England* (commonly known as the Newbolt Report). London: His Majesty's Stationery Office.
Board of Education (1944) *The Education Act* (commonly known as the Butler Act). London: His Majesty's Stationery Office.
Burgess, Tony (2009) 'Harold at the Institute'. *Changing English*, 16:1, pp. 39–49.
Burt, C. (1955) 'Juvenile Delinquency'. *British Medical Journal* 3: 2, p. 604.
Cushing (2023) 'Word Rich or Word Poor? Deficit Discourses, Raciolinguistic Ideologies and the Resurgence of the 'Word Gap' in England's Education Policy'. *Critical Inquiry in Language Studies*, 20:4, pp. 305–331.
Hardcastle, J. and Yandell, J. (2018) "Even the Dead will not be Safe': The Long War Over School English'. *Language and Intercultural Communication*, 18:5, pp. 562–575.
Harris (2009) 'Language and Social Class: A Rosen Contribution'. *Changing English*, 16:1, pp. 81–91.

Hill, M. (2006) 'Bio-Bibliography: John Barron Mays (1914–1987)'. *Sociological Origins*, 4:Spring, pp. 111–114.

Holbrook, D. (1979) *English for Meaning*. Slough: National Foundation for Educational Research.

Jackson, B. and Marsden, D. (1962) *Education and the Working Class*. London: Routledge and Kegan Paul.

Labov, W. (1972) *Language in the Inner City: Studies in the Black English Vernacular*. Philadelphia: University of Pennsylvania Press.

Lambirth, A. (2011) *Literacy on the Left: Reform and Revolution*. London: Continuum International Publishing Group.

LATE (1958) *Secretary of Studies Report 1957–58*, held in the LATE archive at the University of London Institute of Education library.

LATE (1962) *Changing Concepts of the Curriculum: The School, Society and the English Teacher*. Conference Report, held in the LATE archive at the University of London Institute of Education Library.

Medway, P. and Kingwell, P. (2010) 'A Curriculum in Its Place: English Teaching in One School 1946–1963'. *History of Education*, 39:6, pp. 749–765.

Rosen (1972) *Language and Class: A Critical Look at the Theories of Basil Bernstein*. Bristol: Falling Wall Press.

Rosen (1975) 'Out there or where the Masons Went.' *Theory Into Practice*, 14:5, pp. 338–342.

Rosen (1982) 'Multicultural Education and the English Teacher' in Richmond, J. (ed.) *Harold Rosen: Writings on Life, Language and Learning 1958–2008*. London: UCL Institute of Education Press.

Rosen, B. (1988) *And None of it was Nonsense: The Power of Storytelling in School*. London: Harper Collins.

Rosen, H. (1986) 'Language and the Education of the Working Class' in Richmond, J. (ed.) *Harold Rosen: Writings on Life, Language and Learning 1958–2008*. London: UCL Institute of Education Press.

Rosen, H. and Burgess, T. (1980) *Languages and Dialects of London School Children* London: Ward Lock Educational.

Chapter 4

Harold Rosen

Language and Learning across the Curriculum

Introduction

It's clear that Rosen's influential contributions to debates and ideas about the education of the working class and multi-, or inter-, cultural education are infused throughout with ideas about language; the language of the working class and the vast range of languages and dialects of the children in London's classrooms. Language, culture and identity are inextricably linked, and this presents one of the challenges in seeking to organise an account of Rosen's work and influence. This chapter will consider Rosen's work on the language of the school and his significant contribution to notions of language across the curriculum, which came to prominence towards the end of the 1960s and which, for many, gained official endorsement in the publication of the Bullock Report in 1975 (Department for Education and Science, 1975). Working with colleagues in LATE and at the Institute of Education, Rosen was critical in driving forward the arguments that put language at the very centre of the school experience, seeking to ensure teachers from all subjects and phases gave language prominence in their thinking. As Rosen explained himself in a letter of application for a post as Chair in Education at Bristol University in 1970, he had by this time been looking beyond the boundaries of English in the school, 'Both my theoretical interests and practical concerns have increasingly drawn me towards a consideration of the role of language in learning and, therefore, the curriculum as a whole' (Rosen, 1970, p. 2).

Language across the Curriculum

Rosen was at the heart of the moves that came in the 1960s and beyond to bring into focus the ways in which language – for speaking, writing and reading – is used in schools. A number of key points were central to working in this area. One general area of interest was the recognition of the divergence between the ways in which language is used in schools within different subject disciplines and the disjunction between these uses of language and the language of pupils themselves. Rosen's work on the language of working-class children demonstrates his sensitivity to the way children from working-class backgrounds are at a potential disadvantage when they encounter the language of the classroom. In the work that pioneered the broader thinking about language across the curriculum, however, the central notion was that essentially the particular ways in which language was used in the different subject areas, including the impersonal style of speech and writing demanded and the specialist vocabulary deployed, were – to a greater or lesser extent – a challenge to all children and one that teachers across different disciplines had not hitherto confronted in any meaningful sense.

Two strands of work, taking place roughly simultaneously, illustrate Rosen's key contributions to debates about language use in school. The first of these was the Schools Council[1] funded research project, undertaken with colleagues at the Institute of Education, that led to the publication of *The Development of Writing Abilities (11–18)* (Britton et al., 1975).

The Development of Writing Abilities (11–18) was a large-scale research project which was led by James Britton, with the initial proposal written by Britton, along with Rosen and Nancy Martin (Britton et al., 1975, p. xi). The project began in 1966 following and, to an extent, growing from previous collaborative work of the three proposers (Britton et al., 1966). This earlier research on the multiple marking of compositions generated a series of questions that Rosen, Britton and Martin wanted to pursue: 'What difference did the kind of writing undertaken by a student make to the quality of work that was achieved, what were the differing orders of difficulty, what were the implications for assessment?' (Burgess, 2009, p. 42). The Development of Writing Abilities project was followed by a funded three-year development project looking at writing across the curriculum, headed by Nancy Martin, the aim of which was to 'investigate in collaboration with teachers in school the practical application of our research' (Burgess, 2009). Thus, the focus on school writing was an important area of Rosen's work for more than a decade. Indeed, during this period, Rosen completed his own doctorate (Rosen, 1969), and this too was focused on the written composition in English of pupils working towards the O level examination (Rosen, 1967). *The Development of Writing Abilities (11–18)* began to take Rosen's work beyond English; though it may have had its origins in work on writing in the subject specifically, with a focus on assessment, it grew to consider the nature of the writing pupils undertook in a range of secondary subjects and the implications of the linguistic demands of these for pupils' learning.

The research for the project initially involved collecting over 2000 pieces of writing completed by pupils across the secondary age range in a variety of subject areas in 65 schools (Britton et al., 1975, p. 13). The research team used this data as the basis for seeking to devise a way of categorising the types of writing children undertook in school, before follow-up work in five schools used the theoretical model proposed to explore how children made progress in their writing. *The Development of Writing Abilities (11–18)* sets out the approach the research team took in analysing the scripts to arrive at two sets of categories – one for the function of a piece of writing and one around the 'sense of audience' (Britton et al., 1975, p. 55). In the writing of the book detailing the project, it was Chapter 4, 'Sense of Audience', for which Rosen took the lead. The project was a collaboration between colleagues at the Institute of Education English department, but in considering this chapter, we can get a sense of Rosen's particular contribution to the critical debates about language across the curriculum that were promoted through the project.

Rosen's chapter begins with a theoretical discussion of audience, drawing on both historical work and that of contemporary sociolinguists, particularly that of Dell Hymes, whose work was well known to Rosen. The conclusion of this opening section leads to what in some ways might be the self-evident declaration that 'We conceive of the audience categories as a relationship between the writer and the reader' (Britton et al., 1975, p. 63). Though perhaps self-evident, the crux of this declaration is the way in which it is experienced by pupils in school, where the 'audience will overwhelmingly be predetermined and sharply defined; the teacher, a known audience of one' (Britton et al., 1975). The writer-reader relationship here is complex, with the reader taking a variety of roles; for example, assessor, which means 'pupils must focus a special kind of scrutiny in order to detect what they must do to satisfy him' (Britton et al., 1975, p. 64).

Rosen goes on to detail the divisions of audience generated by the project team – self, teacher, wider known audience, unknown audience and additional (Britton et al., 1975, p. 66), exploring in particular the audience of teacher in the various forms it may take since this is the predominant audience for the child as writer. These various audiences are used as a framework for the presentation in Chapter 8 of the text, which details the findings about audiences that children write for in school, and this sits alongside the analysis of the functions of writing defined by the project team (here the notions of transactional, expressive and poetic are employed along with the ideas of the participant and spectator role). These are all ideas developed by James Britton in other areas of his work.[2]

The findings presented in *the Development of Writing Abilities (11–18)* offer a fascinating picture of the types of writing undertaken in the secondary school, and in doing so they made a significant contribution to the developing initiatives around the emergence of language across the curriculum policies. By the time of its publication (1975), these initiatives, begun through LATE as described below, were reaching a seminal moment. The findings show very starkly how the audience of teacher as examiner is the most predominant in pupils' writing experience and that the vast majority of pupils' writing is transactional in nature. The project data indicate that, even from very early in the secondary school, the range of writing pupils undertake 'reflects information in the form in which both teacher and textbook traditionally present it' (Britton et al., 1975, p. 197). For the project team, a key point to emerge is the problem that comes from the fact that so little expressive writing is undertaken by pupils, and where it does happen, it is only ever in certain subjects (in this case, English and Religious Education). It is when undertaking writing in the expressive mode that pupils are using linguistic resources with which they are familiar and as the project team suggest:

> It is language that externalizes our first stages in tackling a problem or coming to grips with experience. Moreover, it represents, we believe, the move into writing most likely to preserve a vital link with the spoken mode in which up to this point all a child's linguistic resources have been gathered and stored.
> (Britton et al., 1975, p. 197)

This line of thinking was to become critical in the development of the ideas around language across the curriculum and was central to Rosen's thinking in the area. It is very likely, too, that it influenced Rosen's thinking on the importance of narrative in education, as will be considered in Chapter 5. The impersonal nature of transactional writing was far removed from children's own language use, and in forcing children to try to adopt this particular style of discourse, they were being prevented from using the linguistic resources in their possession to develop their understanding. Elsewhere Rosen took up the argument as to how far the kinds of impersonal, transactional discourses demanded by subjects were, in any case, seen as valid by schools intellectually rather than merely stylistically. The ways in which schools prevented children from using their own voice in their writing were a significant problem for Rosen, potentially severing the link with talk and jeopardising the intractable links between language and learning.

The second strand of work that Rosen was critically involved in was that being undertaken by LATE on language use in school. By the 1960s, LATE activity was diversifying. The focus on English curriculum and, particularly, assessment in the form of examinations had dominated the Association's activities in its first decade, but as the sixties progressed, LATE moved into other areas. Some of these, under the influence of Rosen, involved – as explored in the previous chapter – explicit consideration of education and class in the context of the comprehensive school, but another key strand was a burgeoning interest in language use more widely – the different ways in which children used language and the varying ways in which children experienced and used language in school, both in speech and writing. As Rosen put it himself when describing the way in which those in LATE were broadening their horizons:

> We stopped minding our own business and ventured into discussing language in education, language and experience, language and thought. For we had begun to realize that some goals could never be reached if we continued to regard language as something which happened only in five or so lessons each week.
> (Rosen, 1988, p. 2)

The idea that language – in the form, for example, of the teaching of writing – was the sole preserve of the English department in a secondary school has historically been used as a reason to explain the difficulty of encouraging teachers from other subject areas to address language in their own disciplines. Rosen and his LATE colleagues, as their thinking on the relationship between language and learning was beginning to be informed by Vygotsky's work, saw how limiting it would be for students if their experience of language was confined to English. An excellent example of the work LATE began to do in this area would be the 'Talk and Talkers' conference that Rosen convened in 1966. At this conference, LATE delegates were invited to explore the different ways in which groups of children used talk in different situations and for different purposes. In remembering his experience of LATE events, John Dixon felt this conference was a particularly critical event in the Association's work, and it was one that demonstrates the importance of Rosen's work. Dixon recalled the conference as one that:

> Harold ran with a great friend who was a primary school teacher and they'd done experiments with this chap's 10 year old class. We heard tapes of them in different contexts. Harold was very interested in language in context and the way it varied. I remember there was one where they'd let them free to share out the food or something and all this uproarious stuff they wouldn't have said with Harold and Martin Richards (that's the teacher's name) there.

The conference demonstrates Rosen's interest in ways that children use language differently for different purposes and how a language user might move across a spectrum of language use depending on the particular context. The ideas here were, of course, pursued later in some senses in Rosen's work on the *Languages and Dialects of London School Children* (Rosen and Burgess, 1980). At the 'Talk and Talkers' conference, as the report of the event details, tape recordings of two days' worth of work with children had been collected:

> Harold Rosen said their plan had been to get several different kinds of talk from the children, in particular they were after chat among the children, decision making talk, talk accompanying action, problem solving talk and talk in a learning situation.
>
> (LATE, 1966a)

This conference was explicitly focused on talk, coming, as the conference programme notes, on the heels of NATE's annual conference on the topic the previous year and at a time when 'oracy has joined literacy and numeracy to make the new educational trinity' (LATE, 1966b). However, it seems altogether sensible that this interest in the different ways in which children use talk, which takes us far beyond simply the work of the English classroom, should lead to questions about the different ways in which children use talk and language more broadly in school. This move towards a fuller consideration of language use across the school by children took its most significant step when Rosen convened the 1968 LATE conference held at Beatrice Webb House, titled 'The Use of Language – making a policy'. In essence, this was the conference that led to the publication of the hugely influential *Language, Learner and the School* (Barnes et al., 1969). As the title of the conference suggests, the aim of the event was to produce 'a straightforward policy document which could be used by any school as a basis for staff discussion' (LATE, 1968). This was the conference at which, according to Rosen, the phrase 'language across the curriculum was born' (Rosen, 1988, p. 3). The phrase has been so commonly used since then that it has become part of standard educational discourse, but the story of the conference and how it ultimately led to the publication of *Language, Learner and the School* is, in some senses, a story of happy accidents and coincidence.

A key contributor to the conference was Douglas Barnes, and his recollections make clear the central role of Rosen in driving forward the language across the curriculum agenda. Barnes' critical contribution to the conference and to the publication that followed actually began some years earlier, following a chance meeting:

> 'I'd met Harold in street in central London and we'd had a chat and he said wouldn't it be fascinating to take a tape recorder and find out just what sort of language washes over kids in their first few weeks in a secondary school? And I thought yes, that's the answer'.[3]

After the chance meeting and conversation, Barnes initiated work, little knowing at the time how important it would prove to be in the language across the curriculum movement:

> So I sent these teachers in this group to go and tape record lessons. I did it for two years and they produced excellent seminars – it was an interesting teaching method I'd stumbled on. I probably wouldn't have done anything more about it but I had a new head of department who came round asking everyone what research they were doing, so I told him about this, and he said marvellous, write it up. So I wrote it up, he liked it, and I sent 50 copies around of what was going to be my contribution to *Language, Learner and the School*, and got answers from two people! One of them was Harold and he was planning the 68 Beatrice Webb Conferences on Language. So I went down and talked about what I had been doing, and in the audience was that chap from Cambridge – Martin Lightfoot – and he suggested we should publish it. As it wasn't long enough for a book we asked Jimmy to write something on small groups and Harold wanted to write about the outcome of the Conference and the policies for language across the curriculum. That was how the book happened.[4]

Barnes further reinforced the importance of Rosen's influence on his work in his chapter on *Language, the Learner and the School*. Quoting from an unpublished paper by Rosen, Barnes indicates the nature of Rosen's insight into the need for attention to the language used across different subjects within the curriculum. Urging for an investigation into the language of different subjects, Rosen had said:

> We should set about distinguishing between the linguistic-conventional and the linguistic-intellectual, so that we can understand that traditional formulations are not sacrosanct.
>
> (Barnes et al., 1972, p. 12)

This was a critical insight by Rosen in advancing the thinking around language across the curriculum. It might have been obvious to anyone in education that individual subjects had their own distinct registers and linguistic differences, but to what extent were these actually rooted in the different conceptual thinking within different subjects that might necessitate different uses of language, and to what extent were they simply accepted traditions and conventions that had become socially established without actually performing an intellectual function? Were schoolchildren being expected to adopt certain linguistic and grammatical conventions purely to reproduce stylistically accepted norms with no actual cognitive benefit? This was a vital question for Rosen, given the effect that the language of the school could have upon children, as Barnes indicates in his further extract from Rosen's unpublished piece:

> Much of the language encountered in school looks at pupils across a chasm. Some fluent children . . . adopt the jargon and parrot whole stretches of lingo. Personal intellectual struggle is made irrelevant and the personal view never asked for. Language and experience are torn asunder.
>
> (Barnes et al., 1972)

Rosen's Walworth syllabus, and indeed the work of LATE as a whole, insisted that learning should begin with the language and experience of the child, and yet his analysis was that this was utterly absent within the discourses of subject specialisms in school, where specialist terminology and particular ways of speaking, and particularly writing, were the expected norms. Not being offered the opportunity to draw on their own language and experience whilst learning in science or history was clearly detrimental to children's access to education, and whilst this might affect working-class children more acutely, given the gulf between their own language uses and the impersonal discourses of the curriculum, it would also affect – to a greater or lesser extent – all children. One can hardly imagine the most sophisticated of users of what Bernstein has claimed was the elaborated code to be using the language of a science report in their interactions at home. Thus, the linguistic demands of school would mean that, potentially, even for children with confidence and understanding, seeking to acquire the impersonal language of subject disciplines would result in resorting to 'desperate mimicry' (Barnes et al., 1972) in order to negotiate the tasks they encountered. Rosen was questioning the nature of language used in the secondary school and its potential negative impact on children's learning. It was not to suggest that there might well be reasons for particular language uses in particular subject disciplines. Rosen was clear, 'Boundaries must be clearly established and a chemistry student should write chemistry not history, autobiography or journalism' (Barnes et al., 1972, p. 120), but there should be proper investigation of this and an explicitness so that children could be empowered to take on these languages of the curriculum disciplines. There ought to be explicit, justifiable reasons for the adoption of certain language uses in certain subjects. And, Rosen was clear, there should be ways in which children's own language and experience, both in talk and writing, should be allowed to play their role as young people seek to understand the content they encounter in the different classrooms of the secondary school.

Following Barnes' study of the language encountered by pupils across a school day and James Britton's chapter on group discussion, 'Talking to Learn', Rosen's contribution to *Language, the Learner and the School* is the chapter titled 'Towards a Language Policy Across the Curriculum'. This piece contributed in significant ways to ensuring that language across the curriculum became a focus for schools; arguably, it was this piece of writing that ultimately led to the calls in the Bullock Report for all schools to adopt such a policy.

Rosen begins by suggesting that, 'In their penumbra of attention most teachers have a kind of concern for language' (Barnes et al., 1972, 119), an acknowledgement expressed in such a way as to make clear that far greater concern was essential. He suggests teachers might well have a sense of the 'linguistic proprieties' of their subject, but even if this is so, this is 'rarely explicit' (Barnes et al., 1972).

The initial sections of Rosen's chapter relate most specifically to the ways in which spoken language is used by pupils and teachers in the school. Referring to Barnes' contribution to the book and to the work of others, Rosen discusses the 'language games' (a metaphor he borrows from the writing of Bellack et al., 1966) that make up a lot of classroom interaction, where children are often led through dialogues with teachers which become increasingly restricted as they are drawn to the idea or answer that the teacher has in mind. For Rosen, the way these sorts of typical classroom interactions between teachers and pupils progress, the sorts of interactions that Barnes clearly details, restrict the language pupils are able to use. The effect of this, however, is not simply linguistic restriction; the limitation on language results in 'a limitation of thinking resources called into play' (Barnes et al., 1972, p. 126). Though uncited, Rosen's reading of Vygotsky[5] is very evident in the comments he makes in this area:

> It is through the enormous variety of dialogue with others that we gather together the linguistic resources to dialogue in our head; there is nowhere else to get them from. Restrict the nature and quality of that dialogue and ultimately you restrict thinking capacity.
>
> (Barnes et al., 1972)

In the lifelong interrelationship between thought and language that Vygotsky posited as being unique to the human condition, the tools of language we develop through speech are internalised to facilitate our thinking.

Rosen's damning assessment of the way language is used in classrooms is that 'out of the vast repertoire which language offers us very few items are left available to the pupil as a speaker' (Barnes et al., 1972). This is, of course, lamentable as Rosen sees that 'School could be a place where pupils enriched their resources, because it would be there that they encountered new verbal strategies and were inspired to more ambitious uses of language' (Barnes et al., 1972). Rosen is not, of course, suggesting that pupils are not taken beyond their own uses of language; as ever, the pupils' language should be the starting point for the move into other areas, illustrated by the extracts of group discussion which feature in Britton's chapter. The plea for children to be allowed to use their own voices is typically passionate:

> We are saying that it is as talkers, questioners, arguers, gossips, chatterboxes, that our pupils do much of their most important learning. Their everyday talking voices are the most subtle and versatile means they possess for making sense of what they do and for making sense of others.
>
> (Barnes et al., 1972, p. 127)

For as Rosen goes on to argue, although the language of subject disciplines as school pupils all too frequently receive them is impersonal and possessing of a 'cold neutrality' (Barnes et al., 1972, p. 133), this 'public discourse is not a record of thinking and talking which brought it into being' (Barnes et al., 1972). At the root of the knowledge that is brought to pupils in school is a personal hinterland 'populated with memories, images, attitudes, feelings and fancies' (Barnes et al., 1972). Rosen argues that pupils need to bring these things to bear in their own language as they come to form new understandings – if they cannot one real risk is that some pupils are simply frozen out of the learning process since they don't possess the necessary impersonal language. As Burgess suggests:

> The argument does more than recommend a place for spoken language in classrooms. It gains its power from its deeper, psychologically oriented focus on the necessity of talk to children making sense and making meaning, and, further, from the recognition of these processes as central to children's development as learners.
>
> (Burgess, 2009, pp. 42–43)

Rosen's argument for the role of everyday language in learning is powerful and persuasive; it makes the case for classrooms alive with the talk of pupils as they work with their peers to grasp new concepts and come to new understandings, finding ways to link new ideas with their own experience through their own words. Pupils will come to make the impersonal language of school subjects part of their repertoire, Rosen argues, through a process of differentiation from their own language use, and, in this way, pupils can make this kind of language their own. If the experience of language offered at school is rich, then pupils will 'reach out for it' (Rosen, 1978, p. 52) and this process of differentiation will take place. If this process does not occur, pupils may well be able to mimic the language of the textbook, 'but this does not make it available for considered, appropriate, individual use' (Rosen, 1978). For Rosen, it was critical for pupils to be able to use their own language first, 'they've got to express themselves in the language they have and not make attempts simply to ape language which has not been made theirs in any kind of way' (Rosen, 1978).

Turning to writing, Rosen returns to the categories of writing determined by *The Development of Writing Abilities (11–18)* research project and points to the ubiquitous nature of transactional writing in the secondary school across the bulk of subject disciplines. However, he argues that this type of writing can only grow from 'expressive language with all its vitality and richness' (Barnes et al., 1972, p. 138). It is in the moving from the expressive to the transactional within a given subject that Rosen makes one of the key arguments within the sphere of language across the curriculum: the questions about what is the 'proper' language of a subject, when it needs to be used and how pupils can be helped to acquire it. He suggests that 'it would be refreshing if specialist teaching included conscious attention to the language of their specialism' (Barnes et al., 1972). Such a conscious attention to language would enable pupils to make the specialist discourse their own so that 'growth towards the appropriate transactional form can be through an understanding by the pupils of when and why he should modify his language from the expressive to the transactional on some occasions and can please himself on others' (Barnes et al., 1972). This has been a lasting influence of the work on language across the curriculum and the encouragement of subject specialist teachers to be attuned to the particular language demands of their subjects and, by extension, to see how the language demands of their subject intersect or overlap with the language demands of other disciplines. This can lead to an explicitness that, in the best outcomes, enables pupils to make the language of a subject their own. Some years later, in an interview, Rosen elaborated on this point: when teachers are not explicit about the ways language is used in the subject, 'teachers are asking pupils to express things in particular forms, and there is no rationality to this from the pupil's point of view; it's simply what teachers want' (Rosen, 1978, p. 51). For the pupils, the writing of a science report in a certain way becomes akin to the fact that there are just certain ways schools have things done – like protocols for walking in corridors.

Furthermore, Rosen argues, given the importance of the expressive mode of language that comes naturally to pupils, teachers of all subjects might be well advised to encourage children to employ it in tasks – he includes poems written by pupils in biology and maths as examples. Rosen draws our attention to the very difficult of writing and the difficult position the writer finds themselves in – particularly the developing writer in school – and poses a series of questions that draw the teacher's attention to consider the different content pupils are asked to write, the contexts in which they do this and the audiences for their writing. Ultimately Rosen makes the critical comparison to speech; our mastery of speech is informed by the multitude of spoken interactions that we hear and engage in; to similarly master the written form of any subject discipline there needs to be a breadth and depth of experience of reading in that subject – a single textbook can simply not provide pupils with the immersion in language that is necessary if the aim is for them to come to own that language.

Rosen's contribution to *Language, the Learner and the School* enshrines many of the key ideas that would go on to inform work on language across the curriculum in subsequent years. Its importance in the subsequent focus on such work in schools, and ultimately government reports, can hardly be overstated. The clarity of thought and expression combine to make what ought to be an irresistible case for all teachers to bring language to the forefront of their thinking about learning.

The final part of the contribution is the inclusion – with some explanatory context – of the draft of the Language Across the Curriculum policy that had been produced at the 1968 LATE conference. The description of the production of this draft policy indicates the sense of importance Rosen and his LATE colleagues assigned to this area: 'It was produced from the heat of our discussions, produced by five working groups in half a morning, typed and duplicated in a lunch hour, finally sewn together and edited by a small committee' (Barnes et al., 1972, p. 148). The description of this almost frenzied collaborative activity underscores how those involved saw that action in this area was needed immediately. In the revised edition of *Language, the Learner and the School* (Barnes et al., 1972), the presentation of the revised suggested policy for language across the curriculum is preceded by a description of some of the activity that had followed the publication of the first edition. The examples given from particular schools, the interest shown by other subject associations and the adoption of the agenda by NATE indicate the impact that the work was already having. The intention of Rosen and his colleagues in LATE had been to stimulate awareness and discussion amongst teachers; the evidence presented suggests that this had been, to some degree at least, achieved.

The suggested policy is clearly the result of collaborative effort, and it articulates much of what Rosen lays out in his chapter for *Language, the Learner and the School*. It stresses the remoteness of the school pupils from the impersonal language of subject disciplines and asserts that pupils will only come to write in this way through 'the confident use of personal expressive language and the thoughtful, conscious consideration of the new language the teacher has to offer' (Barnes et al., 1972, p. 163). There is a powerful call for the role of group talk in children's learning and for a broad range of reading material to be offered to pupils, going far beyond the use of a single textbook. The policy invites schools not to take on the document wholesale but to use it to inform their own reading, research and investigations so that each school can come to its own policy on language use across the curriculum.

Evidence in the LATE archive points to the immediate impact of *Language, the Learner and the School*. A 'Language Policy Across the Curriculum' working group continued to meet within LATE in the years following the Beatrice Webb conference and in their annual report for 1969 recorded that 12,500 copies of the text had been sold and that it had already been reprinted (LATE, 1969). This is a genuinely remarkable figure for an educational publication and one many education academics could only dream of. In addition, 3,500 copies of the draft policy had been distributed to schools, and, in the first indication of the ideas spreading internationally, 'Nancy Martin discussed the ideas at a seminar in the summer of 1969 with teachers at Branston High School, Illinois' (LATE, 1969).

The LATE work on language across the curriculum, in which Rosen took such a leading role, was to have a significant impact in ways that can be seen in subsequent publications. Often cited as the most notable example of the way in which ideas about language across the curriculum gained official endorsement is the publication in 1975 of the Bullock Report (Department for Education and Science, 1975). The committee responsible for this report had terms of reference that ostensibly seemed related purely to the teaching of English. They were to consider:

(a) all aspects of teaching the use of English, including reading, writing, and speech;
(b) how present practice might be improved and the role that initial and in-service training might play;
(c) to what extent arrangements for monitoring the general level of attainment in these skills can be introduced or improved; and to make recommendations.

(Department for Education and Science, 1975, p. xxxi)

However, and perhaps the presence of James Britton on the Committee was important here, they went beyond this, with Chapter 12 of the report focused explicitly on language across the curriculum. The influence of LATE's work is inescapable when one reads the report, as it states:

> we must convince the teacher of history or of science, for example, that he has to understand the process by which his pupils take possession of the

historical or scientific information that is offered them; and that such an understanding involves his paying particular attention to the part language plays in learning.

(Department for Education and Science, 1975, p. 188)

The case is made for the use of small group exploratory talk as the means for pupils to come to understanding, and there is a strong argument made too for expressive writing to have its position in all curriculum areas – at this point in the text of the Bullock Report, findings from *the Development of Writing Abilities (11–18)* are referenced, and an example of pupil work from *Language, the Learner and the School* is used. Rosen's comment in that text on the need for transactional writing to grow from expressive writing is quoted directly in the Report. The Report indicates the impact of the work of LATE in the subsequent direction taken by NATE and in the Writing Across the Curriculum research project but acknowledges that the important ideas of language across the curriculum have not taken root in large numbers of schools. With this in mind, the Report's fourth recommendation states that 'Each school should have an organised policy for language across the curriculum, establishing every teacher's involvement in language and reading development throughout the years of schooling' (Department for Education and Science, 1975, p. 514).

To assess the actual impact of this recommendation on schools is not easy. As Rosen later reflected any recommendation in a government report can have a negative impact – Rosen and his colleagues wanted teachers and schools to have agency in generating their own policy, but 'some authorities, in their eagerness to toe the line, made peremptory demands that schools hand over a language policy in short order' (Rosen, 1988, p. 4). Such a response would doubtless be counterproductive and result in the hasty production of something that would probably only ever exist as a document rather than a working policy to inform teaching and learning. The imposition of policy in this way might result in teachers seeing it as yet another thing they have to do, just the latest new initiative, and consequently not engaging with the substance of the matter. Rosen's vision was that teachers would discuss language together, and through this, understand its importance in learning. In that way, teachers would see attention to language not as an additional demand on their time, but as something that would enhance learning in their subjects. Notwithstanding the problems associated with authorities seeing the adoption of a language policy as something to be ticked off as done, Rosen did feel that the impact of the chapter in the Bullock Report 'was enormous. It stimulated discussion at all levels and set in train many initiatives in many schools' (Rosen, 1988, p. 4). In referring to the original draft policy Rosen included in *Language, the Learner and the School*, it has been claimed that

> The initial discussion document, and the key principles it enunciated, were to prove a catalyst for change. Schools in Britain, other countries in the

British Commonwealth, and in North America, began to develop their own school language policies, drawing on the original document as a model.

(May, 1997, p. 230)

This would suggest that the impact of the language across the curriculum work that Rosen was so influential in spearheading spread across the English-speaking world.

One assessment has it that in England language across the curriculum work, 'developed slowly and steadily into and through the 1970s. This development was characterized by rich infusions of practical work done in schools, of classroom research (including action research by teachers) and of theory building' (Parker, 1985, p. 174). This approach is contrasted with that of Canada and Australia, where 'writing and talking have been the concern, with reading and literature taking a back seat' (Parker, 1985, p. 174), and the United States, where 'people have been quite exclusively concerned with writing; other uses of language have been totally neglected' (Parker, 1985, p. 174). The focus may well have been different in these jurisdictions, but the evidence certainly points to the genuine impact of the work of Rosen and his LATE colleagues in instigating this focus on language use across the curriculum on a global scale.

By the time *Bullock Revisited: A Discussion Document* was published (Department of Education and Science, 1982), there was central acceptance of the limits to the impact the calls for language across the curriculum work in schools had reached. One reason cited for this was the possible sense amongst teachers of other areas that they were being asked to take on work that was not their concern but which belonged in the realm of another subject discipline. This sense was enhanced by school language across the curriculum policies that were imposed 'top down' from senior leaders in schools.

The rapid generation of school language policies that were unlikely to have any impact on teachers' work and pupils' learning was not what Rosen and his colleagues in LATE wanted when they had begun their work on language across the curriculum. Their work was intended to turn teachers' attention to matters of language and to explore for themselves the importance of language in their subjects. As Nancy Martin wrote in an article emerging from her Writing Across the Curriculum Project, 'If Recommendation 4 of the Bullock Report means anything, it must mean consultation, revision and reformulation by groups of teachers as school personnel changes and educational events occur' (Martin, 1976, pp. 211–212).

Where it might be the case that some schools did effectively pay 'lip service' to the recommendations of Bullock, there are notable examples that point to the impact of the work of Rosen and his colleagues. One of these examples would be Forest Gate Community School, the work of whose Language and Learning committee over an extended period led to the publication of *Teachers, Language and Learning* (Hickman and Kimberley, 1988). This book is essentially a collection of presentations made by teachers at the school to the Language and Learning Committee there, which look at language as a cross-curricular concern. It is not about enacting a particular policy around language across the curriculum – the explicit purpose of the Committee was to 'explore processes rather than write a policy' (Hickman and Kimberley, 1988, p. 24). Rosen himself wrote the introductory chapter to the text, offering a strong validation of the work that lay behind it. Here was a group of teachers doing exactly as he would have wanted with the language and learning agenda – exploring its practical implications, investigating the realities of their own classrooms and their own pupils. It is an example of the direct impact of the work of Rosen and his LATE colleagues in the late 1960s, and his endorsement is ringing: 'Had we known at that weekend conference that what we were saying would make a contribution to the coming into being of this book we would have been incredulous but thrilled' (Rosen, 1988, p. 9).

John Hickman, who led the work of the Language and Learning committee at Forest Gate School along with his colleague Keith Kimberley, had, significantly, completed the Role of Language in Education course at the London Institute of Education. Rosen was instrumental in the introduction of this highly innovative course of professional development for teachers, and it was a course that could be said to have grown naturally from the concern of Rosen and his collaborators at the Institute of Education with language use in the classroom and across the curriculum and out of Rosen's work on linguistic diversity. It was a course 'for experienced teachers from all levels of schooling to come together to engage with the new research in sociolinguistics and in the continuous development of children's language' (Meek, 2009, p. 52). Rosen had been instrumental in gaining funding from the Department for Education and Science for the new course, which offered teachers the opportunity to take a year's sabbatical to be seconded to the Institute.

Hickman's memory of the ROLE course is a fascinating insight into a form of professional development the like of which is seldom seen, at least not in England:

> it was certainly one of the best years of my professional life and it had been set up in a very Institute-English-Department fashion. I think it was the baby of Margaret Spencer and it was apparently the only course at the Institute at the time that didn't require a final exam (why I chose it!). The rumour was that she got it through the Academic Board by waiting until the very end of a very long and boring meeting – just as people were preparing to leave – before she raised the idea and just – exploiting the exhaustion around the table – slipped it through without any dissent. When I did the course, she was helped by Josie Levine with occasional input from Tony Burgess, Bernard Newsome, Alex McCleod and Heather Kaye who ran the regular drama component. There were two essays to be completed (I think 10,000 words) and one final "Report" (15000 words?) and every week there was a discussion on two "set" texts led by one of us "students"

(we'd all read the text) . . . a sort of glorified seminar on books by people like Vygotsky (obviously), Joan Tough, Kuhn, Polanyi, Inglis, Frank Smith etc etc. It was all very much led by "students" with Margaret and Josie chipping in occasionally. There were also a number of drama presentations and poetry readings which Harold often attended with a fair amount of post-session drinking going on. We were also required to go into a school weekly to help a student who was struggling with reading and to report back on our findings. Most people had been seconded for a year to do it so it was all done in a sort of escape-from-the-classroom euphoria. Much idealistic nonsense was articulated during the year as well as useful explorations of racism, sexism and class. It was an unforgettable experience and all, no doubt, supported by Harold who – as Head of the Department – was a kind of distant guru throughout.[6]

There is no doubt that Rosen's work, along with his colleagues, on language across the curriculum has continued to have enduring impact, resurfacing in different ways in the decades since the publication of *Language, the Learner and the School*. When the New Labour government in Great Britain launched the secondary school age phase of the National Literacy Project in 2001, a significant priority was given to what it was calling Literacy Across the Curriculum. Despite the change in the name, this was in all other ways a renewed attempt to put language across the curriculum back at the forefront of secondary school teachers' thinking. Training materials were published and delivered by an army of key stage 3 National Strategy consultants, and these were intended to offer professional development on areas such as the use of talk in subjects. Subject-specific materials were subsequently made available – *Literacy Across the Curriculum in Science, Literacy Across the Curriculum in Geography* and so on. With the money the government invested in these training materials and consultants, it is safe to say that this was by far the most heavily funded attempt to embed language across the curriculum. Again, though, the impact of this work was undoubtedly limited – as someone who worked as a consultant for the strategy and delivered whole-school professional development days on literacy across the curriculum, I can attest to this from personal experience. The National Strategy was the ultimate in top-down policy initiatives, and I certainly experienced first-hand the response from subjects outside of English that this training was not really their concern (the change of language to literacy was particularly unhelpful in this regard, in my view; whilst a teacher from a practical subject might be persuaded that language had a role to play in their classroom, literacy – with its narrower implications of simply reading and writing – is a far more tricky sell).

Attempts to focus attention on language across the curriculum have continued, even if the impact of the National Strategies was perhaps negligible in the area. In 2021, in the final report of the Oracy All-Party Parliamentary Group, the evidence submitted by Robin Alexander is quoted:

There is a strong case for revisiting the 1975 Bullock Report's advocacy of 'language across the curriculum' in order to underline the argument that educationally productive talk is the responsibility of all teachers, not just those who teach English.

(Oracy All-Party Parliamentary Group, 2021, p. 44)

Rather than simply revisiting Bullock, however, I would argue that the stronger case is to revisit the work that informed the advocacy of that report, for it is in doing this that the power of the argument for the critical role of language in learning is made plain.

A Note on the Teaching of Standard English

It would be difficult to conclude a chapter focused on Rosen's work on language without at least some consideration of his thinking on Standard English. The desire of the institution to equip students with Standard English has been ever-present in policy documents, articulated in the Newbolt Report and in every incarnation of the National Curriculum in English. As Rosen put it in his characteristically blunt way: 'It is a well-known fact that Standard English is the official dialect of the British state. Judging by the way some people speak of it, I think it must also be the chosen dialect of God' (Rosen, 1991, p. 169).

Inevitably in the importance Rosen placed on schools inviting pupils to use their own speech and dialects, with this being critical to their learning and their sense of identity, there would be potential conflict in the face of the need to acquire a Standard. For working-class children and those from different ethnic backgrounds, this conflict would likely be particularly felt. Even as Rosen saw that attitudes in education towards dialect speakers were becoming more tolerant and the discourse around linguistic deprivation and underachievement was shifting, there was still an:

> ever-powerful drive to teach standard English and Received Pronunciation, usually on the benevolent grounds of wider communicative intelligibility. This is presented innocuously as 'adding to the repertoire', 'making a child bilingual', etc. But there are enormous difficulties which cannot be evaded.
> (Rosen, 1974, pp. 48–49)

For Rosen, the risks of imposing Standard English were various; in forcing it upon pupils, he believed:

> there is a good chance that you will teach children to be silent. You run the risk that they will lose confidence in the old without gaining confidence in the new. Alternatively they may end up with a grammar which you find more acceptable but with which they have little or nothing to say.
> (Rosen, 1974, p. 49)

When the teaching of Standard English became mandatory in the first incarnation of the National Curriculum for English, Rosen was at his most critical in his piece titled *The Nationalisation of English* (Rosen, 1991). He sardonically questioned the nature of such a mandate to teach a particular dialect, 'Since English teachers are now saddled with this legal obligation, I presume that if they failed to meet it they could face some dire sanction, dismissal, fine, or even prison' (Rosen, 1991, p. 170). It's tempting to believe that Rosen might have quite relished being the teacher jailed for dereliction of duty in respect of teaching Standard English.

Rosen called in to question exactly what was meant by Standard English anyway:

> What, for example, unambiguously defines what is and what is not Standard English? Since it is acknowledged that written Standard is in a constant process of change, often borrowing from the very dialects from which it is supposed to be sharply distinguished, it is clear that we do not have the tidy category which the name implies.
>
> (Rosen, 1991, pp. 170–171)

This was a critical question; as Rosen observes, policy documents had for decades been calling for the teaching of Standard English, yet there was little or no attempt to offer a definition or relate the use of the Standard to dialects. In the first National Curriculum statements, Rosen argues that there is a complete lack of attention to the dialect continuum along which speakers may move, and that they may do this for particular reasons – the work on the *Languages and Dialects of London School Children* offered ample evidence for this.

Rosen reiterates the problematic nature of asking children to take on a new dialect; it's barely feasible that this can be done without communicating something to the child of the inferiority of their own language use, irrespective of what sensitivity may be shown. Rejection by pupils of the imposition of a new dialect was ignored in the curriculum document but was something that had to be addressed:

> What we need is a totally honest appraisal of what it means to take on board spoken Standard English and to understand why the effort to impose it meets with such resistance.
>
> (Rosen, 1991, p. 176)

Rosen rightly acknowledges – citing himself as example – that there are those who do move into the use of the Standard, but this has little to do with the direct teaching of the dialect but instead with a whole set of circumstances affecting the life of the speaker that give direct motivation to take on the Standard. Such a transition is not even then unproblematic:

> That said, we ought to note that even in these propitious circumstances, there is usually a price to be paid for acquiring spoken Standard English. Converts usually lose their first dialect. Or perhaps it would be more accurate to say they bury it deep in the recesses of their psyches. They develop a special set of anxieties from the way they have to monitor their own speech, unlike a native speaker of Standard. They are par excellence victims of hypercorrection and linguistic anxiety.
>
> (Rosen, 1991, p. 177)

Rosen also invites us to consider the issue that in sociolinguistics is termed 'covert prestige', so that although speakers of, say, a working-class dialect may feel their language use is in some way inferior:

> they also in practice will show hostility to Standard English and RP. It turns out that prestige and status (the usual terms) can be accorded to non-Standard speech and that stigma (another favourite word) can be attached to Standard English.
>
> (Rosen, 1991, p. 178)

For as Rosen points out:

> There are many contexts where the speaker of Standard is the odd man or woman out, inviting ridicule, mockery and downright hostility in such places as assembly lines, building sites, working men's clubs, pubs, etc.
>
> (Rosen, 1991, pp. 178–179)

Rosen also quite rightly questions the process by which it is envisaged that teachers will actually do this teaching of Standard English. The curriculum document makes the unsupported assertion that in some way use of the written standard will feed into the learning and deployment of the spoken standard. It also suggests that, given the right sorts of opportunities, pupils will be motivated to learn to use the Standard, but as Rosen points out:

> I repeat, the point is precisely that many will, reasonably enough, not be motivated. The scrabbling around for curriculum suggestions smacks of desperation, for it is exactly those 'experiences and opportunities' which the promoters of novel schemes are under an obligation to set out for us. The underlying idea seems to be that spoken Standard will be acquired by a relatively spontaneous and indirect process.
>
> (Rosen, 1991, p. 178)

Politically, Rosen was against the imposition of a national curriculum per se – or he was at least against the imposition of the national curriculum as the process was enacted in England and Wales in the early 1990s. However, his critique of the place of Standard English within the curriculum was not simply a revulsion to central imposition. Rosen wants us to ask the critical question about Standard English – what actually is it? And even if we might find it easier to land on a definition for written Standard English, then this does not resolve the question of spoken Standard, for the two things are quite evidently not the same thing. The curriculum did acknowledge the differences between spoken and written standards but failed to offer meaningful definitions. And other critical questions were absent. For example, how far are arbiters' judgements about spoken Standard English actually to do with dialects and how far are they actually matters about accent? And even if a curriculum document might be at pains to make clear that the recommendation of the teaching of Standard English is not the same as saying this is 'good' English, as – to be fair – the Cox curriculum did at least try to assert[7] – is it ever possible to mandate the teaching of a particular dialect without that action in itself reinforcing a prestige and status already felt acutely by speakers of other dialects? Standard English is a particular site of conflict, but the central issues remain for Rosen across his work on the language of the working class and the language and dialects of those from diverse backgrounds: the language of the child is central to their identity, their family and their community and this must therefore be the language that is central to their school experience if they are to be offered the hope of success. One could argue that the National Curriculum did try to take this view, stating, for example, 'Standard English has to be treated very sensitively in schools, since dialect is so closely related to pupils' individual identity' (Department for Education and Science, 1982, p. 67) and explicitly acknowledging 'A child's native language (including his or her native dialect) is an intimate part of individual and social identity' (Department for Education and Science, 1982, p. 67) whilst urging that 'schools should teach it in ways which do not denigrate the non-standard dialects spoken by many pupils' (Department for Education and Science, 1982, p. 67). Whilst statements like these may have made the curriculum's mandating of Standard English palatable to many English teachers, they were simply not good enough for Rosen, who clearly saw them as lip service – blithe calls without proper recognition of the complexity of these issues. For Rosen, issues of language and identity could not be dealt with in a couple of easy sentences. These are critical things to remember whenever arguments circulate – as they will likely continue always to do – about the necessity for all children to become users of the standard dialect.

Conclusion

Rosen was always profoundly concerned with the role of language within English; his work on the formulation of the new English and the priority given to language in the Walworth syllabus attest to this. As Rosen observed, 'Schools are language saturated institutions. . . . Teachers explain, lecture, question, exhort, reprimand and make jokes. Pupils listen, reply, make observations, call out, mutter, whisper and make jokes' (Rosen, 1972, p. 119). It's therefore unsurprising that his work, often in collaboration with his LATE and Institute of Education colleagues, took him beyond English to consider language issues across the secondary school. Rosen's contributions to *The Development of Writing Abilities (11–18)* and *Language, the Learner and the School* helped to shape an agenda for thinking about children's language and learning that was new. It was, for Burgess, within these two 'founding texts':

> A knot of interconnected themes was seen as central to re-thinking pedagogy and taken forward as key issues for research. The focus was on language, but the approach was educational and developmental. Priority was given to the place of talk in pupils' learning and development, and this was followed by attention to relations between speech and writing and to differences between them, with a further concentration on the varying difficulty of uses of different kinds both in speech and writing.
>
> (Burgess, 2009, p. 42)

It was Rosen who was particularly attuned to the difference in language use between pupils and school; this came from his upbringing and his experience teaching in an experimental comprehensive school in central London, and it was he who was particularly concerned to ensure that the pupils' own uses of language were made the foundation for their school learning and not excluded from the classroom. He wanted children to become fluent in the language of school when this was to their benefit, so amongst his collaborators, for Burgess, Rosen's 'focus is distinctive, for the question Harold asks is not "whether" pupils should engage with the concepts and the modes of communication within curriculum subjects, but how in doing this their own voice is to be preserved' (Burgess, 2009, p. 43).

Language, the Learner and the School remains a core text on every beginning teacher education programme on which I have taught, and, when I recommend it to the new teachers I meet every year, I am able to tell them with the utmost sincerity that it was, for me, the single most important text I read on my own PGCE training year. It was my introduction to the work of LATE, one that inspired me to join and take an active part in the Association for much of my professional career, and it was my introduction to the work of Harold Rosen. It might be said that in many ways it was my encounter with that text that ultimately has led to me writing the words that appear here. The evidence is clear that Rosen's contribution was essential for the emergence of the language and learning across the curriculum agenda, and it is equally arguable that without his particular influence, the work may not have moved in the particular directions that it did. Rosen's contribution to the work serves to remind us always that the language with which children come to school is the language that has facilitated all their learning up to that point, and it must therefore be the language they are empowered to use as we, as educators, strive to expand their experience, knowledge and language.

Though the bulk of Rosen's thinking and writing on language focused on the secondary phase, it is worth pointing out too that he made a significant contribution to thinking about language in the primary phase with his role in the writing of The Language of Primary Children (Rosen and Rosen, 1973). This fascinating text was published as a result of Schools Council Funded project led by Connie Rosen. Its chapters on 'Talking', 'Writing', learning to read and drama contain an abundance of material taken directly from primary classrooms, collected primarily by Connie Rosen on her multiple visits to schools as part of the project. The book makes a significant contribution to debates about the ways children use language in classrooms and the ways in which it is critical in their learning. It's impossible to declare with any certainty exactly which aspects of the text can be attributed to Rosen – indeed as the introduction declares after detailing the collaborative writing process that took place that the text is partly written by one author, partly by the other and partly jointly, and that reading the text there would be 'difficulty in distinguishing which is which' (Rosen and Rosen, 1973, p. 19). And though the introduction points to the help that was needed in writing the text in 'matters of language theory and research' (Rosen and Rosen, 1973, p. 18), the assumption that Rosen simply added a theoretical layer is 'at most only partly true' (Rosen and Rosen, 1973, p. 19). Certainly, Rosen's voice is distinct in the closing chapter of the book when the works of Bernstein and Labov are cited, but throughout the writing, the constant interchanging of the personal pronoun from 'I' to 'We' points to a genuinely collaborative enterprise. The book underscores the importance of Rosen's work on language for teachers' right across the age phases of education.

Rosen's interest in language never left him, as an anecdote from Douglas Barnes confirms. Barnes sought Rosen's advice, just a couple of years before his death, as he was teaching a University of the Third Age course on 'How Language Works':

> He suggested that I should begin with my group of students, older people with many years of diverse experience, by giving them briefly my linguistic autobiography, and then inviting each of them to do the same. I am now teaching the course for the third time, and on each occasion the advice has been wonderfully effective, for without it I might have missed much of the experience that my students brought with them.
>
> (Barnes, 2009, p. 356)

This recollection highlights perfectly the interrelatedness of language, experience and identity in what is referred to as a 'linguistic autobiography'. It throws a light, too, on to Rosen's interest in autobiography, which was an important element of his work on narrative, which the following chapter will go on to consider.

Notes

1 The Schools Council was a body that existed in Britain from 1964 to 1984. Partly government funded, the Schools Council was led by a combination of teachers, academics, local authority representatives and civil servants. Amongst its activities, it funded educational research projects. In an age before increased centralisation of educational policy, the work of the Schools Council gave teachers the opportunity to play a part in developments in curriculum and assessment.
2 James Britton had first used the concepts of language in the participant and spectator roles as early as 1962 (Britton, 1984). The idea of language in the spectator role would appear to bear some relationship with the British psychologist Denys Harding's notion of the onlooker articulated much earlier (Harding, 1937), but according to Britton, he only discovered this work when he met Harding at Dartmouth in 1966.
3 Comment taken from an interview with Douglas Barnes conducted by the author as part of PhD research.
4 Comment taken from an interview with Douglas Barnes conducted by the author as part of PhD research.
5 Although the work of Vygotsky is not referenced in Language, Learner and the School, it is clear that when Vygotsky's work in translation – particularly Thought and Language (Vygotsky, 1962) – came to the attention of Rosen and his colleagues in LATE and the IoE, it was used to support the theoretical arguments used to support the calls for making talk absolutely central to pupils' experience in the classroom. This line of thinking can probably be summed up most succinctly when Britton wrote, 'The implications of these ideas for pedagogy are, of course, enormous. If speech in childhood lays the foundations of a lifetime of thinking, how can we continue to prize a quiet classroom?' (Britton, 1987, p. 26).
6 This is taken from an email exchange between the author and John Hickman in which the author asked Hickman to reflect on his experiences of having taken the ROLE course in 1979.
7 In English for Ages 5–16 Department for Education and Science (1989), the comment is made that 'Nor should Standard English – a technical term to refer to a dialect which has particular uses – be confused with "good" English' (p. 64).

References

Barnes (2009) 'Learning from Harold'. *Changing English*, 16:3, pp. 355–356.
Barnes, D., Britton, J. and Rosen, H. (1969) *Language, the Learner and the School*. Harmondsworth: Penguin.
Barnes, Britton and Rosen (1972) *Language, the Learner and the School, Revised Edition*. Harmondsworth: Penguin.
Bellack, A., Kliebard, H., Hyman, R. and Smith, F. (1966) *The Language of the Classroom*. Columbia University: Teachers College Press.
Britton, J. (1984) 'Viewpoints: The Distinctions between Participant and Spectator Role Language in Research and Practice'. *Research in the Teaching of English*, 18:3, pp. 320–331.
Britton, J. (1987) 'Vygotsky's Contribution to Pedagogical Theory'. *English in Education*, 21:1. pp. 22–26.
Britton, J., Burgess, T., Martin, N., McLeod, A. and Rosen, R. (1975) *The Development of Writing Abilities (11–18)*. London: Schools Council Publications.
Britton, J., Martin, N. and Rosen, H. (1966) *The Multiple Marking of English Composition*. London: Her Majesty's Stationery Office.

Burgess (2009) 'Harold at the Institute'. *Changing English*, 16:1, pp. 39–49,

Department for Education and Science (1975) *A Language for Life*, commonly known as The Bullock Report. London: Her Majesty's Stationery Office.

Department for Education and Science (1982) *Bullock Revisited: A Discussion Document*. London: Her Majesty's Stationery Office.

Department for Education and Science (1989) *English for Ages 5–16 Proposals of the Secretary of State for Education and Science and the Secretary of State for Wales*. London: Her Majesty's Stationery Office.

Harding, D. (1937) 'The Role of the Onlooker'. *Scrutiny*, 6:3, pp. 247–259.

Hickman, J. and Kimberley, K. (1988) *Teachers, Language and Learning*. London: Routledge.

LATE (1966a) *A Fresh Look at Talk and Talkers: Conference Report*, held in the LATE archive and the University of London Institute of Education library.

LATE (1966b) *A Fresh Look at Talk and Talkers: Conference Programme*, held in the LATE archive and the University of London Institute of Education library.

LATE (1968) *The Use of Language – Making a Policy Conference report*, held in the LATE archive and the University of London Institute of Education library.

LATE (1969) *Language Policy Across the Curriculum: Report for 1969*, held in the LATE archive and the University of London Institute of Education library.

Martin, N. (1976) 'Language across the curriculum: A paradox and its potential for change'. *Educational Review*, 28:3, pp. 206–219.

May, S. (1997) 'School Language Policies' in Wodak, R. and Corson, D. (eds.) *Encyclopedia of Language and Education Volume 1: Language Policy and Political Issues in Education*. Dordrecht: Kluwer Academic Publishers.

Meek (2009) 'Harold on Memory'. *Changing English*, 16:1, pp. 51–53.

Oracy All-Party Parliamentary Group (2021) *Speak for Change: Final Report and recommendations from the Oracy All-Party Parliamentary Group*, available at https://www.education-uk.org/documents/pdfs/2021-appg-oracy.pdf accessed on 12th March 2025.

Parker, R. (1985) 'The "Language across the Curriculum" Movement: A Brief Overview and Bibliography'. *College Composition and Communication*, 36:2, pp. 173–177.

Rosen, C. and Rosen, H. (1973) *The Language of Primary School Children*. Harmondsworth: Penguin.

Rosen, H. (1967) 'Progress in Composition in the O Level Year: Some Disturbing Evidence'. *The Use of English*, 18:4, pp. 299–304.

Rosen, H. (1969) *An Investigation of the Effects of Differentiated Writing Assignments on the Performance in English Composition of a Selected Group of 15/16 Year Old Pupils*. Unpublished PhD Thesis, held at University College London Institute of Education Library.

Rosen, H. (1970) *Application to the post of Chair of Education*, University of Bristol, held in the Harold Rosen Archive at the University College London Institute of Education library.

Rosen, H. (1972) 'Towards a Language Policy Across the Curriculum' in Barnes, D., Britton, J. and Rosen, H. (1eds.) *Language, the Learner and the School: Revised Edition*. Harmondsworth: Penguin.

Rosen, H. (1974) 'Language and Social Class' in Richmond, J. (ed.) (2017) *Harold Rosen: Writings on Life, Language and Learning 1958–2008*. London: UCL Institute of Education Press.

Rosen, H. (1988) 'Language Across the Curriculum: A Changing Agenda' in Hickman, J. and Kimberley, K. (eds.) *Teachers, Language and Learning*. London: Routledge.

Rosen, H. (1991) 'The Nationalisation of English' in Richmond, J. (ed.) (2017) *Harold Rosen: Writings on Life, Language and Learning 1958–2008*. London: UCL Institute of Education Press.

Rosen, H. and Burgess, T. (1980) *Languages and Dialects of London School Children*. London: Ward Lock Educational.

Rosen, L. (1978) 'An Interview with James Britton, Tony Burgess and Harold Rosen'. *The English Journal*, 67:8, pp. 50–58.

Vygotsky, L. S. (1962) *Thought and Language*. Cambridge MA: MIT Press.

Chapter 5

The Importance of Story, Narrative, Autobiography and Memory

Introduction

Of critical importance to Harold Rosen was the significance of narrative, or story, and his thinking and writing in this area has potentially profound messages for educators at all stages of education. In terms of his own written output, it was towards the latter part of his life that Rosen focused particularly on narrative and story, as his good friend John Richmond observed:

> The topic which dominated the last period of Harold's intellectual life was narrative – or, put even more simply – story. Stories – factual and fictional, autobiographical and concerning the world beyond the self, traditional and contemporary, fabulous and realistic, oral and written, permanent and ephemeral – seemed to Harold a fundamental, essential element of our humanity, both as individuals and as social beings.
>
> (Richmond, 2017, p. 382)

Richmond's final comment here is crucial; for Rosen, narrative and stories were central to the experience of thinking and of being, both individually and as a member of a family, community and society. In his recollection, however, when asked about the enduring importance of his father's professional work, Michael Rosen – whilst admitting he couldn't be certain – suggested that Rosen himself would say that story was not an interest that simply came to him towards the end of his career:

> He would start off with his commitment to literature. I think he would start there and say his major commitment throughout his teaching career – both in schools and in teacher training – was to what we call books, literature, which he ultimately started calling story and narrative. . . . Later that was refined when he got interested, if you like, in the language of narrative, narratology and so on and he produced essays like 'Stories and Meanings', where he's saying the most powerful pedagogic tool for all human beings as part of cognition is narrative. That's how we come to understand the world.[1]

Although in a later conversation, Michael Rosen somewhat amended this view,[2] there's certainly strong evidence to suggest that Rosen's interest in story and narrative was there from the very beginning of his career. Rosen convened the 1959 LATE conference on 'Narrative, in School and Out', which began with a session where attendees listened to a range of tape recordings of 'yarns' told by country people and an ex-sailor as a way to explore ideas about narrative and storytelling (LATE, 1959, p. 1). The use of tape recorders was a new innovation for educational purposes in the 1950s, and the material used at this conference would have been unusual for a gathering of English teachers.[3] However, this use of tape recordings of so-called 'yarns' is indicative of the kinds of narratives that Rosen tended to focus on in his thinking and writing. He was, of course, interested in the written narrative, and indeed wrote many narrative pieces himself, but in his theoretical writing, the concern was often for oral narrative, storytelling and retelling, and the personal, autobiographical narrative of the anecdote of personal experience. Such dimensions of narrative as these have traditionally attracted little theoretical consideration; certainly, the early academic work that led to the development of narrative theory centred on genre such as the folk tale,[4] and 'serious' consideration of autobiography was reserved for fully fledged life stories or the fictional autobiographies of great literature. It's fair to say that there was a thrust in the work of LATE, reflected in James Britton's work on language in the spectator and participant roles that is integrated into the model of English articulated in *Growth through English* (Dixon, 1967), which argued that the language of children in their talk and writing was on a continuum with the great works of literature. Such conceptual thinking drew scorn from some (see, for example, Whitehead, 1976), but Rosen's focus on oral narrative, story, autobiography and anecdote is in an established tradition of thinking that he helped to found with those collaborating in LATE. His work on narrative took him beyond thinking about the particular use of language in operation to explore the intellectual and cognitive importance of narrative, and therefore the importance he believed it should have in the educational experience of young people in school, right across the curriculum.

A prominent speaker at the 1959 LATE conference on 'Narrative: In school and out' was Barbara Hardy, then a professor at the University of Birkbeck, and her ideas about narrative were undoubtedly influential on Rosen's thinking. Her view was that

> narrative, like lyric or dance, is not to be regarded as an aesthetic invention used by artists to control, manipulate, and order experience, but as a primary act of mind transferred to art from life.
>
> (Hardy, 1968, p. 5)

Hardy's notion that narrative is fundamental to the way that we think and is central to the essence of being human was one that certainly influenced Rosen. Through his own thinking and writing, Rosen developed ideas about the importance of narrative and storytelling, literature and autobiography. He explored the ideas of narrative theorists as the 'science' of narratology developed in the 1960s and 1970s, and he considered the contributions of the structuralists and post-structuralists. This central idea, however, that narrative is a primary act of mind, remained critical to his thinking at all times.

Rosen and the Importance of Narrative, Story and Autobiography

As indicated, Rosen was no stranger to the work of the narratologists – he knew very well the works of Propp, Todorov and Genette – but their work did not explore narrative in the more general way that he wanted; they did not adequately consider its importance to us as individuals and societies, nor did they explore its cognitive significance. The narratologists' work at the time did not 'offer psycho-social explorations of what narrative means to all of us' (Rosen, 1985, p. 11) rather, applying itself to written narrative, it was essentially a form of literary criticism that was seeking to reveal the underlying workings and systems that govern the narrative form, 'Dominating the analysis of narrative is the attempt to reveal the physiology and anatomy of the text' (Rosen, 1985, p. 24). Such work did not only not consider the possible centrality of narrative to the human condition, but it also did not engage with the types of narrative in which we all participate as part of our daily lives. Rosen's view was that, rather than seeing stories as removed to books, stories in fact more often come to life 'in the ebb and flow of leisurely talk and most of all in the mind with its eternal rummaging in the past and its daring, scandalous rehearsal of scripts of the future' (Rosen, 1985, p. 12).

For Rosen, 'narrative will always be there or thereabouts, surfacing in the daily business of living' (Rosen, 1985), and therefore

> we might be disposed to take stories much more seriously if we perceived them first and foremost as a product of the predisposition of the human mind to narratize experience and to transform it into findings which as social beings we may share and compare with those of others.
>
> (Rosen, 1985).

Similarly, elsewhere, Rosen suggested: 'Since we dream in narrative and speak to ourselves in narrative (inner narrative speech), these are pointers to its profound relationship to thought. The narrative forms we master provide genres for thinking with' (Rosen, 1986a, p. 425).

One can clearly hear echoes of Hardy's 'narrative as a primary act of mind' here, but Rosen was interested, too, in the ways in which we construct the stories that we tell. To construct our narratives out of the multitude of things that we experience,

The unremitting flow of events must first be selectively attended to, interpreted as holding relationships, causes, motives, feelings, consequences – in a word, meanings. To give an order to this otherwise unmanageable flux we must take another step and invent, yes, invent, beginnings and ends.
(Rosen, 1985, p.13)

For Rosen, then, the construction and retelling of stories was essentially a process of meaning-making and in narrative, 'We transform raw events and actions into causes, consequences and point' (Rosen, 1988, p. 460).

The stories we tell are often autobiographical, and autobiographical has a particularly prominent position for Rosen within the sphere of narrative. Autobiographical talk is ubiquitous:

Just as it is difficult to pay attention to the very air we breathe or to observe what makes up our culture, so it is difficult to notice what goes on in conversation. If we listen carefully to intimate, friendly, relaxed talk (or eavesdrop, I might almost say) or better still attend closely to tape and transcript of such talk, we shall always find that the participants offer each other moments of their pasts, recent or distant.
(Rosen, 1993, p. 133)

The fact that so much of what goes on in conversation is exchanging of personal stories – 'what happened to me this morning, last week, last year, when I was little' (Rosen, 1993, p. 147) – means the significance of this kind of talk can go unnoticed, but for Rosen it is from this type of discourse that 'storytelling begins and the very fact we do so much of it points to its importance' (Rosen, 1993, p. 148). In drawing attention to how we all use autobiography in our talk, Rosen essentially argues for a change in our understanding of the word itself, away from the 'portentous sense of autobiography' (Rosen, 1993, p. 133), where it is used purely to describe the extended written life story, to an acknowledgement of autobiography as part of the way in which we interact with others in our daily lives. Rosen suggests that 'To understand autobiography we get beyond illustrious writers (Rousseau, Gorki, Gosse) and hundreds of lesser writers and try to perceive the essential processes which lie beneath their discourse' (Rosen, 1994, p. 188). It is only when this shift beyond the renowned autobiographers of history is made that the key insight can be made. This, for Rosen, is that these writers are in fact 'practising a common art which historically preceded them and which can be heard in the buzz of everyday talk' (Rosen, 1994). If we accept this, then we see how Rosen makes his argument for the significance of the stories we share in conversation with one another, for 'Lurking beneath the surface of anecdotes, the telling of moments of disaster or delight, recollections of childhood, crises, turning points are the great themes of memory, identity and the making of meaning' (Rosen, 1994). If memory, identity and the very act of making meaning are embedded in what happens in the ebb and flow of apparently everyday conversation, then the argument for the importance of this kind of talk for children – both in school and out – is made.

The great theme of memory referred to here became an increasing focus of Rosen's work as he pursued his reading, thinking and writing on the importance of autobiography. Personal stories are, of course, inextricably linked to memory, and as Rosen put it succinctly, and deceptively simply, 'Autobiography is the rendering of memory into discourse' (Rosen, 1998b, p. 99). Rosen offers this definition of autobiography so that it can encompass both the work of the great writers and thinkers and the everyday talk in which we all engage.

Much is said in education about the role and importance of memory, but, particularly in recent years, this has very often been seen to belong in the domain of the cognitive scientists, where the committing of knowledge from working memory to long-term memory in the form of schemata is seen as a plausible theory to explain how learning happens. Rosen's interest in autobiographical memory goes far beyond this somewhat mechanistic dissection of memory, which, in a sense, sees the mind as processing data to be stored in memory banks. Rosen was interested in the ways that, 'Memory is implicated in personal-experience stories in different ways' (Rosen, 1993, p. 140). Rosen explains what he sees as these different ways, which include the distinction between what actually happens and what we recall immediately, and the further distinction between that and how we may remember it years later. Then there is the importance of the use of language, 'the telling of the memory' (Rosen, 1993). In constructing a memory into words, one is not merely finding the words but the particular ways of telling within our communities and cultures, 'which we have learned from others since our earliest years as surely as we have learned "Once upon a time. . ."' (Rosen, 1993). In the telling of a memory, then, we are putting to use our knowledge of the narrative genres that are part of the fabric of the community in which we have been raised. Then there is a collection of questions that, for Rosen, it would be natural for a teacher, in fact anyone, to give important consideration to; such questions would include why the person is recounting the memory and what the importance of the story is to the teller. Answers to these questions allow the listener to learn about the storyteller from the story being told, as we have an interest in 'how that person's memory is working' (Rosen, 1993). In the construction of autobiographical stories, Rosen sees:

> a mind ceaselessly reviewing the past to confront its riddles, to rework it, to resavour it, to celebrate it, to mourn it. In a word, to wrest a huge array of meanings from it. Raw events and actions, lingering images of places and people, are transformed by memory into causes, motives, consequences and point.
>
> (Rosen, 1993, p. 141)

A description like this is suggesting that what we are doing in the telling and retelling of our lives through autobiographical anecdote is a continual attempt not simply to make meaning but indeed to make our lives mean something, to make our existence make sense. Through autobiography, the attempt is made to impose a sense of meaning on the course of events that befall us through our lives. Such a search for meaning may be uniquely human; for Rosen, its importance should not be overlooked.

As he became increasingly focused on ideas about autobiography and memory towards the end of his life, Rosen set about the task of creating a framework for what he termed autobiographical discourse, which he initially defined in the following way:

> Autobiographical discourse is to be found in all those texts or parts of texts, spoken or written, in which the speaker or author represents his or her own life, or parts of it, by a presentation of episodes in it (i.e. it is narrative in mode).
>
> (Rosen, 1994, p. 189)

It was his interest in the importance of autobiography and memory that led Rosen to write his longest sole-authored text and the text which, on the face of it at least, takes him further from the classroom than any of his other writing, *Speaking from Memory*.

Speaking from Memory

In *Speaking from Memory* (Rosen, 1998b), Rosen significantly amended his earlier description of autobiographical discourse to encapsulate what he saw as the pervasiveness of autobiography in everyday human behaviour to the following:

> all verbal acts, whether they be whole texts or parts of texts, whether they be spoken or written, in which individual speakers or writers or two or more collaborators attempt to represent their lives through a construction of past events and experiences.
>
> (Rosen, 1998b, p.12)

Speaking from Memory is a hugely impressive work, revealing a remarkable breadth of reading across literary and narrative theory, linguistics, psychology and philosophy. It is an enormously ambitious enterprise; Rosen's view is that though many different theorists have written from different perspectives and in different ways about autobiography and memory, there is a sense of people working in particular domains so that the opportunities to bring together ideas about autobiography, memory and life history are not explored in the ways they might be. As he suggests: 'It is though excited thinkers and investigators have entered the autobiographical arena through different doors and have not noticed each other's entries' (Rosen, 1998b, p. 2), and so his stated aim is to invite around the table 'guests who should speak to one another but have not yet managed to do so' (Rosen, 1998b, p. 3).

In the second and third chapters of *Speaking from Memory*, Rosen sets out to create a map or framework – or what he called a landscape – of autobiography. His landscape of the written word ranges from the major literary autobiography right through to the personal curriculum vitae, taking in memoirs, diaries, letters and journalism in between. The oral landscape – and it is in this that Rosen is most interested, since it is the everyday autobiographical acts that have been overlooked in terms of the study of the central importance of autobiography to the human condition – is more difficult to map since 'speech is less susceptible to control'. Rosen's suggested categories in this domain are therefore 'looser and more easily mixed' (Rosen, 1998b, p. 52). Finding their place on this landscape are what Rosen calls the 'minimal autobiographical utterance', the utterances that pepper everyday conversation. Rosen wants to assert the importance of these apparently throwaway examples, as for him they demonstrate 'the human disposition to narratise personal experience' and contribute to the creation of 'nothing less than a cognitive, emotional, moral and social world' (Rosen, 1998b, p. 60).

The centre of the text, as I read it at least, is Chapter 5, 'Autobiographical Memory', in which Rosen seeks to interrogate and explore the concept that fascinated him most towards the end of his life. In the chapter, Rosen reveals frustration at the sorts of empirically based psychological research that offers explanations of the way short- and long-term memory function, bemoaning therein the 'lack of concern with memory as meaning-making, that is the organisation of our pasts as our richest resource for making sense of our lived worlds' (Rosen, 1998b, p. 102). He considers the philosophical writing of Mary Warnock[5] but feels it focuses too much on the artistic autobiography and also fails to acknowledge relationships between self, class and society. Moving from philosophy, Rosen turns to the work of neuroscientist Steven Rose[6] and considers what his experiments on the memory of one-day-old chicks might helpfully reveal about the workings of human memory. It is a fascinating turn, and what Rosen takes from Rose's insights into the working of memory in one sense is the idea that memory is not something neatly stored in a particular part of the brain like some sort of filing cabinet. It is dispersed across the brain and is complex and dynamic, so for Rosen, memory is 'a property of the whole organism' (Rosen, 1998b, p. 111). Perhaps most importantly, in drawing on Rose's ideas about what makes memory different in animals and humans, it is in the retelling, and here, 'there is the immense significance of language' (Rosen, 1998b). In considering the turn of psychologists to give serious consideration to autobiographical memory, Rosen quotes extensively from Marigold Linton's[7] work in which she put forward a structure of memory and then turns to the re-evaluation of Frederick Bartlett's[8] writing on the reconstructive nature of memory. Rosen grapples with ideas about what some have called 'flashbulb' memories – those that seem to remain preserved and obtain canonical status for individuals, the memories that are told and retold through a person's life. Finally, Rosen turns to consider the shift to thinking of memory not as exclusively individual but as social and collective. Rosen suggests that 'Memories must be saturated with social meanings as soon as they are turned into texts, social or written' (Rosen, 1998b, p. 132) and that 'Every text is a complex intertwining of social meanings encoded in language' (Rosen, 1998b) and ends the chapter by considering two of his own autobiographical pieces with these notions in mind. The chapter as a whole stands out as a complex consideration of the thinking and writing about autobiographical memory from different fields and how it might be possible to draw them together to illuminate this most human of shared endeavours.

Purists in the fields of psychology, philosophy or neuroscience might well question the ways in which Rosen delves into their respective specialisms to synthesise some overarching ideas about autobiographical memory. Whether Rosen is able to achieve cohesion in this attempt at synthesis is open to interpretation, of course, but one's view on this is perhaps less important than the impetus the work might give to experts in the various fields to consider talking to one another. The desire for this to happen seems to me to be a key motivation for Rosen in writing *Speaking from Memory*.

One might also question to what extent *Speaking from Memory* has something to say to English educators – a reasonable question given that, as I write, my intention is to evaluate Rosen's standing as a key thinker in English Education and the Language Arts. Perhaps it is unlikely that *Speaking from Memory* will be read by many teachers of English, but this seems to me to be something of a shame. In its concerted attempt to draw together ideas from literary theory, philosophy and psychology, it underscores the complexity of autobiography and the cognitive processes at work in the retelling of memory. And it makes a strong case for the place of oral autobiography, from the briefest anecdote or utterance, as having central importance to us as individuals and members of societies and communities. It also underscores the centrality of language to what we do when we engage in telling our stories: language as intrinsic to our cognitive processes and language as a social process. For teachers who advocate for the importance of young people being empowered to share their stories in classrooms, a reading of *Speaking from Memory* invites us to more fully consider what it is that we are enabling students to do. It helps to support the argument for the importance of everyday talk in the classroom. It also forces us to be wary of accounts of memory that neatly align learning with memory as if we were all highly functioning machines equipped to transfer knowledge in some unproblematic way to our mental storage systems, ever to be recalled in unproblematic ways. Teachers know that learning is complex; the seductive arguments that seem to offer simple ways to explain the role memory plays in learning are undoubtedly called into question by a reading of *Speaking from Memory*.

Speaking from Memory also, of course, enhances a reading of Rosen's own autobiographical writing. For example, it is difficult to read through the autobiographical accounts collected in *Troublesome Boy* (Rosen, 1993) without recourse to Rosen's thinking about how memory works and what is involved in the process of retelling. Rosen takes his own critical thinking about autobiographical memory to his recount of the events of the East End anti-fascist march in which he took part in 'A Necessary Myth: Cable Street Revisited' (Rosen, 1998a). Cable Street for Rosen is one of those 'flashbulb' memories, and in reflecting on how he recalls and retells the events of the day, in the light of alternative 'facts' that are to some extent at least at odds with his own recollection, he is able to critically explore the ways in which memory creates and recreates the myths by which we live, endowing certain events and moments with particular significance. This takes him back to thinking of the classroom. He had been innovative and pivotal in the moves to invite pupils to tell their own stories in the classroom from his time as a teacher in the 1950s, but with the depth brought to his thinking by the study of autobiographical memory, he is able to make an even more powerful call for space to be made in the classroom for young people's stories and for how they are treated. Rosen suggests that the autobiographical storytelling that teachers encourage their pupils to do:

> could now include considerations of the mythical elements in these stories. Everywhere there are Cable Streets in local memory, which need to be evoked, valued and scrutinised thoughtfully and positively.
> (Rosen, 1998a, p. 34)

Such work would bring greater depth to such activity, encouraging the exploration of the values and beliefs of individuals, families, community and society. The invitation for young people to share their, and their community's, stories promises the opportunity for those young people to consider their own identity in relation to their historical and contemporary context.

Narrative and Culture

A further dimension of the importance of narrative, story and autobiography for Rosen is the cultural dimension. There exists, of course, what might be called the naïve view that the inclusion of narrative from diverse cultures and traditions is itself a relatively straightforward way to contribute to a curriculum in the effort to make it multicultural. The fact that there are stories that seem – at first glance perhaps – to be global might suggest that importing stories from other cultures into the English curriculum could be unproblematic. As touched on in the third chapter of this text, Rosen saw through the problems inherent in this kind of simplistic approach to diversity in the curriculum. Although there may be some underlying structures to narrative which mean that stories can travel between countries and languages, and although there may be some themes that apparently transcend geographical boundaries, each narrative comes into being in a particular culture and society, and this can have a profound impact, given the cultural assumptions and beliefs that might be at work within the stories. Rosen's own memories of the stories that played their part in his own formal education point to the potential difficulties very powerfully. He remembered that:

> At school, I was repeatedly confused, baffled and alienated by a totally opaque Anglo-Christian universe. A pervasive allusiveness – references, images, assumptions, citations and the taken-for-granted of a Christian world – permeated the literature we studied.
> (Rosen, 1999, p. 554)

Remembering studying Chaucer's *The Prioress's Tale*, involving the murder of a character by Jews in the ghetto of Lincoln, Rosen points out that as the teacher drew attention to the literary merit of the work, 'he was oblivious to (or at least silent about) the seething rage inside me' (Rosen, 1999). Rosen was silent at the time, and it is this experience that leads to his insight that

> There are classes today which are full of children who are Muslims, Hindus, Buddhists, etc. and who must be undergoing very similar experiences as they encounter the assumptions and racism which disfigure the narrative repertoire of our schools. The very universality of the narrative mode is ironically a guarantee that this will be so.
> (Rosen, 1999)

In recalling his experience as a Jewish child in a classroom filled with narratives imbued with the values of Anglo-centric Christianity, Rosen reaches the conclusion that 'While narratives may cross cultural boundaries, they may at the same time be culturally oppressive, offensive and threatening' (Rosen, 1999). There is a prescient warning here to the well-meaning English teacher seeking to embrace multicultural literature as a means to celebrate and champion diversity.

Rosen therefore argued that 'We need to understand better what happens to stories when they travel, when a story from one culture finds itself in another. What do the new receivers make of it?' (Rosen, 1999, p. 552). In his piece 'Narrative and Intercultural Education', Rosen poses teachers many questions about the ways in which stories from other cultures may profitably be employed in the multicultural classroom. He questions, for example, the extent to which a story coming from a different place may tell us anything about the culture of that place (or even to what extent it may simply confirm existing stereotypes). He questions the ways in which narratives may lose potential impact if encountered by readers who lack understanding of the cultural undertones implicit in the stories, asking whether it is the case that certain narratives could in fact cross cultural boundaries. Whilst raising these important questions, however, Rosen importantly asserts that 'narrative has the potential to be the supreme mode for intercultural communication' (Rosen, 1999, p. 555), and this is rooted in the belief that narrative is central to thinking, central to being a member of the human race, whatever one's cultural background or upbringing. For Rosen, this centrality of narrative to human experience means, 'The power of narrative to give coherence to the world as it is lived and by implication how it might be lived is, as far as we can tell, universal' (Rosen, 1999, p. 556).

Referring to work undertaken by teachers in his London Narrative Group,[9] and drawing on Bruner's ideas (Bruner, 1986) about the way culture is not a fixed thing but it is recreated and renegotiated by its members, Rosen suggests that it is in the telling, retelling and interrogation of narratives from other cultures and traditions that there is the potential for narrative to be central to a classroom forum where meanings and understandings are made and remade. For Rosen, 'The narratives of the classroom must not be fossils or holy relics of the past presented as inviolable or represented as the culture of the pupils, who may not recognise it as their own' (Bruner, 1986, p. 558). Instead, the telling and retelling of stories in the classroom should prompt questions and enquiry so that ideas about culture and identity can be part of a debate. In bringing stories from different cultures into the classroom and in inviting young people to share their own stories, teachers need to be asking:

> When do you tell these stories in Nigeria? In Iran? In Trinidad? All stories are there to be challenged and changed. What does a little Indian girl make of the Ramayana here and now? How does a story about then become a story about now?
>
> (Bruner, 1986, p. 558)

Implications for Teaching and Learning of Rosen's Work on Story

Rosen's thinking and writing on narrative, story and autobiography left him in no doubt that they should have a central part in the educational experience of children in school. For him, the argument was clear:

> all storytelling is an essential part of the functioning of the human mind. It is a major means of thinking and communicating our thoughts. That is why room must always be found for it in schools, for pupils of all ages, and why adults will listen entranced to old folktales.
>
> (Rosen, 1993, p. 149)

If the argument that narrative is central to the way that we think holds validity, it seems self-evident that pupils coming to understanding of school content knowledge should be allowed, or more than that, empowered to use story as a means for developing their understanding. This view was contained within the thinking on language across the curriculum, as the previous chapter showed, and Rosen's later thinking and writing on story brought more power to the argument. However, Rosen's thinking was contrary to the 'common sense' view that storytelling was the domain of the child and that progression up the educational ladder ought to see children progressing to other ways of using language, moving towards abstraction in their thinking and language, and to the impersonal discourse of the essay or report. Such thinking inevitably means that narrative and storytelling disappear from the classroom, residing only – and even there in a diminishing importance as pupils move up the school years – in the English classroom. Whereas this might be highly predictable when it comes to young people writing in schools and was vividly illustrated by *the Development of Writing Abilities (11–18)* (Britton et al., 1975), Rosen saw this absence of narrative firmly embracing the realm of the spoken word too, as he regretfully noted, 'The further up the school system we go the less likely is it that spontaneous, pupil-made narrative will be able to insert itself comfortably and naturally into the flow of talk' (Rosen, 1985, p. 18).

The highly structured and impersonal uses of language across the school curriculum were, as explored in the previous chapter, called into question by Rosen. Such uses of language, particularly when not justified on an intellectual basis, in effect marginalise young people. As Myra Barrs observed in her introduction to 'Stories and Meanings':

> Rosen analyses the elitism that underlies this concept of a progression towards abstraction, and shows how narrative, given proper status and respect, may prove to be good for more than has been generally thought.
> (Rosen, 1985, pp. 4–5)

In arguing for the place of narrative in the classroom, Rosen directly confronts what he implies is a false conception of science, for example, being characterised by formalised, abstracted uses of language and an absence of narrative and story. Reflecting on his reading of an academic paper written by his son Brian, Rosen suggests that:

> If I have understood the drift of one part of his argument, it is that if you aspire to becoming an invertebrate palaeontologist you must be someone given to story-telling. What is geology but a vast story which geologists have been composing and revising throughout the existence of their subject?
> (Rosen, 1985, p. 16)

He extends this argument to encourage us to question whether the arguments over conflicting theories of evolution are in fact an example of 'two stories competing for the right to be the authorized version, the authentic story, a macro-narrative?' (Rosen, 1985). Everything from the creation of human life – 'a fundamental story in which sperm and ovum triumph at the denouement of parturition' (Rosen, 1985) to each car that 'speeds down the road by virtue of that well-known engineer's yarn called the Otto cycle' (Rosen, 1985) is to be understood for Rosen as narratives rather than scientific reports. In recalling his father's thinking in this area, Michael Rosen remembered that even in looking at something apparently as numerical as equations, this sense of narrative might apply, because with an equation, 'when you work it through, it's like a story . . . you do this, then you put this with that. Chronology and narration are incredibly closely related'.[10]

A scientist might well argue with this line of thinking as the attempt to impose story structure on chemical reactions or physical processes, but the result for Rosen is that when we consider the body of knowledge that constitutes science, we ought to consider both how to become a scientist it is necessary to master a set of stories and that scientific discoveries themselves might be the act of an 'innovator constructing a plausible story' (Rosen, 1985).

To invite pupils to consider the content of subjects as the emergence of dominant narratives is to invite thinking about narrative into the curriculum. Allowing pupils to consider the stories of science and of mathematics has the potential to unlock their own narrative thinking for the purposes of understanding. We might even say that engagement too is a result of being able to use narrative to think and to come to understanding; I can't be alone amongst former A-level chemistry students in remembering the discovery of the structure of the benzene molecule through the story of August Kekule's dream of the snake eating its own tail. In all honesty, everything else I learned in studying chemistry for seven years has long since disappeared. What benzene is, what it does and why it might be important are lost to me. The narrative of the dream of the snake is the only memory that remains.

Arguably, Rosen's interest in narrative was in part fired by his passion for the education of the working class, since he knew – and the very first LATE conference on narrative in 1959 demonstrated – how important the form was to this group, 'Consider narrative in the widest and deepest sense of the word. What do we do with it in schools compared with its role in cognition and its pervasiveness in working-class culture?' (Rosen, 1986b, p. 135). Rosen's reading of William Labov and Shirley Bryce Heath underlined the crucial role of narrative and storytelling in the lives of the working class, but this focus is rarely explicit in his writing on the subject, as he feels that the primacy of narrative as a way of thinking is not reserved for particular classes or cultures. Personal narrative, anecdote or autobiography was something that Rosen powerfully advocated for inclusion in education for all children, as forms of talk that merited particular attention. As he observed:

It has been a hard struggle over the years to convince others that common or-garden talk, everyday, messy, interminable chatter, easily engaged in by everyone, navvies as well as Nobel Prize winners, needed to be given full scope. The battle is far from won. We need, nevertheless, to extend the argument and to create an awareness of the significance of the anecdotal tissue of conversation.

(Rosen, 1993, pp. 144–145)

In making his argument for the role of autobiography, Rosen drew heavily on the work of Bruner. Rosen returns on several occasions to Bruner's claims relating to what he saw as the two ways in which the mind works:

There are two modes of cognitive functioning, two modes of thought, each providing distinctive ways of ordering experience. The two (though complementary) are irreducible to one another. Efforts to ignore one at the expense of another inevitably fail to capture the rich diversity of human thought.

(Bruner, 1986, p. 11)

Rosen explains that these two ways are 'paradigmatic (i.e. logical and scientific) and narrative' (Rosen, 1993, p. 138) and this 'places narrative firmly in the cognitive domain, as a way of ordering experience' (Rosen, 1993, p. 138). Though Bruner concentrated on the analysis of fictional narrative in his writing on these two modes of cognitive functioning, he did then move into the consideration of autobiography and personal anecdote, and it is in doing this that Rosen sees the importance of the ideas for teachers and pupils. The challenge that Bruner's ideas pose to educators comes if we accept the idea that:

the way we know about the physical world is not the same as the way in which we develop and refine our knowledge of ourselves and others and the way in which we construct and represent human interaction.

(Rosen, 1993, p. 138)

The reasoning goes that we learn about ourselves, others, society and our place in it through thinking in narrative. This kind of thinking, which manifests itself in the kinds of personal anecdotes and autobiography that are the stuff of everyday conversation, is eschewed in schools as pupils are forced to use language in different ways in the discourse of the classroom. The result, Rosen claims, is a sobering thought for educators, particularly those in secondary schools:

We might almost say that in higher education the guiding principle is 'Forget the stories, learn to generalize, learnt to be theoretical, be impersonal'. If Bruner is even halfway right then I think he is saying, 'Sacrifice your autobiographical thinking and telling and you sacrifice a major form of learning'.

(Rosen, 1993, pp. 138–139)

Primary act of mind or not, Bruner's ideas reinforce the central idea that narrative is not simply a way of telling; it is a way of thinking; it is critical for cognition.

In the telling of personal stories, too, indeed any narrative, there is both the cognitive work and the linguistic challenge. This, too, justifies the place of autobiography and narrative in the classroom, as it is developing the language skills and resources of pupils. Rosen seeks to demonstrate this in his piece 'Stories of Stories' (Rosen, 1988) by elaborating on the processes that a narrator must go through in constructing a personal anecdote from a series of events that have taken place (in this particular case, the fixing of a hook to a garden door). Rosen talks of the series of boundaries that need to be constructed in the formation of the story to be told – the boundaries that create a beginning and an end, that sequence and prioritise events and which ensure the story fulfils the cultural expectations the listener has of a narrative. If we begin to consider the endeavour that goes into the constructing of a personal story, we can hardly avoid the question, 'What are our pupils doing when they take up for themselves the role of narrator?' (Rosen, 1985, p. 24). In constructing a story and in rendering the events to a listener, the teller of the anecdote is drawing on different linguistic resources, leading Rosen to claim that, 'narrative, more than any other mode, produces the highest levels of linguistic performance' (Rosen, 1985, p. 24). This consideration of the cognitive and linguistic processes at work when constructing a personal anecdote leads Rosen ultimately to conclude that: 'Personal storytelling then calls for an active, exacting attention both to the world and the word, the very kind of attention which should be at the heart of all learning' (Rosen, 1993, p. 144).

This is a bold statement and one that many teachers might find difficult to countenance. Teachers of all subjects – not just those whose default discourse might be the scientific – have traditionally thought of anecdote and personal storytelling as, at best, at the periphery of learning. Before reading a piece of gothic horror, an English teacher might invite pupils to share personal experiences of feeling scared themselves, but this is invariably as a prelude to the 'real' work of reading the text and analysing it for the way in which it creates a sense of horror. Here, the impersonal language of literary criticism will assert its preeminent place as the proper discourse of the subject. The anecdote becomes a warm-up or a starter activity when, in fact, for Rosen, it is what more properly should be considered to be the most important part of the learning process.

Conclusion

Rosen's thinking and writing on narrative, story and autobiography is extensive and wide-ranging. To engage in narrative thinking and telling is to be human, so it's little wonder Rosen saw story as essential to education and that this insight was consistent through his professional life. Ideas about narrative and story ebb and flow and intersect and overlap with his thinking in other areas. Establishing a place for narrative in the English curriculum and across the curriculum is entirely consistent with the call for pupils' own language to be the foundation of learning and teaching and for pupils' own voice in speech and writing to be heard across subject disciplines rather than the imposed and impersonal discourses of the conventional curriculum. It aligns precisely with the arguments made as part of the language across the curriculum agenda that young people should have the opportunities to use their own language and their own experiences when striving to develop understandings of subject-specific content. Rosen's preoccupation with narrative, autobiography and storytelling as he reached the last years of his life might, one could suggest, simply be the result of the ageing process. It might be considered natural to reflect on memories and past experiences, as one has little choice but to confront the inevitability that our own life story must have an end. It may equally have been, as John Richmond has suggested, that at a point in his life when he was at some significant remove from the classroom that Rosen turned to this area as something that he 'could get his teeth into theoretically'.[11] In a sense, though, there is a feeling that in spending his latter years exploring narrative, autobiography and memory, Rosen had identified something that brought all areas of his interest together in some way. Indeed, whilst in his remarks at the book launch of Rosen's collected writings, Richmond discussed five key areas of Rosen's thinking; he did reflect that the last of these, the 'centrality of narrative in all learning'[12] might be one that 'encompassed all the others'.[13]

There will undoubtedly be those who question the priority and pre-eminence Rosen would have for the place of narrative and story in the experience of school students. Certainly, the evidence of curriculum documents does not suggest that policymakers, even those responsible for the English curriculum, have any real regard for narrative as a way of thinking and a way of learning. Policymakers may be able to avoid it, but what is difficult, arguably impossible to ignore, is that story, anecdote and autobiography are part of the fabric of our everyday conversations and the way we interact with the world. Story and narrative surround us and are within and without us. That being the case, it seems unavoidable that educators need to at least engage in serious discussions about the potential role of narrative in formal learning contexts. At the very least, the scope of Rosen's writing makes it hard for any serious educationalist not to take narrative seriously. Rosen undoubtedly made a significant and original contribution to debate in his field. As his colleague Tony Burgess suggested:

> The educational argument is a bold one, informing both the narrative and the work on autobiography. This is a claim for narrative and autobiography as the focal point for living language, and therefore as founding principle for a curriculum that seeks to put learners' experience at the centre. The

theoretical work is grounded in his reading of narratology and literary theory, forming a parallel with the early generative reading in sociolinguistics, which introduced the work on language and social class undertaken in the seventies. The approach is, nonetheless, distinctive.

(Burgess, 2009, p. 47)

Burgess' argument here demonstrates how Rosen's thinking about narrative in his later years takes us right back, in a sense, to his starting point as an educator; making the language and experience of learners the foundation of the curriculum. In their exploration of his work in the field of narrative and storytelling, Doecke and Parr suggest that the distinctiveness of Rosen's thinking 'derives from the way Rosen uses literary theory and specifically the new field of inquiry of "narratology" to argue the central role that narrative should play in curriculum and pedagogy' (Doecke and Parr, 2009, p. 64). In *Speaking from Memory*, Rosen, in fact, draws also from psychology and philosophy to further argue the case for this central role for narrative. The result is indeed a distinctive, arguably unique, contribution to the field, and one that ought at least to promote further questioning and research.

That the work on story and narrative dominated the final years of Rosen's work, in what Burgess called 'an astonishing and creative period' (Burgess, 2009, p. 47), seems entirely fitting. Finding a place for narrative in the curriculum is the means by which to construct a curriculum that starts with the child, with her language and her experience; for Rosen, this was ultimately what the English curriculum, at least, should do. It's been suggested that granting narrative and storytelling a preeminent place in education has the potential to be genuinely transformative:

> Conceived in this sense, story-telling provides a lever for transforming curriculum and pedagogy, making schools into places where children and adults might engage in rich forms of communication and meaningful activities.
>
> (Doecke and Parr, 2009, p. 66)

In a system where many pupils will be heard frequently to ask, 'What is the point?' when undertaking a task the teacher has set them, the idea that storytelling could have this transformative effect to create meaningful activities sounds perhaps like utopian thinking. Rosen was clear, however, that storytelling belonged in the classroom, part of what he suggested might be 'a kind of self-made curriculum' (Rosen, 1993, p. 145). And whilst he accepted that there might be disbelief in the notion that a child's anecdote had such potential in the education experience, it was not the individual story in isolation that imbued it with such importance. Rosen saw that each story a child told was part of what he called the 'intricate web of narratives' (Rosen, 1993, p. 145), so that

Autobiographical stories, both in and out of school, are best regarded as a set of social practices which belong inside the larger set of narratives in general. They should find an honourable place in the narrative culture of the classroom.

(Rosen, 1993, pp. 145–146)

Reaching the end of a chapter on narrative and autobiography insists on some form of closure. Inevitably, this ending is only another beginning; I now can't help but return to the personal flashbulb memory with which I began Chapter 1 and reconsider the importance of that evening in Corsica Hall when I first heard Harold Rosen speak. How much of what I think I know about the importance and influence of that event is influenced by the contemporary context and by future experiences and events? How much of its significance is being remade and reinvented even as I write these words? There may be no definitive answers, but asking the questions invites consideration of self and others as I try to make meaning of my own professional and personal being.

Notes

1. The author had a series of conversations with Michael Rosen, facilitated by Frances Gilbert from Goldsmiths, University of London. In the interview quoted here – available on YouTube at https://www.youtube.com/watch?v=nZLMVd1LLQ8 (accessed 17th March 2025) – Michael reflected on what his father might believe would be his enduring legacy in terms of the importance of his work in English in education.
2. In a subsequent interview with the author conducted as part of the research for this book, Michael Rosen talked about various interests at different points in his father's professional life, beginning with his focus on language. He suggested that his turn to narrative and story in his later years was in part as a result of a sense that the battles around language had, to some degree, been lost in the context of policy developments around curriculum. Notwithstanding this, however, the view he originally offered of the overarching importance of story to Harold Rosen is one that, I think, holds significant weight.
3. Although it is not clear from the records of the conference itself, it's very possible that the link here is with the work of BBC radio producer Charles Parker. The series he co-produced with Ewan McColl, Radio Ballads, was groundbreaking in its presentation of the recorded songs and experiences of, for example, those in fishing communities. In an interview with the author, Michael Rosen talked of his father's links with Parker and McColl and how Rosen invited Parker to the Institute of Education to play the raw recordings used for his radio show Singing the Fishing with the student teachers.
4. Vladimir Propp is often seen as a key figure in the birth of narrative theory; his key work, Morphology of the Folktale, was originally published in 1928 but only translated into English in 1958 – coincidentally, perhaps, a year before the LATE conference on Narrative.
5. The British philosopher Helen Mary Warnock (most commonly known as Mary Warnock) wrote extensively on the philosophy of mind, for example, *Memory* (1987). She has a background in education and is well known in the field for

having chaired the committee that produced the landmark report on special education needs (Department of Education and Science, 1978) that became known as the Warnock Report.
6 Well-known British neuroscientist Steven Rose was known to Rosen through his book *The Making of Memory: From Molecules to Mind* (1992).
7 Rosen drew on Marigold Linton's chapter 'Ways of Searching and the Contents of Memory'. Linton broke new ground in terms of the education of Native Americans (see http://www.planningcommunications.com/jf/linton_pr.htm, accessed on 25th March 2025).
8 Frederic Bartlett was a British psychologist. In his work Remembering: A Study in Experimental and Social Psychology (1932), he outlined his ideas of memories as mental reconstructions.
9 The London Narrative Group was an initiative set up by Rosen and his second wife, Betty. Running from 1998 into the 1990s, the group 'held evening meetings, often including workshops, to which teachers and professional storytellers were welcomed.' (Dunning, 2009, p. 77)
10 Comments taken from an interview with the author conducted as part of research for this book.
11 Comment taken from an interview with the author as part of research for this book.
12 Comment taken from John Richmond's unpublished remarks at the launch of *Harold Rosen: Writings on life, language and learning 1958–2008* (Richmond, 2017). A text of this talk was generously provided to the author by Richmond.
13 Comment taken from an interview with the author.

References

Bartlett, R. (1932) *Remembering: A Study in Experimental and Social Psychology*. Cambridge: Cambridge University Press.
Britton, J., Burgess, T., Martin, N., McLeod, A. and Rosen, R. (1975) *The Development of Writing Abilities (11–18)*. London: Schools Council Publications.
Bruner, J. (1986) *Actual Minds, Possible Worlds*. Harvard University Press: Cambridge, Massachusetts.
Burgess (2009) 'Harold at the Institute'. *Changing English*, 16:1, pp. 39–49.
Department of Education and Science (1978) *Report of the Committee of Enquiry into the Education of Handicapped Children and Young People* (commonly known as The Warnock Report). London: Her Majesty's Stationery Office.
Dixon, J. (1967) *Growth through English*. London: Penguin.
Doecke, B. and Parr, G. (2009) "Crude Thinking' or Reclaiming Our 'Story-Telling Rights'. Harold Rosen's Essays on Narrative'. *Changing English*, 16:1, pp. 63–76.
Dunning, J. R. (2009) 'The Man who could Tell Stories' in 'More Memories'. *Changing English*, 16:1, pp. 77–79.
Hardy, B. (1968) 'Towards a Poetics of Fiction: 3) An Approach through Narrative'. *Novel: A Forum on Fiction*, 2:1 pp. 5–14.
LATE (1959) *Narrative in School and Out Conference Report 8th–10th May 1959*, held in the LATE archive and the University of London Institute of Education library.
Richmond, J. (ed.) (2017) *Harold Rosen: Writings on Life, Language and Learning 1958–2008*. London: UCL Institute of Education Press.
Rose, S. (1992) *The Making of Memory: From Molecules to Mind*. London: Bantam Press.
Rosen, H. (1985) *Stories and Meanings*. Sheffield: National Association for the Teaching of English.

Rosen, H. (1986a) 'The Importance of Story Language' in Richmond, J. (ed.) (2017) *Harold Rosen: Writings on Life, Language and Learning 1958–2008*. London: UCL Institute of Education Press.

Rosen, H. (1986b) 'Language and the Education of the Working Class' in Richmond, J. (ed.) (2017) *Harold Rosen: Writings on Life, Language and Learning 1958–2008*. London: UCL Institute of Education Press.

Rosen, H. (1988) 'Stories of Stories: Footnotes on Sly Gossipy Practices' in Richmond, J. (ed.) *Harold Rosen: Writings on Life, Language and Learning 1958–2008*. London: UCL Institute of Education Press.

Rosen, H. (1993) *Troublesome Boy*. English and Media Centre: London.

Rosen, H. (1994) 'The Whole Story?' in Richmond, J. (ed.) (2017) *Harold Rosen: Writings on Life, Language and Learning 1958–2008*. London: UCL Institute of Education Press.

Rosen, H. (1998a) 'A Necessary Myth: Cable Street Revisited'. *Changing English*, 5:1, pp. 27–34.

Rosen, H. (1998b) *Speaking from Memory: The Study of Autobiographical Discourse*. London: Trentham Books.

Rosen, H. (1999) 'Narrative in Intercultural Education' in Richmond, J. (ed.) *Harold Rosen: Writings on Life, Language and Learning 1958–2008*. London: UCL Institute of Education Press.

Warnock, M. (1987) *Memory*. London: Faber and Faber.

Whitehead, F. (1976) 'The Present State of English Teaching: Stunting the Growth'. *The Use of English*, 28:1, pp. 11–17.

Chapter 6

Harold Rosen

Activist and Advocate for Teacher Agency

Introduction

Significant dimensions to Rosen's professional life were his own activism and campaigning and his enduring commitment to encouraging teacher autonomy and teacher agency. It seems to me sensible to link these two aspects in this consideration of Rosen as a key thinker, as there is some shared ground here if we want, as I would hope all teachers do, to see the practice of education not as enacting the whims of the current policymakers, but as a profession peopled by individuals committed to a vision of what they want to achieve and a desire to exercise some independence in the pursuit of this vision. Rosen was, as I have previously sought to argue (Gibbons, 2016), a radical in approach and outlook. One might look at this in a number of ways. In one sense, Rosen was certainly a campaigner, actively arguing against things like curriculum and assessment practices that he saw as iniquitous in terms of how they served the needs of children and young people. He made no secret of his left-wing political beliefs, but he was not a man who would tow a party line; his strong socialist principles meant he would always champion the cause of the working class, and in reality this resulted in frustration at governments of different political persuasions, both those on the right and those who at least claimed to be on the left. Rosen powerfully believed that English is a subject that can and should empower young people, particularly those young people from marginalised or disadvantaged groups. For Rosen, to teach English is to engage in what is, or should be, a political activity.

It seems only natural that alongside such strong beliefs about the potential of English, Rosen should be a staunch advocate for classroom practitioners and for the primacy of their capacity to affect the lives of young people. Rosen always promoted the agency and autonomy of teachers, believing that teachers should be active professionals, engaging with and, whenever possible, taking ownership of their own professional development and destinies, trusted with the freedom to respond to the challenges of their classrooms. John Richmond remarked about Rosen that 'I've never

DOI: 10.4324/9781003588917-6

met a man who more clearly exemplified Marx's comment that the point is not to interpret the world, but to change it'.[1] This seems a wholly apposite observation to make, as there is little doubt that Rosen's own politics inspired his approach to his work in education. Rosen believed that teachers should work to change their worlds through their professional endeavour, and he believed that with the help of their teachers, young people, too, would have the chance to change their own worlds. This was, ultimately, the goal of education.

Politics

Rosen's left-wing politics infused his professional thinking and practice, and he never shied away from the fact that the teaching of English is always a political activity. Any attempt to pretend to oneself that education could be viewed as some kind of benign, apolitical activity was at the very least blissful naivety and at worst an act of self-deception. The teaching of English, whatever one's preferred model, will have at its heart issues of language, literature and identity; the curriculum choices made and the opportunities young people are offered carry values and ideas. Politics, whether one wants to acknowledge it or not, is never far from the surface in the English classroom.

In considering Rosen's work, it's very hard not to come to the conclusion that for Rosen, 'debate about the teaching of English is another front in the class war of ideas' (Yarker, 2018, p. 144). Throughout his writing and thinking, Rosen's Marxist philosophy is very often unashamedly front and centre. From a Marxist perspective, state education in a capitalist society is part of the superstructure; it acts in a hegemonic way to reinforce the established norms of society and to ensure that the working class are trained to accept their appropriate roles and that there is no challenge to the ruling class, who educate their own to fill the positions of power. It reinforces a sense that the status quo is the best way that things have been, or could ever be, organised. This maintenance of the status quo and, in effect, subjugation of the working class is enacted not only through the official curriculum but through the hidden curriculum, too, the ways, for example, in which pupils in school learn the importance of discipline, how they conform to expectations of behavioural norms and how they are inducted into an acceptance that authority, status and power should be respected.

For Rosen, however, it was not merely a case of the hidden curriculum working its influence on the development of the young; to his mind, he saw overt and explicit inequity enshrined in the very visible pronouncements on English curriculum. Perhaps the most obvious manifestation of this is the ways in which Rosen saw language being controlled and the ways in which certain kinds of language are suppressed in the school. Rosen's interpretations of a succession of government reports clearly illustrate his reading of the political forces at work in the effort to eradicate working-class language from the school.

From his disdain at the comments on working-class language in the Newbolt Report (see, for example, Rosen, 1982, 1991, 1994) to his view of the 'social coercion' (Rosen, 1991, p. 173) implicit in the recommendations around the teaching of Standard English in the first National Curriculum (Department for Education and Science, 1989), Rosen's view was that the State's official pronouncements on education were working to ensure that the norms of existing power structures were preserved and protected from the potential threat of 'the other'. In his inaugural lecture as Professor of Education at the Institute of Education, Rosen claimed that 'the teaching of English was shaped by the class divisions of the educational system, proposing nothing less than the abolition of working-class language' (Rosen, 1981, p. 73).

One can easily enough take an alternative perspective to that of the Marxists on the functions of state education. Many do. It would probably not be unreasonable to suggest, too, that Rosen's often polemical writing style was intended to challenge and provoke. However, Rosen's overt political stance means at the very least that as educators, particularly as educators involved in a politically charged subject like English, we hide our heads in the sand if we refuse to engage with the arguments about what it is that education, and an education in English, is doing. Rosen ceaselessly asked English teachers to confront the difficult political questions of the effects of the way in which English is taught, insisting that English teachers become sensitive to the underlying belief systems at work in the organisation and functioning of schools, curriculum and assessment. In his inaugural lecture just cited, titled 'Neither Bleak House nor Liberty Hall', Rosen is hugely provocative in the observations he makes on the functioning of schools:

> Schools are sorting mechanisms which in a very rough and ready way supply different kinds of cohorts to the work force. They are also inevitably one powerful agency which in visible and invisible ways transmits the dominant ideas, values and attitudes of our society.
>
> (Rosen, 1981, p. 85)

In 'The Politics of Writing' (Rosen, 1993), Rosen turns his attention to the ways in which young people are taught to write in English and how this may similarly be working to reinforce the existing norms and values. He asks us to question the assumption that in inducting pupils into the world of literacy, we are simply bestowing an unquestionable benefit. Writing, Rosen claims, is in fact 'A socialisation into a specific kind of literate culture' (Rosen, 1993, p. 115). Through a focus on writing, the essay in fact allows Rosen to insist that we must question the whole model of a society with established norms and values, into which we are all seemingly destined to be inducted. He insists that as teachers we question to what extent certain practices (for example, certain types of writing) simply exist as they are endorsed by those with power, and to realise that 'many of the most important practices in the culture help to keep the powerful powerful though they are never presented that way but rather as universal or value free' (Rosen, 1993, p. 115). Rosen invites us to question this value-free status when it comes to the way writing is approached in the classroom and to confront the capitalist notion that the established rules and norms represent an evolved state of societal perfection. Addressing the ideas of genre theory, with its conception of finite fixed genres to which all writing ultimately conforms, Rosen illustrates how the evolution of language and the playfulness of writers undermine the notion of this fixed system. Rosen does not avoid the difficult question for teachers of English, however – given that we do want our pupils to succeed in the system as it exists (be able, for example, to pass exams and write job application letters), how do we give them the space to escape the norms and rules? In search of an answer, Rosen turns to the work of Bakhtin and considers the notion of authoritative discourse – the language, for example, of the textbook and examination. Though he acknowledges that escape from this discourse can never be totally achieved, he implores teachers to square up to 'the oppressive power of authoritative language' (Rosen, 1993, p. 125). The writing of children in essays and examinations is evidence of 'the forced labour of submission' (Rosen, 1993), and Rosen insists that as teachers of English we should 'emancipate ourselves from the notion that there is only one good and proper way, and that that way is quite rightly prescribed by others, because they are paying the piper or because we have bowed before their assured authority without question' (Rosen, 1993). It is a powerful and passionate call to action for teachers to find ways to allow students' own voices into their writing in the classroom.

Throughout Rosen's writing, the bleak vision of the maleficent influence of education in a capitalist society can be seen. Rosen was not defeatist, however; it's scarcely credible to believe he would have embarked on the huge endeavours of 50 years working in the system if he did not believe that change was possible, and it is this possibility of change that his professional practice and writing encourage all teachers to see.

Rosen's hope and belief in the power of teachers to fight against the system and to put education genuinely to the public good are derived from various wells of strength. We know, for example, that Rosen saw the shortcomings of the ruling class and the flaws inherent in the argument that the state was manipulating the masses, using education to supply cohorts to the workforce. Rosen was very clear that it simply wasn't viable to suggest that schools and teachers could be controlled as part of an elaborately functioning state apparatus designed to ensure the status quo. During an interview with a Canadian academic and a doctoral student in the early 1980s, Rosen remarked that although school systems may be set up in any society to reinforce that society's norms, 'fortunately for us the system is too big, too untidy, too shoddy, in many respects for anyone to totally succeed in doing what they want to do' (Anderson and Butler, 1982, p. 28).

Rosen's commitment to fight for change and to empower teachers to see themselves as potential agents of change meant that, in Richmond's view, he was:

> as impatient with voices on the extreme left which said that nothing can be done, that teachers and schools are the helpless dupes of an oppressive system designed to replicate existing power relations, as he was active in opposing the increasingly detailed and reactionary control of teachers' working lives that some governments, especially that in England, were taking.
>
> (Richmond, 2017b, p. 4)

Specifically in the English curriculum, Rosen saw opportunities for teachers to enable young people to question and challenge established rules; narrative writing and retelling were essential vehicles for this, as he suggests in 'The Politics of Writing' (Rosen, 1993). Rosen's calls in this essay invite the political dimension of having narrative at the heart of the curriculum. In their exploration of Rosen's insistence that narrative be at the heart of the English curriculum, Doecke and Parr suggested that

> debate about English curriculum and pedagogy is nothing if not a debate about the social uses of literature and the role that a rich language and literacy curriculum might play in enabling students to participate more fully in a democratic society.
>
> (Doecke and Parr, 2009, p. 65)

In 'The Politics of Writing', Rosen asks us to look specifically at the way the teaching of writing is part of the mechanism of reinforcing established values and norms, but ultimately in asking us to think of ways in which we can change this, he is insisting that our teaching 'should do far more than induct young people into existing culture. It should enable them to imagine the future differently and to work together to bring about social change' (Doecke and Parr, 2009, p. 65).

Rosen spent his career fighting the system in various ways and working with like-minded individuals who were doing the same, so he believed that schools were not sites of compliant teachers educating compliant pupils as if they were factories functioning as part of a seamless system. Schools, existing in an untidy and unwieldy system, are themselves complex and messy institutions. And whilst there might be well-publicised examples of individual teachers standing up to the system, one could think of Chris Searle in Stepney as the obvious example, the important story for Rosen was not of individual high-profile battles between English teachers and the system; it was the fact that in most schools:

> there is a never-ending series of small but important skirmishes and incursions. They arise because so many teachers cannot fail, to some extent at

least, 'to suspect the work the system asks them to do' and to confront its contradictions and tensions.

(Rosen, 1981, p. 84)

For Rosen, schools are sites of 'movement, conflict, imperfect control which make it possible, inside limits which are always shifting and need therefore to be discovered in practice, to contest the terrain' (Rosen, 1981, p. 85). Rosen's work with his colleagues in LATE and the Institute of Education, and his work with teachers on research projects on writing, dialect and language in the inner-city schools supplied ample evidence of ways in which teachers were challenging and questioning the system. Rosen felt that the potential for this kind of challenge was most possible for English teachers in inner-city schools, for in such schools:

> English teachers are more likely to perceive the collision between the time-honoured practice and the needs of their pupils; the need to use language to articulate significant and urgent meanings, the need to use language to formulate in new ways their experience and understanding, the need to find in literature an illumination (not a reflection) of their lives.
>
> (Rosen, 1981, p. 76)

Rosen's experience, too, told him that it was not just so-called left-wing progressives that were trying to find space in the curriculum for ways to change the lives and hopes of children, for just as 'there are many teachers of quite differing philosophies who to their credit are against corporal punishment, so there are just as many who are opposed to the intellectual and cultural punishment of English-for-working-class-dunces' (Rosen, 1981, p. 83). Optimistically, Rosen saw that English teachers from across the political spectrum with very different visions of the subject might share common goals, but this was justifiable optimism given, for example, the kind of consensus that had emerged from the disparate group of educators at the Dartmouth Conference.

The politics that infuses much of Rosen's writing acts as a challenge to English teachers and to educators more broadly. In urging us to confront the idea that the education system, and English teachers within it, are parts of the machine that perpetuate established norms, Rosen inevitably invites us to question the veracity of claims about social mobility in a system and wider society that seem designed to allow only so many people to achieve certain levels. He offers hope and a call to action in his reading of such a system as vulnerable to the professional endeavours of committed teachers and gives evidence to empower teachers. 'The Althusserian view'[2] (Rosen, 1981, p. 85) that Rosen referred to in his inaugural professorial lecture, where schools are firmly part of the ideological state apparatus, is only one he shares up to a point, since he rightly observed that the critical question is 'how the system is supposed to work as against how it actually works and how people actually respond to it' (Rosen, 1981).

Rosen did not believe, nor did he deceive others into thinking, that working for change was anything other than a constant struggle. Even writing before the advent of the National Curriculum and the first state-led moves to genuinely control what English teachers taught, Rosen knew that the gains he felt had been made by teachers working in collaboration through organisations like LATE were themselves fragile, as 'Spaces do not simply exist in the system; they have to be won, defended and extended' (Rosen, 1981, p. 86). Interestingly, John Richmond, one of the teachers Rosen would no doubt be thinking of when citing the progressive work of those in the inner-city schools, when recalling his work in the 1970s that led to the publication of Becoming our Own Experts (Eyers and Richmond, 1982), confessed to a political naivety, the belief that 'ground won by proper intellectual effort and practical effort and collaborative effort is ground gained forever'[3] Rosen, in his writing at least, never had this optimistic naivety; he knew the battle was unceasing. It was a battle that had to be taken up by teachers, the foot soldiers in schools; it would not be won by generals. For this reason, it was so important to Rosen that teachers should have professional agency and autonomy, and through his career, he undertook work and research that sought to engender these things in the professional lives of the teachers with whom he collaborated. This commitment to teacher autonomy and to teacher agency is evident throughout Rosen's career; it is essential to his importance as an educator and demonstrated in numerous ways in the work that he undertook.

Encouraging Teacher Agency and Autonomy

Rosen's commitment to teacher agency and autonomy spanned his professional life. There is ample evidence of this in the different contributions he made to the work of LATE in its first two decades. In a sense, LATE's entire modus operandi centred on fostering teacher agency and teacher autonomy through networking and collaboration. One could argue that at the time English teachers had, to a large extent, a kind of forced autonomy; most were probably working independently in schools (the notion of the 'English department' as a collaborative enterprise not really existing in the sense we know it today) with minimal central intervention. Examination syllabuses wielded influence over what was taught to certain pupils at certain ages, but beyond this, there was no national curriculum to define content. And there was certainly no sense in which policymakers actively sought to influence the way teachers went about their work in the classroom, no centrally recommended pedagogies and no centrally driven accountability frameworks, the architecture, intended and unintended consequences of which have become so familiar in the last few decades. This was a kind of 'left to their own devices' autonomy for the profession, but only really of use to those who knew what they were doing – and potentially dangerous in the hands of those who didn't. This was what no doubt prompted many London English teachers to engage with the work of

LATE – to seek solutions to the problems they were facing in their classrooms through collaboration with colleagues facing those same problems. LATE work was always about teachers, perhaps inexperienced and undertrained and certainly faced with children they would previously not have been expected to teach, seeking their own solutions, developing genuine, meaningful agency and autonomy as a result of collective endeavour. Colleagues with greater experience, perhaps with more obvious subject expertise, would work with those less experienced and knowledgeable in what appear to have been genuinely non-hierarchical ways.[4] It was the way, ultimately, that Rosen considered academics and practising teachers ought best to work together, as co-workers engaged in a joint enterprise.

Rosen's contribution to enabling teachers to develop as active professionals, taking control of their professional lives and working to improve their own practice and the experience of young people, runs through the evidence of the LATE archive. A very early instance, for example, can be seen in the contribution Rosen made to a 1954 LATE conference on 'Books in the Life of the Teacher and the Pupil'. In a report of the Conference, the *Times Educational Supplement* made reference to what Rosen had claimed to be the importance of reading in supplying the four main needs of the English teacher. These were English teachers: 'needed to read to "recover from the training college course"... "to survive as teachers" ... they would hardly 'stay adult or human' without the refreshment of books, and reading was necessary 'to know the world of the school and change it' – a continuously necessary process' (report cited in Gibbons, 2009, p. 97). In this powerful advocation of the value of reading, there are perhaps echoes of Matthew Arnold or F. R. Leavis, but Rosen's closing comments here go far beyond any supposed humanising effect of literature. 'To know the world of the school and change it' introduces a more distinctive political edge, with Rosen urging teachers to take on the responsibility for necessary improvements in the system. This is a call for teachers to take action. It's very tempting to assume that in choosing the phrase 'know the world of the school and change it', Rosen was intentionally echoing Marx's words on changing rather than interpreting the world, though even if this were the case, how many of his audience would have been sensitive to such an echo is questionable (one can speculate it would have been very few given what is known about the LATE membership of the time). What is clear is that even in these early years of LATE activity, Rosen was urging colleagues to challenge and change the status quo, to develop and cultivate their own agency and autonomy through developing themselves professionally.

The importance of the autonomy of the English teacher is writ large in the LATE document *The Aims of English Teaching*, published at this time, to which Rosen contributed significantly. Whilst LATE had been asked by the British Council to produce a document that would be used to inform the teaching of English, and the teaching of English teachers, in overseas jurisdictions, the document unashamedly eschewed the notion that a single version of the subject could be put down on paper. Pointing to the fact that there are different models of what the aims of English should be and different ways in which English was enacted in classrooms, the document makes no apology for singling out:

> 'one of the most jealously guarded of the conditions' under which the teacher works, that is the freedom to construct his own scheme of work in fulfilment of the aims he believes in: and his continued freedom to adapt his plans, and even his objectives, in the light of changing conditions, new needs, unforeseen difficulties.
>
> (LATE, 1956, p. 1)

It is a bold statement – one could almost say it sits paradoxically in a document that ostensibly sets out the aims of English. The freedom the document refers to is, of course, meaningless unless the teacher knows what to do with it; that is to say that the teacher needs to exercise autonomy and agency in any meaningful sense, an understanding of the subject and a knowledge of the children. LATE's collaborative approach was enabling English teachers to acquire this understanding and knowledge through their study groups, research projects and conferences. Interestingly, though, for at least one eminent colleague of Rosen, it was in the planning of conferences, as much as the conferences themselves, that this empowerment was taking place. In remembering being part of the working parties planning LATE conferences, Douglas Barnes recalled:

> Harold saw to it that we argued through the nature of the learning that was going to be offered to the teachers who attended, so that we had a clear idea of what was required before we chose speakers and set up activities. On one occasion, I remember thinking I had learnt more from the working party than from the conference itself.
>
> (Barnes, 2009, p. 355)

The LATE way of working was aligned with Rosen's principles. Working in their own classrooms, with their own children, then collaborating with colleagues, teachers should have the power to make changes to curriculum and to pedagogy. This power should come from the bottom and inspire meaningful change. It was a democratic process and one that, on a larger scale perhaps, informed Rosen's views when the proposals came forward for the founding of the National Association for Teaching of English in 1963. An account of the formation of NATE (see Gibbons, 2014) reveals how there were tensions evident from the beginning as English teachers coming from different perspectives argued over how best such a new national association might be constituted and what its purposes might be. The group was formed through an alliance between Use of English study groups – primarily associated with the Cambridge model of English and associated with the journal of the same name – and LATE and other local groups that LATE had been instrumental in supporting (LATE had, for example, supported the founding of similar groups in Essex, Leicester and Bristol (LATE, 1963c)). The general view of the teachers and academics coming from the Use of English groups, represented by Denys Thompson[5] and Boris Ford,[6] was that a new national body should be one that had authority and prestige, one that was able to speak directly to ministers, 'a pressure group' (The Use of English, 1963, p. 1). Douglas Barnes, who was the LATE representative at the initial meetings that led to the formation of NATE believed this to be the reason that Bors Ford was the preferred choice as first chair, as he was someone with the profile that meant he could offer 'a push at a high political level, someone who could actually meet the minister'.[7]

When Barnes reported back to LATE on the initial proposals for the national organisation, there was a good deal of scepticism, in part, Dorothy Barnes remembers due to the fiercely independent spirit of LATE, as members felt 'they were going to be taken over, rules were going to be made and they were going to become part of it'.[8] Rosen's view was informed by his belief that the power should be with the members, not in the hands of a ruling committee and was indicative of his democratic ideals and his commitment to strengthening teacher agency and teacher autonomy. He told the LATE meeting that 'if we were to have power at the centre and function democratically, the centre must grow out existing groups' (LATE, 1963c, p. 2), a view supported by James Britton, who warned against a national organisation that 'gave prestige but nothing else and did not encourage local activity' (LATE, 1963c, p. 2). At the NATE launch, the details of the way the new organisation would work – through the use of study groups to stimulate discussion and collaborative study (LATE, 1963a) echoed very closely the sentiments of the original LATE constitution (LATE, 1947), in a clear indication that Rosen's view – which was supported by John Dixon and others – was definitive in deciding how NATE would run. It would be a bottom-up, rather than top-down, organisation, just as Rosen had insisted it should be; for LATE members, the terms of joining NATE 'had been specifically tailored to fit LATE requirements' (LATE, 1963b). The influence of LATE in the way that the new national association was founded, which Rosen played a significant role in, was ultimately bemoaned by Frank Whitehead, who claimed that very quickly 'the London Association for the Teaching of English and its acolytes took over key positions of power' (Whitehead, 1976, p. 11).

Just as Rosen was centrally involved in the activity of LATE, championing the approach of teachers collaborating to improve their practice and be empowered to have agency, so in his 'day job', he was instrumental in developing a culture of self-development and improvement. Of his time as head of department at Walworth, Hardcastle and Medway suggest that, 'Harold's leadership represented a new professional self-confidence that encouraged teachers to take it upon themselves to introduce innovations and forge new associations' (Hardcastle and Medway, 2009, p. 5).

As Hardcastle and Medway's study of three schools in post-war London suggests (Medway et al., 2014), the 'English Department' was something of a new phenomenon at the time – the idea of teachers working collaboratively in their school was not widely practised. Rosen was pioneering in this regard during his short time as the head of English at Walworth School, but his influence was profound and far outlasted his time at the school. As detailed in Chapter 2 of this text, the commitment to working collaboratively and to introduce innovations inspired those that came after him – John Dixon, Simon Clements and Leslie Stratta – to continue the developments he set in motion, inspiring them to develop the fourth- and fifth-form syllabus that resulted in the publication of *Reflections* (Clements et al., 1963). There is perhaps no more striking practical example of teachers taking control of developing and designing their own model of English than *Reflections*, and it was facilitated by the culture Rosen installed at Walworth.

Rosen's commitment to teacher agency and teacher autonomy was critical to much of the work he undertook at the Institute of Education. The projects in which he was involved himself were, more often than not, founded on the idea that teachers themselves should be actively engaged in interrogating and researching their own practice. Academics would not treat schools as sites of data collection or see teachers as objects of research; joint enterprise was the most productive way to facilitate positive change.[9] An excellent example would be the work that, in one sense, ultimately led to the publication of the *Language and Dialects of London School Children* (Rosen and Burgess, 1980). One account of the genesis of the work that culminated in this publication begins with the interest Rosen showed in a group of teachers working at the south London girls' comprehensive school, Vauxhall Manor. At the school, a young John Richmond was working collaboratively with colleagues from across the school on an innovative project, as described in *Becoming our own Experts* (Eyers and Richmond, 1982):

> Between 1974 and 1979 a group of teachers at Vauxhall Manor School, a girls' comprehensive in south London, shared insights and experiences, offered statements and speculations, about the language which was actually going on in their classrooms and their school. 'Language' here includes the language of the teachers, the language of the school as an institution, the language of educational resources and materials, and, most important, the language of the pupils. At the beginning of 1976 we gave ourselves a name: the Talk Workshop Group.
>
> (Eyers and Richmond, 1982, p. 2)

Rosen heard about the work of the group in the school, and Richmond remembers that 'One Tuesday afternoon he came down with Tony Burgess and sat in the classroom where we had our regular Tuesday afternoon meetings and he was very, very interested'.[10] As a young English teacher, Richmond might have been forgiven for being taken somewhat aback by the presence of such an established authority, but in fact he remembers 'what was so impressive about him was an absolute lack of grandeur and a forensic interest in what we were doing'.[11] This was precisely the kind of work Rosen wanted to see teachers undertaking, and he offered his support, ultimately helping the group to secure an interest-free loan of £4000 from the Schools Council to publish *Becoming Our Own Experts*. The connection established, Richmond went on to work with Rosen and colleagues at the institute in the setting up of a series of conferences called Language in Inner-City Schools. Rosen convened the first conference, titled 'The Language linked difficulties of inner-city schools'. During that first conference,

> a loose co-ordinating committee was formed, and the plenary session of the conference established its first priority: the development of ways and means for studying the linguistic diversity of London schools, which was recognised collectively as a productive and important object for enquiry.
> (Burgess, 2009, p. 46)

Richmond remembers that the bi-annual conferences, which ran for a decade, were 'major events' which would attract 'up to five or six hundred people'.[12] They brought together

> mainstream English teachers and those whose interests were in the teaching of English as an additional or other language, or in mother-tongue teaching, or work on Afro-Caribbean language – related enterprises but often conducted discretely. The central aim and principle was to encourage research at school and institutional level.
> (Burgess, 2009, p. 46)

This central principle was essential to Rosen, and the flourishing of the language in inner-city schools initiative must have given him hope for the kinds of changes he wanted to see. His affirmed belief was that positive and actual change would come from teachers working on areas of their own interest and of importance to their own professional development and working collaboratively with like-minded colleagues. In telling a group of his students at the Institute of Education about the Language in the Inner-City school project and conferences, Rosen wrote to his wife Betty, saying, 'it was all founded on notions of teacher initiative. Did they want to join in? In what ways?'.[13] It was an approach that was at the heart of the decades of work in LATE and in the spirit of the English department at the London Institute of Education: an absolute commitment to the realisation of teacher autonomy and to the power of teacher agency. This commitment was shared by colleagues in LATE and at the Institute, but the importance of Rosen's staunch advocacy of this approach was critical to the impact of the Language in Inner-City Schools project:

> Harold's vision for the work reflected his commitment to teachers taking into their own hands the study of issues in their professional lives. While the work was co-ordinated from the Institute English department, he was determined that directions taken should reflect the work of teachers, and teachers played a strong role on the organising committee, including acting as chair, and in convening working groups.
>
> (Burgess, 2009)

This commitment to the principle of teachers making decisions about their work is evident again in the development of the innovative Role of Language in Education Course at the Institute of Education (see Chapter 4 for one teacher's recollection of this programme). Margaret Meek, a co-founder of the course that saw teachers taking a year's secondment to pursue study and research, recalled Rosen's telling intervention as she and colleagues were discussing planning for elements of the course:

> One day, irritated no doubt by our persistent tutorial threnody, Harold stopped what he was doing and said: 'You've already chosen a group of experienced teachers you think will be able to cope with what you want to do. Let them do it!'.
>
> (Meek, 2009, p. 53)

It was a pivotal intervention in what was to become an influential course of study for the teachers who were lucky enough to pursue it. Rosen's insistence on the teachers themselves taking control of their own development was critical:

> His principal concern was that the teachers could, should 'become their own experts'. Their experience would be a major part of the course content. It was a moment that still vibrates in the social memory of this undertaking. As the years passed and our experience of the course increased, we saw how important that intent had become.
>
> (Meek, 2009)

The commitment to teacher autonomy and the encouragement of teacher agency were not unique to Rosen, but his conviction and his seemingly boundless enthusiasm and energy were critical in ensuring that the spirit of this approach was sustained through the endeavours of the colleagues at the Institute of Education and, previously, in LATE. In his commitment to teacher agency, it could be said that Rosen was fundamental to a critical shift in the mindset of teachers, in thinking about themselves, their subject and their teaching. His colleague and close collaborator at the Institute of Education, Tony Burgess, believed that in the way that Rosen worked:

> Expectations of what might be involved in a subject – and what might be on offer to teachers – were steadily transformed. It was not Harold alone who supplied the engine for all this, but he provided a continuing impetus through his commitment to the work of teachers and of schools and through his own continuing spirit of enquiry.
>
> (Burgess, 2009, pp. 41–42)

Campaigning against National Agendas

Agree or disagree with Rosen's politics, it is beyond doubt that his beliefs were the engine behind his professional endeavours over so many decades, and his deeply and passionately held views for the potentially emancipatory nature of education, and of English within that, meant he was a genuine champion of the rights of children and a powerful advocate of teachers. As he came towards the end of his official working life, the educational context in which he found himself was one of increasingly centralised control of curriculum, assessment and – ultimately – pedagogy. The National Curriculum, standardised attainment tests and the National Literacy Strategy were all part of the neoliberal standards-driven education policy world. For all the politicians' rhetoric of improving outcomes, closing attainment gaps and enhancing social mobility for young people, it hasn't been hard to see the policy agenda as one driven by marketisation and competition on a global level. The standards-based agenda gathered huge momentum in the last decades of the twentieth century and the first of the twenty-first. Typically, Rosen was not shy of tackling the policymakers and their methods in direct and explicit terms. Whilst he was not necessarily in principle against some form of curriculum framework, the nature of centrally driven curriculum development was anathema to the way Rosen felt change should happen, with its wilful sidelining of teacher expertise. When the first National Curriculum was presented to the profession, Rosen's principal objection was to the way it had been written:

> We have a fine tradition of English teachers talking to each other, advisers who know the need for participation of teachers. So the central point is that matters of the curriculum have to emerge from what is essentially a democratic process – consultations and participation.
>
> (Teaching London Kids, 1990, p. 24)

For Rosen, the active engagement of the profession in curriculum change was critical, and this meant a genuinely bottom-up process of reform, not the often spurious consultative approach that Rosen saw, in the years of the Conservative government, for what it was. When Rosen was belatedly invited to offer his views to the Kingman Committee,[14] a Committee he later cited as one of those that had been 'blatantly rigged' (Rosen, 1994, p. 185), the letter he sent in reply (Rosen, 1988) is a withering indictment of both the policymakers' aims for education and their efforts to offer these aims as a result of consultation. The membership of the Kingman committee was, according to Rosen, 'a calculated insult to the English teaching fraternity' (Rosen, 1988, p. 150) and 'a planned attempt to exclude the vigorous and sustained presentation of certain points of view' (Rosen, 1988, p. 150). It was, in Rosen's view, a committee set up to deliberately exclude the very people who might offer something approaching a sensible view about language in the curriculum, and he was not minded to risk the potential consequences his involvement might suggest:

> I have no knowledge of how any submission by me might be treated but I do have some unhappy past experience of the use of selective citation of my work. I do not want to risk being singled out in that way, however slight the risk. I much prefer to present my views, unfiltered, in a public forum and eventually in print.
>
> (Rosen, 1988, p. 152)

Rosen knew that to engage with the consultation process risked, ultimately, to be implicitly or explicitly identified as someone who agreed with the ultimate conclusions. The dilemma has faced many in education in the past 40 years at least (and I include myself in this number): whether to engage in government consultation exercises on the basis that one has to be in the conversation to have any hope of influence, or to stand outside them to avoid assumed complicity in a process that you have, in all honesty, little realistic chance to impact. Rosen, referring to Urzula Clark's account of involvement in the National Curriculum review (Clark, 1994), made clear his own thoughts on this dilemma facing the profession:

> I am not saying that no involvement whatever with government machinery can be countenanced, but at least there should be some principles on which it should be based. First, clear, explicit, publicly available terms of participation. Second, written guarantees of openness and the right to make public matters of concern. Third, noisy withdrawal at the first signs of double-dealing.
>
> (Rosen, 1994, p. 186)

Rosen spoke for many when he made his stance against the invitation to submit his view to the Kingman Committee, and in any case he sincerely doubted that the report would achieve its aims, for he knew that for change to happen, teachers needed to be involved: 'To win assent for innovation means appealing to teachers' intellect and imagination and never flying in the face of their experience and commitment' (Rosen, 1988, p. 161).

By the time that Rosen addressed NATE's annual conference in 1994, the then Conservative government, nearing the end of its lengthy term in office, was ratcheting up still further its interventionist tendencies and its attacks on what it claimed to be a progressive educational establishment (a line of thinking returned to two decades later when Michael Gove branded academics who dared to question the new national curriculum as the new enemies of promise).[15] In his speech, Rosen, in a typically uncompromising fashion, branded the then Secretary of State for Education, John Patten, 'a midget', making clear his view that:

> I think the time has come in the battle against the idiocies of the National Curriculum and the subject orders for English to say unequivocally that we are in contention with a government of unashamed lies, obscene secrets, shady fiddles, and impenetrable cabals.
> (Rosen, 1994, p. 184)

Rosen's response to the workings of government committees of enquiry and to the central policy interventions like the National Curriculum can certainly be seen to be politically motivated. Although it might be self-evident that a socialist would stand in opposition to an English curriculum introduced by a Conservative government, a key element of Rosen's objection to the way the curriculum came about was its top-down construction. Central policy initiatives and directives were antithetical to Rosen's career-long held commitment to the importance of teachers having a voice and taking control over the direction of this work. Teachers, not policymakers – and not even educational academics, even with the best interests of the profession at their heart – should be the key agents in the development of pedagogy, curriculum and assessment. It is little wonder, then, that he was particularly despairing as he witnessed the introduction of the New Labour government's primary Literacy Strategy and Secondary National Strategy. Though these in fact included some content, for example, training on literacy across the curriculum, that Rosen might have been broadly sympathetic to, their entirely top-down implementation, with consultants delivering training material to schools, was starkly at odds with Rosen's thinking on teacher development. Rosen apparently observed these initiatives with 'mounting despair' as he saw that they were 'abandoning any idea that professional development might be something to do with a partnership between equals, some with more knowledge and experience certainly, but all involved in a common pursuit'.[16]

Conclusion

When considering Rosen's political activism, his campaigning and his championing of teacher agency and autonomy, it is worth noting John Dixon's view of the role that Rosen often took up in discussions in LATE committees and meetings, that 'Harold was a great activist and was into argument, putting a contrary position, stirring us up a bit'.[17] It might be worth saying that this was not always well received within LATE; Rosen recalled a particular battle when 'when there were big economy cuts, I wanted LATE to pass a resolution saying as English teachers these affect us, can't buy books, etc, etc, and I was terribly attacked for trying to bring politics into LATE'.[18] Rosen never sought to bury the politics of what was at stake in the education of young people, even if others tried to do so.

Often, Rosen's writing is polemical, but it in no way suffers for this. Rather, the strength of feeling he reveals is indicative of his passion and of his belief in the potential power of education for young people. His communist background meant he was all too familiar with the argument about the functioning of state education in a capitalist society, but he did not allow this to lead to defeatism; through his writing, he actively campaigned for ways in which the system might be changed. He believed it was necessary for teachers to 'know the world of the school and change it' and he believed that with the right kind of teaching the world of literacy, or reading and writing, could be opened up for all pupils, offering them the weapons to fight for change for themselves. He was no idealist, however; he recognised the challenge that teachers and pupils – particularly those from certain backgrounds – faced, and he knew that any advances made under the banner of progressivism were not just hard-fought, but were fragile and their permanency could not be taken for granted. As Richmond wrote in the introduction to the collection of Rosen's writings, Rosen knew that 'ground gained is not ground won forever; that the forces of ignorant, retrospective reaction can and will take that ground back, given that they have the power to do so' (Richmond, 2017b, p. 3). It's probably fair to say, in fact, that Rosen always took a very realistic view of the extent to which the advances he pioneered and fought for from the 1950s to the 1980s had actually changed the practice of schools widely. In the transcript of an undated interview in the archive of material at the University of London Institute of Education library, an interesting perspective emerges. When asked how he felt about the resurgence of textbook use in the wake of all the developments (the interviewer calls them 'thrusts') he had led on language use in schools through the 1960s and 1970s, Rosen candidly responded:

> If you look at the boom period, the utopia of the 60s and early 70s, the thrusts that you mention were never a mass phenomenon among teachers. Even in primary schools it was the minority. It had a big effect, as in LATE and NATE, but the exact degree of permeation was very, very limited. You must always be careful not to get a London view of things.[19]

Although this is perhaps an honest evaluation, and it may certainly be true that teachers in London made the most profound changes to their practice, it risks undervaluing the huge development Rosen was in part responsible for bringing about. Rosen was not simply a man of ideas; he was a man of action. In Richmond's view, 'Harold knew that a person's achievement is only meaningful to the extent that it changes the lives of other people, the lives of organizations (like schools) and the life of society as a whole, for the better' (Richmond, 2017b, p. 4). In one particularly striking anecdote about Rosen's intervention to aid a PGCE tutee who had been arrested after a false accusation of violence on an anti-Vietnam War demonstration, the student assessed Rosen as an academic who 'put their money where their mouth is' (Lamb, 2009, p. 61) – quite literally in the sense of the memory recalled as Rosen lent his own money to cover the bail fee. For this particular student, his experience of Rosen led him to the conclusion that his most important quality 'was his ability not to separate the heart and the head, emotions and intellect, sense and sensibility. For me he showed in his life and work that if your heart is right, your politics and social action will follow in consequence' (Lamb, 2009, p. 61). This seems a fitting description. In his own activism and in the support and urging of this in others, Rosen coupled his passionately held personal beliefs with a sharp intellectualism. In promoting teacher agency and in encouraging autonomy, both in his words and in his professional practice, he inspired many to confront the challenges always associated with the task of teaching.

Notes

1 Comment taken from an interview with the author. The quotation Richmond refers to, 'The philosophers have only interpreted the world, in various ways; the point is to change it', comes from Marx, K. (1888) Theses on Feuerbach No. 11 available at https://www.marxists.org/archive/marx/works/1845/theses/theses.htm, accessed on 14/2/ 2025.
2 The French Marxist philosopher Louis Althusser posited that a capitalist society reproduced its norms and values in part through schools, which were part of the ideological state apparatus. Although Rosen doesn't directly cite Althusser in his inaugural professorial lecture, he does list Althusser (1971) in the references.
3 Comments taken from an interview with the author.
4 In the history of LATE (Gibbons, 2014), there are a number of comments made by members of the Association in its earliest days that attest to the strikingly un-hierarchical nature of the group.
5 Denys Thompson had been a student of Leavis at Cambridge and co-wrote *Culture and Environment* with him (Leavis and Thomspon, 1933). He was an influential figure in the development of English in the secondary school, as detailed in Doyle (1981).
6 Boris Ford had been a student of Leavis at Cambridge and went on to become a distinguished academic and writer. At the time of the formation of NATE, he was Director of the Institute of Education at the University of Sheffield.
7 Comments taken from an interview with the author undertaken as part of a PhD study.
8 Comments taken from an interview with the author undertaken as part of a PhD study.

9 In his remarks at the launch of the collection of Rosen's writing (Richmond, 2017a), John Richmond referred to a letter Rosen wrote to his second wife, Betty, in which he affirmed that 'We must turn research upside down. No more pirate raids for "data"' (Richmond, 2017a).
10 Comments taken from an interview with the author.
11 Comments taken from an interview with the author.
12 Comments taken from an interview with the author.
13 This comment is taken from unpublished correspondence between Harold and Betty Rosen and was quoted by John Richmond at the launch event for the publication of Harold Rosen: Writings on life, language and learning 1958–2008 (Richmond, 2017a). The launch was held at University College London on 20th March 2017. Richmond kindly gave the author a copy of his talk at this event.
14 The Kingman Report was, in essence, a precursor to the National Curriculum. The Committee behind the report had been tasked to 'recommend a model of the English language as a basis for teacher training and professional discussion, and to consider how far and in what ways that model should be made explicit to pupils at various stages of education' (Department of Education and Science, 1988, p. 1).
15 On the 20th March 2013, The Independent published a letter signed by 100 leading education academics which criticised aspects of the new National Curriculum. Three days later, Michael Gove, then Secretary of State for Education, writing in the Daily Mail, branded the signatories of the letter as 'Marxists' and the 'new Enemies of Promise' (Gove, 2013).
16 John Richmond made this remark at the launch event for the publication of Harold Rosen: Writings on life, language and learning 1958–2008 (Richmond, 2017a). The launch was held at University College London on 20th March 2017.
17 Comments taken from an interview with the author undertaken as part of a PhD study.
18 Comment taken from an interview with Harold Rosen conducted by John Hardcastle and Peter Medway as part of research for Medway, P., Hardcastle, J., Brewis, G., and Crook, D. (2014) *English Teachers in a Postwar Democracy: Emerging Choice in London Schools, 1945–65*. New York: Palgrave Macmillan.
19 Comment taken from a transcript of an interview with Harold Rosen held in the University College London Institute of Education library. The transcript is undated and it is unclear to whom Rosen was speaking (the interviewer is simply given the title 'Q' in the transcript) but references contained within to organisations such as the Assessment and Performance Unit (APU) would indicate the interview took place in the early to mid-1980s.

References

Althusser, L. (1971) 'Ideology and Ideological State Apparatuses' in Cosin, B. (ed.), *Education, Structure and Society*. Harmondsworth: Penguin.
Anderson, S. and Butler, S. (1982) 'Language and Power in the Classroom: An Interview with Harold Rosen'. *The English Journal*, 71:3, pp. 24–28.
Barnes (2009) 'Learning from Harold'. *Changing English*, 16:3, pp. 355–356.
Burgess (2009) 'Harold at the Institute'. *Changing English*, 16:1, pp. 39–49.
Clark, U. (1994) 'Bringing English to Order: A Personal Account of the NCC Evaluation Project'. *English in Education*, 28:1 pp. 33–38.
Clements, S., Dixon, J. and Stratta, L. (1963) *Reflections*. Oxford: Oxford University Press.
Department of Education and Science (1988) *Report of the Committee of Inquiry into the Teaching of English Language* (commonly known as The Kingman Report). London: Her Majesty's Stationery Office.

Department of Education and Science (1989) *English for Ages 5–16 Proposals of the Secretary of State for Education and Science and the Secretary of State for Wales*. London: Her Majesty's Stationery Office.

Doecke, Brenton and Parr, Graham (2009) "Crude Thinking" or Reclaiming Our 'Story-Telling Rights'. Harold Rosen's Essays on Narrative'. *Changing English*, 16:1, pp. 63–76.

Doyle, B. (1981) *Some uses of English: Denys Thompson and the Development of English in Secondary Schools*, University of Birmingham Centre for Contemporary Culture Studies, available at https://core.ac.uk/download/pdf/83925959.pdf accessed on 1st March 2025.

Eyers, S. and Richmond, J. (1982) *Becoming our own Experts*. Trowbridge: Talk Workshop Group, also available online at https://www.becomingourownexperts.org/ accessed on 25th July 2025.

Gibbons (2009) "To know the world of the school and change it' An Exploration of Harold Rosen's Contribution to the Early Work of the London Association for the Teaching of English'. *Changing English*, 16:1, pp. 93–101.

Gibbons, S. (2014) *The London Association for the Teaching of English 1947–67: A History*. London: Trentham Books.

Gibbons, S. (2016) 'W(h)ither the Radicals?'. *English in Education*, 50:1, pp. 35–43.

Gove, M. (2013) *I Refuse to Surrender to the Marxist Teachers Hell-Bent on Destroying Our Schools: Education Secretary Berates the New 'Enemies of Promise' for Opposing his Plans*, available at https://www.dailymail.co.uk/debate/article-2298146/I-refuse-surrender-Marxist-teachers-hell-bent-destroying-schools-Education-Secretary-berates-new-enemies-promise-opposing-plans.html accessed on 1st March 2025.

Hardcastle, J. and Medway, P. (2009) 'In His Own Words: Harold Rosen on His Formative Years, with Speculations on Working-Class Language'. *Changing English*, 16:1, pp. 5–14.

Lamb, I. (2009) 'Old Students Remember'. *Changing English*, 16:1, pp. 55–62.

LATE (1947) *LATE Constitution*. Paper from the LATE archive, held at the University College London Institute of Education Library.

LATE (1956) *The Aims of English Teaching a document prepared for the British Council for use in study boxes sent to training colleges in India*. Paper from the LATE archive, held at the University College London Institute of Education Library.

LATE (1963a) *Advice from Ministry of Education Solicitor on the Foundation of NATE and Draft Programme for Inaugural NATE Conference*. Paper from the LATE archive, held at the University College London Institute of Education Library.

LATE (1963b) *Our Approach to the National Association*, Paper from the LATE archive, held at the University College London Institute of Education Library.

LATE (1963c) *Report of Emergency LATE Meeting 1st July 1963*. Paper from the LATE archive, held at the University College London Institute of Education Library.

Leavis, F. R. and Thompson, D. (1933) *Culture and Environment: The Training of Critical Awareness*. London: Chatto and Windus.

Medway, P., Hardcastle, J., Brewis, G. and Crook, D. (2014) *English Teachers in a Postwar Democracy: Emerging Choice in London Schools, 1945–65*. New York: Palgrave Macmillan.

Meek (2009) 'Harold on Memory'. *Changing English*, 16:1, pp. 51–53.

Richmond, J. (2017a) *10th Harold Rosen Lecture, to Mark the Launch of Harold Rosen: Writings on Life, Language and Learning 1958–2008*, Unpublished text of speech given at University College London on 17th March 2017.

Richmond, J. (ed.) (2017b) *Harold Rosen: Writings on Life, Language and Learning 1958–2008*. London: UCL Institute of Education Press.

Rosen, H. (1981) 'Neither Bleak House nor Liberty Hall' in Richmond, J. (ed.) *Harold Rosen: Writings on Life, Language and Learning 1958–2008*. London: UCL Institute of Education Press.

Rosen, H. (1982) 'Multicultural Education and the English Teacher' in Richmond, J. (ed.) (2017) *Harold Rosen: Writings on Life, Language and Learning 1958–2008*. London: UCL Institute of Education Press.

Rosen, H. (1988) 'Struck by a Particular Gap' in Richmond, J. (ed.) (2017) *Harold Rosen: Writings on Life, Language and Learning 1958–2008*. London: UCL Institute of Education Press.

Rosen, H. (1991) 'The Nationalisation of English' in Richmond, J. (ed.) (2017) *Harold Rosen: Writings on Life, Language and Learning 1958–2008*. London: UCL Institute of Education Press.

Rosen, H. (1993) 'The Politics of Writing' in Rosen, H. (ed.) *A Suitable Boy*. London: English and Media Centre.

Rosen, H. (1994) 'The Whole Story?' in Richmond, J. (ed.) (2017) *Harold Rosen: Writings on Life, Language and Learning 1958–2008*. London: UCL Institute of Education Press.

Rosen, H. and Burgess, T. (1980) *Languages and Dialects of London School Children*. London: Ward Lock Educational.

Teaching London Kids (1990) *Language, Culture and the National Curriculum: An interview with Harold Rosen*. London: The English Centre.

The Use of English (1963) 'Editorial'. *The Use of English*, 15:1, pp. 3–4.

Whitehead, F. (1976) 'The Present State of English Teaching: Stunting the Growth'. *The Use of English*, 28:1, pp. 11–17.

Yarker, P. (2018) 'Review of Harold Rosen: Writings on Life, Language and Learning 1958–2008'. *Forum*, 60:1, pp. 142–146.

Chapter 7

The Enduring Importance of Harold Rosen's Work

Introduction

Up to this point, this text has endeavoured to offer an overview of Harold Rosen's contribution to the field of English in education and the language arts and, I've suggested, to the field of education more broadly. This contribution has had a national and international impact. In seeking to offer this overview I have, as a consequence of the kinds of conventions that hold sway in a work such as this, attempted to detail Rosen's contribution in a number of key areas: the development in the post-war years of the new, progressive English; class and culture; language and learning; narrative and autobiography and teacher agency and activism. In each of these areas, there is ample evidence of the extent to which Rosen can be viewed as a key thinker in English in education. However, if I have gone even part-way towards achieving my aims, then it will be obvious that there is an inherent problem with this kind of division. Rosen's views on class and culture, and language and learning, are of course essential elements of the progressive model of English he was critical in developing, and the telling and retelling of personal anecdote, memory and story are core ways in which young people most profitably engage with this model of the subject in classrooms. The model was developed by way of Rosen's powerful campaigning and advocacy and – when and where it has taken root – has been sustained by teachers acting with agency, taking responsibility for the development of their own practice and professional identity. All, ultimately, in the aim of having an education system, and within that an English curriculum and pedagogy, that enables all children to succeed and empowers them with the tools they need to change their selves, their communities and their world for the better. English curriculum, class, culture, language, story and identity constantly overlap in Rosen's work, working within and alongside one another so that the attempt to contain any of these elements in a single chapter was always, in some respects, bound to fail. I hope, though, in whatever ways the structure I chose to adopt, and the consequent choices of material for inclusion that resulted, have been doomed to failure, they have, at least, succeeded in demonstrating the scope of Rosen's immense contribution to the field.

In this concluding chapter, I want to offer a view, or more accurately views, as to both why Rosen's work should be remembered and why it should have importance to those working in education, not only but most importantly, English in education, today. In seeking to offer a view on that question, I think it is necessary to reflect briefly at least on the educational macro-climate in which those working in much of the so-called developed world currently find themselves.

To say the educational climate today is different from that which Rosen found on entering the profession in the 1940s is to do little more than to state the blindingly obvious. The past, as what has now become a cliché goes, is another country where things are done differently. In the aftermath of the Second World War, in the context of a London Plan for renewal and social cohesion, and with the birth of the welfare state, it's perhaps easy to imagine the optimism with which a young educator might be inspired with hope for change and empowered to take on the challenges needed to be overcome in the effort to improve education and the teaching of English, and particularly to seek to improve the life chances of the disadvantaged. And there was the freedom for teachers to take the initiative, as Peter Medway noted when remembering his own time as a teacher at Walworth, 'The curriculum wasn't anyone's anyway, it was up for grabs. . . . It was very much the case we were saying we are in charge of this, we will take hold of it'.[1]

In the years following the Dartmouth Seminar, the progressive model of English that Rosen had been instrumental in shaping took root in many English-speaking jurisdictions across the globe. In the United States, after Dartmouth, 'the force of the student-centred argument offered by the British' (Simmons et al., 1990, p. 110) significantly influenced the work of teacher educators. In Australia, by the 1970s, this model of English was the 'supreme orthodoxy' (Reid, 2003, p. 99). The influence of London English in Australia was catalysed by the work of Garth Boomer,[2] and by the 1970s, curriculum documents in various Australian states meant that 'Dixon's personal growth model had received official endorsement' (Davis and Watson, 1990, p. 159). Rosen would have seen progress in the period from the 1960s to the 1980s; what had begun as collaborative work with colleagues in LATE and was first articulated in the Walworth English syllabus was a version of English that was taken up with enthusiasm by English teachers and, in some jurisdictions, policymakers across the world.

The world, and education within it, has changed, and if the first decades of Rosen's professional life were characterised by a sense that humane teachers could drive their own agenda for reform and by evidence of the growth model of English growing globally, he witnessed in the latter years of his career a different reality emerging, and one which is in many ways hostile to the things Rosen wanted to do and the ways in which he wanted to do them. In my own account of the development of subject English from 1966–2016 (Gibbons, 2017a), I characterised those 50 years as comprising two periods: the first up to the Education Reform Act of 1988 (Department of Education and Science, 1988) I termed the 'Age of Invention'; the second from 1988 onwards, the 'Age of Intervention'. It is this second age that saw Rosen become increasingly frustrated and angered at the way in which apparent gains made in the education of young people were being threatened or lost altogether. It is the age in which we still currently live, and it has particular aspects that, I want to argue, make a restoration and re-evaluation of Rosen's ideas so important.

The educational age in which we live, as I suggested in the introductory chapter to this text, has been, for nearly 40 years now, dominated by a neoliberal agenda. In essence, this has manifested itself across much of the globe in education systems that are characterised by increased competition of schools as education becomes a marketplace with, notionally, greater choice for parents as consumers. National education systems are driven by a standards-based reform agenda that includes an accompanying emphasis on high-stakes assessment and stringent accountability frameworks in the forms of published school league tables and external inspection processes. The arguments given for the education reforms of the 1980s and beyond have been driven by the imperative for developing national economies capable of competing in global terms; the rhetoric of ratcheting up standards was offered to produce skilled workforces to enable a country to become an economic powerhouse. The pronouncements of policymakers pursuing standards-based reform are often infused with what appear to be the noble aims of closing attainment gaps and ensuring that education works for groups like the economically deprived so that the system can facilitate social mobility.[3] Such a neoliberal agenda might be conveyed by its supporters as in some way non-political; surely it is simply common sense to want to generate more wealth, to have greater freedom and to improve outcomes for disadvantaged students? In this kind of rhetorical discourse, the kind of education proposed by a progressive like Rosen would be seen to have failed those underattaining groups. An argument about the supposed failures of progressive education was, of course, already being made in England as far back as the late 1960s in the infamous *Black Papers* (see, for example, Cox and Dyson, 1969), but from the publication of the Education Reform Act of Margaret Thatcher's government (Department of Education and Science, 1988), successive administrations have relentlessly pursued standards-based reform in one guise or another, with impacts on the organisation of local authorities and schools and curriculum and assessment. Whether one chooses to take policymakers at their word or not, the evidence is that despite decades of standards-based reform, the promise of social mobility, in England at least, has not been delivered with the socio-economically deprived groups still failing in the system (Tahir, 2022) relative to their more affluent peers. It was these disadvantaged children – what for simplicity can be called the working class – that had driven Rosen's passion for changing education; it is little wonder that he 'fiercely resented' (Richmond, 2017, p. 3) the attacks on progressive education that peppered the policies of the governments of Margaret

Thatcher, John Major and Tony Blair. It may be a blessing that Rosen was not able to witness the intense ferocity of those attacks that emerged in the wake of the election of the Conservative/Liberal Democrat coalition government in 2010, when the Education Secretary, Michael Gove, trained his sights unremittingly on the so-called progressives.

Under the wider umbrella of standards-based reform, the teaching of English has always been at the centre of the storm, and in the last two decades of his life, Rosen witnessed successive policies and curriculum and assessment rewrites that threatened the very existence of the progressive English he had pioneered, and it is in considering the state of subject English in England today that the imperative for Rosen's work to reemerge becomes most acute.

In terms of the subject matter of English, at least so far as it is outlined in official documents, the National Curriculum has become increasingly narrow and, in its current format, traditional. One might grant an honorary exception to the version of the National Curriculum that emerged in the final years of the New Labour government, which could be viewed as a more progressive model of the subject, using, as it did, the concepts of 'competence', 'creativity', 'cultural understanding' and 'critical understanding' to frame its subject matter (although questions were raised at the time (see Gibbons, 2007) about the extent to which this was a genuine progressive rethinking of the subject rather than simply a repackaging of more traditional ideas). Certainly, the version of the English curriculum, as I write, for secondary students (Department for Education, 2013, 2014), is about as traditional as one could imagine. The introduction of this curriculum followed a grandly titled expert report (Department for Education, 2011) which, in the best traditions of standards-based reform, examined the curriculums of so-called high-performing jurisdictions across the globe. In terms of content of the curriculum, the teaching of Standard English, a dialect which is presented as wholly unproblematic in form and nature, is forefronted. Spoken language is given scant consideration beyond its use for presentations and drama; there is a brief mention of discussion, but no genuine consideration of the importance of talk in the classroom and of the critical links between language and learning. Specified reading is highly canonical and highly Anglo-centric; writing is, in the main, reduced to a set of products in which students deploy devices accurately and use grammar with precision. The grammar content, the bulk of which pupils are expected to learn before the age of eleven, follows a traditional, prescriptive model of the English language. One need not think too hard to imagine what Rosen would have made of the impoverished version of English contained within its handful of pages.

The way that English has been assessed over the course of the past 30 years has similarly impacted upon the experience of English for young people. Following the introduction of the National Curriculum, standardised attainment tests (SATs) were introduced for children at ages 7, 11 and 14. Though the tests for 14-year-olds were withdrawn in 2009, the SATs remain as a key indicator of primary school standards at the end of Key Stage 2, and a phonics test has been introduced for children at the age of 6. The spelling, punctuation and grammar test for pupils at the end of Key Stage 2 is an extraordinarily blunt instrument designed to assess language use in very traditional, formulaic and very arguably wrongheaded ways. The evolution of the GCSE examination has seen the removal of coursework and a return, in the name of rigour and reliability, to terminal examination.

The Current State of English Curriculum, Assessment and Teaching: Influences and Impact

Within the overarching narrative of the drive to ratchet up standards in English, a number of factors have been highly influential in determining the content of the English curriculum and the way it has been taught and assessed in England. Through the years of New Labour's literacy strategy, the work of the genre theorists was highly significant in the model for the teaching of writing – and to a degree, reading – advocated. Coming from the work of the Australian New South Wales Disadvantaged Schools Project (see Cope and Kalantzis, 1993), this model promoted a pedagogy for writing that involved the explicit identification of the conventional features of different writing genres and the adoption of these conventions by students in their own writing. Through mastery of generic conventions, young writers become competent to produce the different texts the curriculum demands. Although it was accompanied by seemingly useful, collaborative pedagogic practices such as modelled and shared writing, the result in classrooms was often an overwhelmingly teacher-led pedagogy with pupils predominantly engaged in the reproduction of non-fiction genres like persuasion, recount or argument. Texts used as examples for pupils would often need to be invented in order to conform to the conventions of the genre to which they belonged,[4] given that in reality, few texts are actually representative of a single genre. The use of writing frames and sentence structures as scaffolds contributed to a sense that there was a single correct way to write any given text. Successful writing was the successful adoption of the conventions of the genre. Student choice and student voice were apparently sidelined.

It is a genre model of teaching writing that has become dominant in much English teaching and, in fact, governs many of the ways in which young people respond to literature, since there has been an adoption of an accepted way in which to write what is, in effect, a 'lit crit' essay. Different structural models are offered to pupils to enable them to frame their responses to texts – most notably the Point, Evidence, Explain (PEE) structure, which is ubiquitous in its many guises (see Gibbons, 2017b) across classrooms. This is driven, it seems, by a view of the sorts of writing that pupils have to produce for GCSE examinations and is where genre teaching of writing intersects with one common – perhaps unintended – consequence of an overarching standards-driven culture. The pressure on teachers to produce results ends up in teaching methods that seek to prepare students for the demands of the examination – the well-known phenomenon of teaching to the test. In the case of English, this has meant making use of the exam specifications' assessment objectives as markers for pupils and using devices like PEE to encourage students to work to a framework that will ensure they produce writing that meets the assessment objectives. Summaries of inspection data (see, for example, Ofsted, 2012, 2024) have clearly detailed how an overemphasis on teaching to the GCSE examination and the focus on a narrow range of approaches, like PEE, to support writing, can negatively impact even the very earliest years of secondary school English teaching.

Whilst the influence of genre theory, introduced through the National Strategies, still holds sway in many aspects of the teaching of writing in English classrooms, the current version of the English national curriculum, introduced in the wake of the expert panel report, owes much, as I pointed out in the first chapter, to those who advocate a knowledge-based curriculum, a curriculum that specifies particular content that pupils should know by certain ages. The work of American educationalist E.D. Hirsch is commonly seen as being the cornerstone for the theoretical thinking behind this approach, and his Core Knowledge Foundation has been highly influential in many jurisdictions beyond his native United States.[5] Nick Gibb, the conservative minister who was significantly involved in the introduction of the new national curriculum, was a devout believer in the value of Hirsch's work declaring that 'No single writer has influenced my thinking on education more than E.D. Hirsch' (Gibb, 2015, p. 12). A knowledge curriculum in English rests on principles like vocabulary instruction so that children's stock of words and phrases is built up from the earliest age, the teaching of phonics, and the specification of particular age-related reading content.

Alongside the growing influence of the knowledge-based approach to curriculum design, pedagogical approaches have been increasingly influenced in recent years by the research emerging from the field of cognitive science and the ways in which, it is suggested, this might be adopted in classrooms. Rooted firmly in notions about the role and functioning of working memory and long-term memory, with the work of Daniel Willingham being influential (see, for example, Willingham, 2009), a number of reviews from the Educational Endowment Foundation (EEF) have highlighted how certain classroom activities may enhance learning (Education Endowment Foundation, 2021a, 2021b). The ideas have been influential and effectively implemented by policymakers through the frameworks that have emerged for those on teacher training courses and for new teachers involved in induction training.[6] In a short space of time, phrases like 'cognitive load' have become part of the discourse of English teachers, and strategies such as retrieval practice, interleaving and spaced practice have been adopted. These become trumpeted as evidence-informed approaches, a phrase which implies that all previous suggestions about effective approaches to teaching were somehow lacking in any concrete support, as if teachers had been doing things on a whim. Advocates of employing teaching strategies that have been informed by cognitive science will often be seen to employ direct instruction, and this can lead to highly didactic approaches in the classroom. Group work, with pupils talking collaboratively together, is often eschewed, as it is suggested that inherent in such activity is an increase in extraneous cognitive load.[7] That the evidence cited in the various EEF reviews is somewhat limited in scope and – more importantly – is seldom drawn from research carried out in English classes or with English teachers (as it relates mostly to subjects like science and maths) appears to be of little consequence for policymakers that have advocated for these approaches to be adopted across the curriculum. It seems that for some, cognitive science has now given us the definitive answer to the question of how children learn, and from that, it is a relatively straightforward path to answer the question of how they should be taught. This thinking is not just dominant in England.[8]

I've attempted to summarise, albeit briefly and with a very broad brush, what has happened to subject English in the final years of Harold Rosen's life and the nearly two decades since. The overarching influence of standards-based reform has had a narrowing effect on curriculum and precipitated an environment in which teachers feel overwhelming pressure to teach in ways that prepare their pupils for the high-stakes assessments, which are used to judge those young people, their teachers and their schools. The influence of genre theory, the knowledge rich-approach and cognitive science have all impacted on what is taught in English classrooms and how it is taught. I've not touched on the ways in which the English curriculum may have been used as a vehicle to transmit a renewed form of 'Britishness' in the ways in which documents like The Newbolt Report did, but there is no doubt an argument to be made there too in the context of rising nationalism and populism. The result of all these influences – on the evidence of many English lessons I see being taught each year – is that the way the subject is enacted in classrooms is at some significant distance, if not in fact utterly removed, from the progressive model of English that Rosen helped to forge, where the experience and language of young people would be the starting point and central focus for work in English. There are, of course, exceptions to these generalisations, pockets of resistance where English teachers pursue a humane version of the subject, but they are the exceptions and they do this by rejecting recommended norms, rather than being supported by the policy context. The current problems of curriculum and assessment in English are writ large in reports such as *Striking the Balance* (Oxford, Cambridge and RSA, 2024). That a curriculum review was launched by the newly elected Labour government in 2024 is encouraging, but how much optimism one can have for such a process on the back of nearly 40 years of reform is to be questioned.

Certainly, some evidence suggests (see, for example, Gibbons, 2017a; Marshall et al., 2018) that the problems described here are not a purely England-based phenomenon; where the standards-based reform agenda has taken hold, English curriculum, assessment and teaching have been impacted by the drive to improve attainment. Writing from an Australian context, Doekce and Parr are forthright in their assessment of what this has meant for the work of those who pioneered a progressive model of English, asserting that the work of Rosen and his colleagues in the London School:

> has largely been forgotten by contemporary policy makers intent on implementing standards-based reforms. This is hardly surprising. Arguments about the centrality of meaning making to school curriculum and pedagogy, including a refined sensitivity to the way that language mediates learning and experience, have been ruthlessly suppressed by neo-liberal ideology for decades.
>
> (Doecke and Parr, 2009, p. 73)

This is indeed a damning assessment of the ways in which current policy direction has marginalised the work of progressives like Rosen. Perhaps if the result of such a direction were improved life chances for all young people, then we might feel obliged, however reluctantly, to accept that the ends have justified the means. However, the effects, in England at least, could hardly, as I've suggested, be said to have succeeded in terms of outcomes, particularly in terms of addressing the gap in attainment that persists between disadvantaged pupils and their more affluent peers. And whilst the goal of closing the attainment gap remains elusive, the impact of reforms on the health of English as a subject may well have been profound. As noted in Chapter 1, attitude surveys suggest that English is a far from popular subject with pupils, and that this is increasingly the case as they move up the years of secondary schooling.[9] Numbers of young people pursuing English studies at post-16 level and undergraduate level have tumbled[10] and whilst we might point to the focus that is placed on STEM education, with the promise of more lucrative prospects associated with an education in the sciences, this is an indicator that English is something that young people are not inspired to study. There is evidence that young people simply don't see the point of English.[11] There are risks of a downward spiral for the subject here; fewer graduates with English degrees means potentially fewer high-quality recruits to teacher education programmes, resulting in problems with the supply of new teachers, and this in turn impacting on how the subject is experienced by young people in schools. With all this in mind, I would argue that a repositioning of Rosen's work to the centre of English teachers' thinking about their subject and their practice is critical for the health of the subject. English, arguably now more than ever, should be a subject that inspires young people, offering the chance to critically engage with a rapidly changing world. One can argue the extent to which being a young person in the twenty-first century is more difficult than at any time before, but the statistics around young people's mental health clearly suggest that young people are struggling in hitherto unseen numbers. Whether it be the climate crisis, global instability and conflict, the impact of technology or a combination of these and other factors, the impact on young people's mental health seems to be profound.[12] Whilst it would be clearly ludicrous to suggest that English teaching alone could provide the solution to this, it is surely not too far-fetched to suggest that an English that engages young people and which offers them the space to explore themselves, their communities, the world and how they negotiate their place within it would surely be a positive force.

The Importance of Remembering Rosen's Work

My argument is that when we look at what the experience of English has become for many pupils in England, and I would posit in many jurisdictions where standards-based reform and ideas about knowledge and cognitive science hold sway, we need to revisit the work of Rosen.

Interestingly, of course, one could argue that taken in isolation, the ideas of the genre theorists and the knowledge curriculum advocates might be seen to be driven by the thrust to secure better educational outcomes for disadvantaged groups. The work of the genre theorists, for example, came from a project specifically intended to improve attainment of pupils from low socio-economic backgrounds in Sydney. The advocates of a knowledge-based curriculum suggest the approach benefits those pupils who come to schools already on the back foot as a result of the broader vocabularies and cultural experience of their better-off peers. Improving the experience of education for disadvantaged groups was precisely Rosen's motivation in seeking to reshape English. However, the evidence is that the current proposed approaches to curriculum and pedagogy have simply not worked in enabling all pupils to succeed. An appreciation of Rosen's work may help us in part to understand why and point us in more profitable directions.

If we consider Rosen's work on narrative, then we are invited to consider the problems inherent in subscribing to a view that there are a fixed set of genres in writing (see, for example, Rosen, 1993b). One effect the narrow view of genre employed in the teaching of writing (in English and in other subjects) has is limiting creativity and acting as a way to simply reinforce the norms and conventions of institutional power. Even if the argument about mastering conventions is offered as a means to ultimately enabling young people to subvert these norms, it's highly arguable to what extent such opportunities are actually offered to young people in classrooms who are being prepared, with the best possible intentions, for the demands of external examinations. Genre approaches to the teaching of writing focus on the kinds of transactional writing associated with the accepted discourses of academic essays, science reports and the like. They promote what is, essentially, a fiction – that writing in the 'real' world is unchanging and unceasingly rule-governed. In drawing on the work of Bakhtin's work on speech genres (Rosen, 1993a), Rosen encourages a far more sophisticated consideration of the notion of genre and its relationship to language and thought. And whilst genre theory, as it has been codified in the teaching and learning of writing, has, it seems by design, sought to cast creative, narrative and autobiographical writing to the sidelines, Rosen's work invites us to consider the potentially endless possibilities of narrative as genre (Rosen, 1994). In seeking to reassert the importance of narrative and autobiography, in both speech and writing, Rosen highlights the paucity of an English curriculum rooted in a narrow pedagogy of genre. Indeed, whilst I would argue that in the context of English curriculums where students are inducted into writing in particular rule-governed forms, any teacher should revisit Rosen's thinking on narrative to consider the potential impact of their practice, since it has been persuasively argued that there is the scope for even broader critique of the contemporary educational context within this work:

> Rosen's essays on narrative are worth revisiting because they provide a valuable intellectual resource with which to challenge the discourse of standards, testing and other neo liberal reforms.
>
> (Doecke and Parr, 2009, p. 64)

When we consider the notion of a knowledge curriculum, one can't really escape the first difficulty, which is that the very concept of a knowledge curriculum in English is, of course, problematic for many reasons (see, for example, Eaglestone, 2020 for a critical look at the impact of ideas about knowledge-rich thinking on English). It's hard to think of a sensible way to reduce the breadth and depth of what might be deemed to be part of the subject into a discrete body of knowledge. Arguably, it may be straightforward in certain other disciplines where knowledge is perhaps more definite and definable. In England, the impact of thinking of English as a knowledge-based subject has been to construct a relatively narrow curriculum, which seemingly limits knowledge as it relates to literature as the traditional canon. The impact has been to push to the sidelines the kinds of non-canonical literature that Rosen and his colleagues had advocated as part of ensuring that children from all backgrounds would find themselves and their lives, communities and experiences reflected back to them.

Whilst the existence of an English curriculum that prioritises canonical texts is itself problematic, meaning that literature from different cultures and traditions disappears, the problem is larger than this. If the goal of an education in English becomes the provision of knowledge or cultural capital through the teaching, for example, of certain texts, then what is deemed to be of value in a given society and culture is simply reinforced as it is passed on. Leaving literature to one side, however, it is perhaps the ways in which arguments about knowledge have affected approaches to language in school that are potentially most insidious in their impact on young people and which most clearly demand a re-evaluation of Rosen's work. Rosen's critique of Bernstein was a powerfully effective challenge to the deficit model of working-class language, but many of the arguments behind advocating a knowledge-based curriculum, as it relates to language, return to the depiction of children from working-class or culturally diverse backgrounds as being somehow lacking when they arrive at school. In the rhetoric around the 'word gap' (see, for example, Ofsted, 2019), the depiction of groups of children entering school as linguistically impoverished is stark. The word gap relates to vocabulary, but there is within the scope of an English language knowledge-based curriculum a heavy emphasis on the teaching and learning of formal grammar, and with that a renewed emphasis on the preeminent place of Standard English. Standard English is given the unquestioned position of the language of power, and it is this that young people from diverse linguistic backgrounds need to acquire in order to bridge the knowledge gap.

The linguist Ian Cushing has written extensively on the ways in which, within the policymakers' discourse of improving attainment for disadvantaged children by ensuring that the word gap is bridged and that Standard English is prioritised in school, there has been an extraordinarily powerful return to the notion of the deficit model of the language of certain pupil groups – those from low socio-economic groups and particularly from racially diverse backgrounds. The deficit model of non-standard uses of English has the effect of marginalising the very children they purport to help (see, for example, Cushing, 2022). Schools, effectively through their policies, police language use. Cushing further suggests (Cushing, 2025) that the policing of non-standard language becomes bound up with behaviour policies, particularly in certain types of academy school that have taken inspiration from the Charter Schools in the United States and the work of Doug Lemov (Lemov, 2015). Such schools adopt zero-tolerance behaviour policies that frame within them not just modes of behaviour but also standardised language use. The effect is to 'locate the root cause of racial and socio-economic injustices not in the unequal distribution of resources, but in the alleged linguistic deficiencies of marginalised children' (Cushing, 2025, p. 13). It is the very position that Rosen's critique of Bernstein sought to challenge head-on. Cushing believes that the various reports and school policies, which ultimately are built on a foundation of knowledge, result in 'a flawed theory of social justice which assumes that if marginalised children make small tweaks to their language, they can dismantle structural barriers and escape their own oppression' (Cushing, 2025, p. 13). Cushing's points are powerful and well-argued and paint a picture of an education system which – though supposedly driven by a social mission to equip children with the linguistic knowledge needed to improve their life chances – results in groups of children marginalised and all the existing social injustices being reiterated. It is a system where schools are again insisting that children leave the language of the home and the street at the school gate. If we are even partly convinced by Cushing's powerful critique of current language policies in schools and the injurious effects they are having on young people from particular backgrounds, then it becomes critical that Rosen's attempts to challenge the deficit model are revisited.

Cognitive Science

As indicated, the evidence emerging primarily from the Education Endowment Foundation (EEF, 2021a, 2021b) has had a significant impact on policy and, increasingly, on teachers' practice. If cognitive science were to provide the definitive answer to how children learn, then perhaps it might be legitimate to cast all previous thinking in the field into the wastebin of history. Cognitive science hasn't – not yet at least – done that. I would posit that it is hardly ever likely to do so. If we are to consider how to draw on the evidence of cognitive science to inform thinking about pedagogy, it seems to me that there is much in Rosen's work that ought to be considered. Elements of Rosen's thinking about learning could inform the extent to which English teachers feel cognitive science has something to offer in the teaching and learning of their subject.

In Rosen's writing on autobiography and personal storytelling, Rosen rightly drew attention to the role of language in the making, telling and retelling of memory. It is the role of language – along with other what might be called affective or emotional aspects of learning – that seems absent in the research and recommended methods of applied cognitive science. Whatever cognitive processes are involved in the development of schema and the transference of knowledge from working to long-term memory, language must play a part in that process. One does not have to be a card-carrying Vygotskyan to adopt a view that language and thought are inextricably intertwined, and any theory of learning that fails to pay due attention to this relationship runs the risk of relegating the status of language work in the classroom. Rosen relentlessly promoted classroom talk, and this must surely remain central to the work of teachers as they are asking pupils to develop new understanding, commit that understanding to memory and then retrieve it at any given moment.

When we add to the consideration of how insights from cognitive science might inform classroom practice the ways in which schools may be asking students to adopt different kinds of language from those in which they habitually talk and think, there is also a potential problem. Rosen wrote about the dangers of imposing the impersonal language of subject disciplines on students at too young an age, with the result that students might ape the language without developing actual understanding of the content at hand. It seems to me that the cognitive scientists may themselves provide an explanation for this – if a student has both the cognitive challenge of mastering a linguistic register alongside the cognitive challenge of a concept or idea being taught, it seems only too predictable that cognitive overload might be the result. The learning of the linguistic register, or at least mastering the ability to mimic it, may well come at the expense of the subject content. If we want a student in English to offer their views on the character of Macbeth, might not the imposition of certain rhetorical devices or structures associated with the literary criticism essay simply create extraneous cognitive load? Given this, it seems all the more important, if we want to take ideas from the cognitive scientists, that we revisit Rosen's ideas about the ways in which pupils engage in talking and thinking and writing in English – and indeed – across the curriculum. There is a strong argument here to support Rosen's views that young people should be encouraged to make use of the language that they have, and the language genres – like narrative – with which they are familiar, when they are developing their understanding, rather than simultaneously being told to adopt the accepted discourses of the subject they are learning.

Teacher Agency and Autonomy

Finally, aside from the subject of English and ideas about curriculum and pedagogy, I would argue there are strong reasons to revisit Rosen's thinking and writing for the ways in which they might inspire teachers to develop a stronger sense of the importance of ownership of their own work and professional development. As the previous chapter highlighted, Rosen was a teacher and academic who was absolutely clear about the need for teachers, working individually and collaboratively, to take control of their own professional development. The belief that Rosen had that teachers needed to 'become their own experts' was integral to the work he drove in LATE and the research in which he was involved as a member of the English department at the Institute of Education. He was insistent that, as an academic and researcher, the goal was to work alongside teachers, enabling them to develop their own practice through involvement in projects, a model described as being one where 'the doers and the supporters of the doers are engaged in mutually supportive enquiry'.[13] There is strong evidence that in England teachers' sense of autonomy, their belief in some sense of agency when it comes to their own professional development, has been eroded over time (Worth and Van den Brande, 2020). It's likely that several factors have played their part in this – the global standards-driven reform agenda, which I've characterised as 'the age of intervention' (Gibbons, 2017a) has seen a succession of centrally driven policy reforms around curriculum and assessment, with English, as has always been the case, at the very centre of policymakers' minds. The rise of multi-academy trusts, where groups of schools have centrally aligned policies and procedures, has also seemingly had a detrimental effect on teachers' sense of autonomy (Worth and Van den Brande, 2020).

Whatever the cause, or causes, of the feeling amongst teachers that they have lost a sense of themselves as professionals, one could argue that there is a potentially huge problem here for the policymakers themselves. Goodson

(2001) has suggested that a problem for those who wish to push through large-scale reform through central policy is that such policies don't take account of 'how seemingly common reforms are refracted through each school context, through the varied micro-politics of schools and through teachers' varying and sometimes resistant personal beliefs and missions' (Goodson, 2001, p. 49). This failure to take account of teachers' own beliefs and ideas means that the changes policymakers wish to effect 'will actually face major problems of sustainability and generalizability' (Goodson, 2001, p. 49). It has therefore been argued that 'for education reform to be effective, teachers must be the enactors of reform rather than recipients' (Friedman et al., 2009, p. 267). This means that teachers themselves need to have an active part to play. Indeed, it has been suggested that the attempt to reform education works successfully when it sees 'personal commitments of teachers as both an inspiration for reform (which works best when carried out by teachers as part of their personal – professional projects) and a necessary object of reform' (Goodson, 2001, p. 60). Policymakers, therefore, if they genuinely want to see the translation of their policies into practice, might do well to learn a lesson themselves from the passionate commitment Rosen always had for teachers to undertake development work rooted in the concerns that came from their own practice in their own classrooms.

I'm not quite deluded enough to believe that policymakers will respond to such a call. However, if they are not influenced by the effect on their intended policy reforms, they would do well to consider the evidence of another potential impact of teachers' lack of sense of professional agency and autonomy in their work. Responding to centrally driven initiatives, rather than having the opportunity to work to their own agenda, can have a significant impact on teachers, meaning that 'the persisting effect is to erode teachers' autonomy and challenge their individual and collective professional and personal identities' (Day and Smethen, 2009, p. 142). When teachers feel little sense of autonomy and agency, the evidence is that they find less satisfaction in their work and are far more likely to consider leaving the profession (Worth and Van den Brande, 2020). The recruitment and retention of teachers is not simply an issue in the United Kingdom; it is a global issue (see, for example, UNESCO, 2024). Given the weight of evidence, it would seem pertinent for policymakers to find ways to ensure that teacher agency and teacher autonomy were given a far higher priority as part of any reform agenda.

Throughout his long career, Rosen inspired teachers to develop autonomy and to work collaboratively, enabling those he worked with to develop a sense of personal and professional agency. His work championed the kind of 'democratic professionalism' (Sachs, 2001, p. 152) that sees teachers working as activist professionals within the notion of 'communities of practice' (Wenger, 1998) so that

> Communities of practice and an activist identity are coextensive; each nourishes and supports each other. These values cannot exist in isolation, nor

without a purpose. The purpose is to revitalize teachers' sense of themselves professionally and personally.

(Sachs, 2001, p. 158)

Colleagues with whom I work see the development of teachers' identity as core to their education as teachers (Rushton and Towers, 2023). For Rosen, the personal and professional were inextricably linked; his political beliefs and passionate desire for a more just and equal society fired the work he undertook and the work he inspired others to pursue. Whilst not all teachers will necessarily share Rosen's political commitments – though I'd warrant schools might be better places if they all did – it seems to me to be essential for individual teachers' well-being and for the well-being of the education system as a whole that if we take nothing else from the life and work of Rosen, we take those core values of the importance of teachers developing that sense of personal and professional autonomy through pursuing their own concerns and with the support and empowerment of collaborative networks within school and without.

One could also argue that an important element of developing teacher identity is autobiography, and this has been taken on by teacher educators as part of their work. I recall myself the influence of Rosen's thinking on the importance of autobiography when I completed the MA in English Education at the London Institute of Education in the mid-1990s. The opening chapter of our dissertation was mandated to be 'the autobiography of the question', where we would, essentially, be asked to tell the story of why the project we were writing about was important to us. The legacy of Rosen's thinking in that programme was clear. Taking their inspiration from Rosen's work, Doecke and Parr encourage their beginning English teachers in Australia to undertake narrative and autobiographical writing as 'a crucial means of developing the reflexivity which all educators require in negotiating social relationships within their classrooms, and within their local and global professional worlds' (Doecke and Parr, 2009, p. 69).

Final Thoughts

If we recall the notion that throughout Rosen's professional life he 'found and promoted the most progressive and innovative work on language, literature and culture' (Miller, 2009, p. 1), then perhaps I need to say no more to support my view that his work should be forgotten at our, and our pupils', peril. Rosen, with his colleagues and collaborators, dedicated his working life to developing a model of English teaching, and indeed a model for teaching, that would offer all young people the chance of success. Within such a model, teachers would be active and engaged professionals, constantly seeking to improve their own work, and thus the experience of their pupils, through individual and collective professional endeavour driven by the challenges they identified for themselves.

Education's function, for Rosen, was to empower young people, to enable them to understand, interpret and use language in all its forms to question, to challenge and to change the world around them for the better. Most, indeed I would venture to say all, people who embark on a career in education believe that what they are doing is in some way altruistic, that they are in some way giving something back, and they want to become a teacher because they 'have the desire to make a difference in some way' (Gibbons et al., 2023, p. 4).

As I conclude, I'm perhaps inevitably drawn to the words John Richmond used in the remarks he made at the launch of the collection of Harold Rosen's writings, 'If Harold were here this afternoon, he would be saying (and I can catch his tone in saying it), "It's all very well going on about my stuff. What are you people doing now?"'[14]

It might be that all I am doing is thinking, writing and offering a view; for Rosen, the point was not to understand the world, but to change it. It's therefore entirely feasible that Rosen might not view the enterprise on which I have embarked as particularly meaningful. It is my hope, however, that a teacher reading this text might be led from this work to the work of Rosen and that, ultimately, the result might be a change in belief and a change in practice.

Notes

1 Comments taken from an interview with the author undertaken as research for PhD.
2 Garth Boomer was an influential Australian teacher educator. In 1972–73, he completed an MA at the London Institute of Education under the tutelage of James Britton, Nancy Martin and Harold Rosen. He took their ideas back to Australia. Boomer is the subject of a volume in this Key Thinkers series (Green, 2024).
3 For a seminal example of the kind of standards-based reform that encompassed the rhetoric of improving outcomes for vulnerable young people, one might point to the No Child Left Behind legislation in the United States in 2001.
4 Working as a consultant for the National Strategies in the early 2000s, I was aware that text examples included in material for the training on the teaching of different writing genres were not, as they seemed on first glance, examples from the real world but specifically written to fulfil generic conventions.
5 Hirsch's work, which can be seen on the website of the Core Knowledge Foundation, which he founded (see https://www.coreknowledge.org/, accessed on 25th April 2025), has been hugely influential in many jurisdictions, for example, in Australia (Australian Education Research Organisation, 2024).
6 In England, the *Core Content Framework* (Department for Education, 2019b) and the *Early Career Framework* (Department for Education, 2019a) the documents that outline what trainee teachers and newly trained teachers, respectively, need to know very heavily draw from the work of cognitive science in the way in which they describe the ways in which children learn and, therefore, how they should be taught.
7 Within the theories about cognitive load, extraneous cognitive load is the term used to describe the demands put on learners' mental faculties that in some way hinder the learning process by making the task that has been set more difficult.

8 The Australian Education Research Organisation has promoted the potential benefits of approaches informed by cognitive science (see https://www.edresearch.edu.au/research/projects/how-students-learn, accessed on 25th April 2025).
9 See, for example, the results of YouGov polling here that indicate young people's attitudes to school subjects: https://d3nkl3psvxxpe9.cloudfront.net/documents/YouGov_Childrens_Omnibus_-_subject_enjoyment.pdf, accessed on 24th March 2025.
10 Data from Ofqual (2022, 2023) indicates the decline in number of English pursuing English studies at post-16 level. Research by the British Academy (British Academy, 2023) shows the decline in popularity of English-related courses at undergraduate level.
11 Along with colleagues at King's College London, I have been conducting some pilot research to investigate why there is such a drop in the number of young people studying English at post-16 level. The initial data from interviews with groups of 17- and 18-year-old students points clearly to the fact that they don't clearly see where the study of English could take them.
12 Research like that undertaken by University College London and the Sutton Trust points to the alarming figures relating to young people suffering from mental health difficulties (see https://www.suttontrust.com/news-opinion/all-news-opinion/almost-half-of-young-people-experiencing-mental-health-problems/?gad_source=1&gad_campaignid=22448929663&gbraid=0AAAAApnz-UuaeeLRlbC3hgBU-NcAgOBzP&gclid=EAIaIQobChMI_M-sg4uRjQMVXopQBh2stxveEAAYAiAAEgLrDfD_BwE, accessed on 1st May 2025).
13 This comment is taken from the unpublished text of the remarks made by John Richmond at the launch event for the publication of *Harold Rosen: Writings on life, language and learning 1958–2008* (Richmond, 2017). The launch was held at University College London on 20th March 2017.
14 This comment is taken from the unpublished text of the remarks made by John Richmond at the launch event for the publication of *Harold Rosen: Writings on life, language and learning 1958–2008* (Richmond, 2017). The launch was held at University College London on 20th March 2017.

References

Australian Education Research Organisation (2024) *A Knowledge Rich Approach to Curriculum Design: A Commissioned Report*, available at https://www.edresearch.edu.au/research/research-reports/knowledge-rich-approach-curriculum-design accessed on 25th April 2025.
British Academy (2023) *English Studies Provision in UK Higher Education*, available at English-studies-provision-UK-higher-education-British-Academy-report.pdf (thebritishacademy.ac.uk) accessed on 25th March 2025.
Cope, B. and Kalantzis, M. (1993) *The Powers of Literacy: A Genre Approach to Teaching Writing*. London: Routledge.
Cox, B. and Dyson, A. E. (eds.) (1969) *Black Paper 2: The Crisis in Education*. London: The Critical Quarterly Society.
Cushing, I. (2022) 'Word Rich or Word Poor? Deficit Discourses, Raciolinguistic Ideologies and the Resurgence of the 'Word Gap' in England's Education Policy'. *Critical Inquiry in Language Studies*, 20:4, p. 305–331.
Cushing, I. (2025) 'The Sound of Misbehaviour: Deficit Thinking and Language Policing in School Discipline Policies'. *International Studies in Sociology of Education*, pp. 1–23.

David, D. and Watson, K. (1990) 'Teaching English in Australia: A Personal View' in Britton, J., Shafer, R. and Watson, K. (eds.) *Teaching and Learning English Worldwide*. Philadelphia: Multilingual Matters Ltd.

Day, C. and Smethen, I. (2009) 'The Effects of Reform: Have Teachers Really Lost Their Sense of Professionalism?'. *The Journal of Educational Change*, 10, pp. 141–147.

Department for Education (2011) *The Framework for the National Curriculum: A Report by the Expert Panel for the National Curriculum Review*, available at https://assets.publishing.service.gov.uk/media/5a7572c5ed915d6faf2b3104/NCR-Expert_Panel_Report.pdf accessed on 20th March 2025.

Department for Education (2013) *English Programmes of Study: Key Stage 3*, available at https://assets.publishing.service.gov.uk/media/5a7b8761ed915d4147620f6b/SECONDARY_national_curriculum_-_English2.pdf accessed on 15th March 2025.

Department for Education (2014) *English Programmes of Study: Key Stage 4*, available at https://assets.publishing.service.gov.uk/media/5a7585a1ed915d731495a9dd/KS4_English_PoS_FINAL_170714.pdf accessed on 15th March 2025.

Department for Education (2019a) *Early Career Framework*, available at https://assets.publishing.service.gov.uk/media/60795936d3bf7f400b462d74/Early-Career_Framework_April_2021.pdf accessed on March 24th 2025.

Department for Education (2019b) *ITT Core Content Framework*, available at https://assets.publishing.service.gov.uk/media/6061eb9cd3bf7f5cde260984/ITT_core_content_framework_.pdf accessed on March 24th 2025.

Department of Education and Science (1988) *Education Reform Act*. London: Her Majesty's Stationery Office.

Doecke, Brenton and Parr, Graham (2009) "'Crude Thinking' or Reclaiming Our 'Story-Telling Rights'. Harold Rosen's Essays on Narrative'. *Changing English*, 16:1, pp. 63–76.

Eaglestone, R. (2020) 'Powerful Knowledge', 'Cultural Literacy' and the Study of Literature in Schools'. *Impact: Philosophical Perspectives on Education Policy*, 2020:26, pp. 4–40.

Education Endowment Foundation (2021a) *Cognitive Science in the Classroom: Evidence and Practice Review*, available at https://d2tic4wvo1iusb.cloudfront.net/production/documents/guidance/Cognitive_Science_in_the_classroom_-_Evidence_and_practice_review.pdf?v=1743760548 accessed on march 30th 2025.

Education Endowment Foundation (2021b) *Cognitive Science Approaches in the Classroom: A Review of the Evidence*, available at https://d2tic4wvo1iusb.cloudfront.net/production/documents/guidance/Cognitive_science_approaches_in_the_classroom_-_A_review_of_the_evidence.pdf?v=1743760548 accessed on 30th March 2025.

Friedman, A., Galligan, H., Albano, C. and O'Connor, K. (2009) 'Teacher Subcultures of Democratic Practice Amidst the Oppression of Educational Reform'. *The Journal of Educational Reform*, 10, pp. 249–276.

Gibb, N. (2015) 'How E.D. Hirsch Came to Shape UK Government Policy' in Simons, J. and Porter, N. (eds.) *Knowledge and the Curriculum: A Collection of Essays to Accompany E.D. Hirsch's Lecture at Policy Exchange*, pp. 12–20. London: Policy Exchange.

Gibbons, S. (2007) 'New Orders, Old Tests: The New English Orders in the Key Stage 3 National Curriculum Review'. *English Drama Media*, 7, pp. 10–12.

Gibbons, S. (2017a) *English and Its Teachers: A History of Policy, Pedagogy and Practice*. London: Routledge.

Gibbons, S. (2017b) '"Death by PEEL?" The Teaching of Writing in the Secondary English Classroom in England'. *English in Education*, 53:1, pp. 36–45.

Gibbons, S., Brock, R., Glackin, M., Rushton, E. and Towers, E. (2023) 'Becoming a Teacher' in Gibbons, S., Brock, R., Glackin, M., Rushton, E. and Towers, E. (eds.) *Becoming a Teacher: Issues is Secondary Education Sixth Edition*, pp. 3–10. Maidenhead: Oxford University Press.

Goodson, I. (2001) 'Social Histories of Education Change'. *The Journal of Educational Change*, 1, pp. 46–63.

Green, B. (2024) *Garth Boomer: English Teaching and Curriculum Leadership*. London: Routledge.

Lemov, D. (2015) *Teach like a Champion 2.0: 62 Techniques that put Students on the Path to College*. New Jersey: Jossey-Bass.

Marshall, B., Gibbons, S., Hayward, L. and Spencer, E. (2018) *Policy, Belief and Practice in the Secondary English Classroom: A Case Study Approach from Canada, England and Scotland*. London: Bloomsbury.

Miller, Jane (2009) 'Editorial'. *Changing English*, 16:1, pp. 1–3,

Ofqual (2022) *Provisional Entries for GCSE, AS and A Level: Summer 2022 Exam Series – GOV.UK* (www.gov.uk) consulted on 10/1/2024.

Ofqual (2023) *Provisional entries for GCSE, AS and A Level: Summer 2023 Exam Series – GOV.UK* (www.gov.uk) consulted on 10/1/2024.

Ofsted (2012) *Moving English Forward*, available at https://assets.publishing.service.gov.uk/media/5a7b44bc40f0b66a2fc0648b/110118.pdf accessed on 1st May 2025.

Ofsted (2019) *Education Inspection Framework: Overview of Research*, available at https://www.gov.uk/government/publications/education-inspection-framework-overview-of-research accessed on 1st May 2025.

Ofsted (2024) *Telling the Story: The English Education Subject Report*, available at https://www.gov.uk/government/publications/subject-report-series-english/telling-the-story-the-english-education-subject-report accessed on 21st July 2025.

Oxford, Cambridge and RSA (2024) *Striking the Balance: A Review of 11–16 Curriculum and Assessment in England*, available at https://www.ocr.org.uk/Images/717919-striking-the-balance.pdf?hsCtaAttrib=177138440350 accessed on 25th March 2025.

Reid, I. (2003) 'The Persistent Pedagogy of Growth' in Doecke, B., Homer, D. and Nixon, H. (eds.) *English Teachers at Work: Narratives, Counter Narratives and Arguments*. South Australia: Wakefield Press.

Richmond (ed.) (2017) *Harold Rosen: Writings on Life, Language and Learning 1958–2008*. London: UCL Institute of Education Press.

Rosen, H. (1993a) 'The Autobiographical Impulse' in Rosen, H. (ed.) *A Suitable Boy*. London: English and Media Centre.

Rosen, H. (1993b) 'The Politics of Writing' in Rosen, H. (ed.) *A Suitable Boy*. London: English and Media Centre.

Rosen, H. (1994) 'How Many Genres in Narrative?'. *Changing English*, 1:1, pp. 179–191.

Rushton, E. and Towers, E. (2023) 'Teacher Identity: Developing a Positive Professional Identity in Your Teaching Career' in Gibbons, S., Brock, R., Glackin, M., Rushton, E. and Towers, E. (eds.) *Becoming a Teacher: Issues in Secondary Education Sixth Edition*. Maidenhead: Open University Press.

Sachs, J. (2001) 'Teacher Professional Identity: competing discourse, competing outcomes'. *Journal of Education Policy*, 16:2, pp. 149–161.

Simmons, J., Shafer, R. and Shadow, L. (1990) 'The Swinging Pendulum: Teaching English in the USA 1945–1987', in Britton, J., Shafer, R. and Watson, K. (eds.) *Teaching and Learning English Worldwide*. Philadelphia: Multilingual Matters Ltd.

Tahir, I. (2022) *The UK Education System Preserves Inequality – New Report*, available at https://ifs.org.uk/articles/uk-education-system-preserves-inequality-new-report accessed on 25th May 2025.

UNESCO (2024) *Global Report on Teachers: Addressing Teacher Shortages and Transforming the Profession,* available at https://unesdoc.unesco.org/ark:/48223/pf0000388832 accessed on March 27th 2025.

Wenger, E. (1998) *Communities of Practice: Learning, Meaning and Identity.* Cambridge: Cambridge University Press.

Willingham, D. (2009) *Why Don't Students Like School? A Cognitive Scientist Answers Questions About How the Mind Works and What It Means for the Classroom.* San Francisco: Jossey Bass.

Worth, J. and Van den Brande, J. (2020) *Teacher Autonomy: How does it Relate to Job Satisfaction and Retention?* Slough: National Foundation for Education Research.

Index

activism 120, 135–137
advocacy 120, 127, 132–133
agency 120–124, 135, 137, 153–155; encouraging teacher agency 126–133
Althusser, L. 125, 137n2
assessment, current state of 145–149
autobiography 100–102, 114–117; implications for teaching and learning 110–114; importance of 102–105; narrative and culture 108–110; *Speaking from Memory* 105–108
autonomy 126–133, 153–155

Barnes, D. 4, 12, 22, 28, 38–43, 80–86, 96, 128–129
Barron Mays, J. 51–52
Bartlett, F. 107
Becoming Our Own Experts (Eyers and Richmond) 126, 130
Bernstein, B. 54–64, 70–71
biography 8–10
Britton, J. 1, 4, 11, 14, 24, 37–38, 41–42, 49, 76–78, 82–83, 86, 97n2, 101, 129
Bruner, J. 110, 113–114
Bullock Revisited (Department of Education and Science) 88
Burgess, T. 4, 22, 61, 64–66, 69, 83, 95, 115–116, 130–133

campaigning 120, 133–135, 141
children, working-class 50–54
Clark, U. 134
class 49–54, 70–72; importance of 54–63; multiculturalism 63–69
Clements, S. 13, 32, 36, 41, 130
cognitive science 152–153

communities of practice 154–155
Cox, B. 17n1, 94
culture/cultures 49–54, 70–72; importance of language and class 54–63; multiculturalism 63–69; and narrative 108–110
curriculum 94–96; current state of 145–149; language across the curriculum 75–91; teaching of Standard English 91–94
Cushing, I. 151–152

Dartmouth Conference (1966) x 38–43, 54, 125, 142
Development of Writing Abilities, The (Britton et al.) 76–77, 84, 95, 111
Dixon 32, 36
Doecke, B. 116, 124, 148, 150, 155

Educational Endowment Foundation (EEF) 146–147
experience of working-class children 50–54

Gibb, N. 146
Goodson, I. 153–154
Gove, M. 135, 144
Greenford County Grammar School 12, 24
Gurrey, P. 10, 24
Gwynne, M. 10, 24

Hardcastle, J. 15, 24, 30, 57, 129–130
Harding, D. 41, 45n20
Hardy, B. 101–102
Harris 65
Hickman, J. 89
Holbrook, D. 66

Jackson. B. 53–54
Jones, K. 23

Labov, W. 64, 96, 12
language 94–96; and Bernstein 54–63; language across the curriculum 75–91; teaching of Standard English 91–94; working-class children 50–54
Language and Class (Rosen) 58, 61–64, 70
Languages and Dialect of London School Children (Rosen and Burgess) 64–65
Language, the Learner and the School (Barnes et al.) 2, 62, 80–82, 85–87, 90, 95
LATE 1–3, 12, 15–17; class and cultures 49, 70; early work of 24–29; enduring importance of Rosen's work 142, 153; language and learning across the curriculum 75–81, 85–89, 95; rise of new English 32–33, 38–43; story and narrative 101, 112; teacher agency 125–132, 136; and working-class children 50–54
learning 94–96; language across the curriculum 75–91; teaching of Standard English 91–94
Leavis, F.R. 10, 22, 33, 127
Lemov, D. 151
Literacy Across the Curriculum in Geography 90
Literacy Across the Curriculum in Science 90
London County Council (LCC) 23
London Day Training College (LDTC) 30, 38
London Institute of Education (IoE) 5, 10–11, 14–15, 24, 62, 75–76, 89, 122, 125, 130–133, 136, 153–155

Maclure, S. 23
Marsden, D. 53
Martin, N. 1–3, 11–14, 24, 42, 49, 76, 86, 88
material 15–17
Medway, P. 14–15, 34, 129–130
Meek, M. 132
memory 1–8, 100–102, 114–117; implications for teaching and learning 110–114; importance of narrative, story and autobiography 102–105; importance of remembering Rosen's work 149–152; narrative and culture 108–110; *Speaking from Memory* 105–108
Miller, J. 5, 39, 155
Muller, H. 40
multiculturalism 63–69

narrative 100–102, 114–117; and culture 108–110; implications for teaching and learning 110–114; importance of 102–105; *Speaking from Memory* 105–108
national agendas, campaigning against 133–135
Nationalisation of English, The (Rosen) 92
National Literacy Project 90
National Literacy Strategy 133, 135
'Necessary Myth, A' (Rosen) 108
'Neither Bleak House nor Liberty Hall' (Rosen) 122
New English 12–14, 42–44, 49–51, 94; and the Dartmouth Conference (1966) 38–42; early work of LATE in developing 24–29; need for 21–24; and the Walworth syllabus 29–38
New Labour government 90, 135, 144–145

Oracy All-Party Parliamentary Group 90–91

Parr, G. 116, 124, 148, 150, 155
personal biography 8–10
PGCE 1, 12–15, 24, 42, 95, 137
politics 121–126
'Politics of Writing, The' (Rosen) 122, 124
professional biography 8–10

Reflections (Clements et al.) 41, 130
Richmond, J. 5, 8–9, 13–15, 17n4, 41, 49, 100, 115, 121–121, 124–126, 130–131, 136–137, 156

Sawyer, W. 33
Simon, B. 8, 23
socialist politics 28, 49, 51, 120, 135
Speaking from Memory (Rosen) 105–108, 116
Standard English 68, 91–94, 122, 151
'Stories and Meanings' (Rosen) 100, 111

story 100–102, 114–117; implications for teaching and learning 110–114; importance of 102–105; narrative and culture 108–110; *Speaking from Memory* 105–108
Stratta, L. 13, 36, 130
syllabus, Walworth 29–38, 41, 81, 94

teacher agency 120–121, 135–137, 153–155; campaigning against national agendas 133–135; encouraging autonomy and politics 121–126
teaching: current state of 145–149 of Standard English 91–94; teaching career 10–15

'Towards a Language Policy Across the Curriculum' (Rosen) 82–83
Troublesome Boy (Rosen) 108

University College London (UCL) 10, 15
Uses of English (Muller) 40

Vygotsky, L. S. 4, 79, 82–83, 90, 97n5, 152

Walworth syllabus 29–38, 41, 81, 94
Warnock, M. 106, 117n5
West, D. 36–38
Whitehead, F. 39–40, 129
Willingham, D. 146
working-class children 50–54

For Product Safety Concerns and Information please contact our EU
representative GPSR@taylorandfrancis.com
Taylor & Francis Verlag GmbH, Kaufingerstraße 24, 80331 München, Germany

www.ingramcontent.com/pod-product-compliance
Lightning Source LLC
Chambersburg PA
CBHW071411300426
44114CB00016B/2262